THE SEX.COM CHRONICLES

The Sex.Com Chronicles
A White Hat Lawyer's Journey to the Dark Side of the Internet

First Edition
Printed in USA
ISBN 1-4392-0101-3

Published by 1 Prime Publishing
For inquiries and comments contact:

1 Prime Publishing
2165 S. Avenida Planeta
Tucson, Arizona 85710
www.1primepub.com

Acknowledgements: The author gratefully acknowledges and thanks the following people for their assistance and contirbutions to the production of this book.

Cover and Interior Design:
Rogue Design Group (www.roguedesigngroup.com)

Proof Reading Assistance:
Maria Carreon

Credits: Alexandre Dumas, Herman Hesse, Sun Tzu, Minamoto Musashi, Niccolo Machiavelli, Balthasar Gracian, The Ramones (all of them), Neil Young.

Disclaimers: Contains logic, satire, and candid assessments of knaves and fools.

THE

sex.com

CHRONICLES

*A white hat lawyer's journey
to the dark side of the internet*

CHARLES CARREON

DEDICATION

To my father and my mother, Conrad and Eloise, who taught me that

justice and kindness are the rewards of courage and strength, and to my

son Joshua, who yearned to attain greatness, and left us all too soon.

TABLE OF CONTENTS

FOREWORD

"It is by his courage, please observe, by his courage alone, that a gentleman can make his way nowadays. Whoever hesitates for a second perhaps allows the bait to escape which during that exact second fortune held out to him. You are young. You ought to be brave for two reasons: the first is that you are a Gascon, and the second is that you are my son. Never fear quarrels, but seek adventures. I have taught you how to handle a sword; you have thews of iron, a wrist of steel. Fight on all occasions. Fight the more for duels being forbidden, since consequently there is twice as much courage in fighting."

THUS DID D'ARTAGNAN, a fictional warrior as real as any history has created, receive his patrimony. For young men without wealth or titles, the only way up was to possess fighting skill, and the courage to apply it. Three hundred years ago, I might have taken the soldier's route to fortune, but since the days of Dumas, we have evolved an alternative to bloody combat in search of profit. Affluent people have decided it is easier to retain wealth when open bloodshed is not the norm. This trend toward non-violent conflict resolution has become popular with almost everyone except gangsters and heads of state. Consider this: However angry Bill Gates ever got at David Boies over the Microsoft lawsuit, it was only in fantasy that Gates may have contemplated putting together a hit squad to kill Boies and his team. With billions of dollars at stake, and the prestige of the richest man in the world on the line, no one pulled a gun, no one detonated a bomb, no one took hostages.

Why? Because the wealth and power at stake were legitimate dollars and socially-approved prestige. If Bill had used homicide to accomplish his goals, he would have forfeited the game; indeed, to the extent that we perceived him as an arrogant man who presumed to write his own rules, he lost prestige. Membership in civilized society was more important to Bill than absolute power, because without the approval of society, he couldn't play in the world's biggest game.

In the legal war over Sex.Com, my client Gary Kremen and I defeated Stephen Michael Cohen, who had leveraged himself into the financial big leagues with a single criminal act—stealing Sex.Com from Gary. He used the money from the theft to buy the appearance of legitimacy. When Gary sued him, he deployed the legal system with merciless effectiveness in an effort to defeat Gary's claims. There was nothing unusual about this. Theft by deception, the laundering of wrongful gains, and the employment of lawyers to make theft secure, are standard operating procedure in the half-world of criminality and business that found a home on the tech frontier. Sometimes CEO's are con men and bankers are thieves. Professionals can be found to defend almost any scheme. What was unusual was that Gary and I fought and won.

On November 27, 2000, Judge James Ware took Sex.Com from Cohen, and gave it back to Gary. On August 30, 2002, with one sentence, the U.S. Court of Appeals for the Ninth Circuit put an end to Cohen's misuse of the courts, dismissing his appeal. The court stated: "In light of Cohen's status as a fugitive from justice and his egregious abuse of the litigation process, we exercise our discretion to dismiss his appeal pursuant to the fugitive disentitlement doctrine." To avoid the effect of a $65 Million judgment, Cohen had moved all of his assets offshore, abandoned a $3 Million home in San Diego, and made his permanent residence in Mexico. He failed to appear in court even when Judge Ware issued a warrant for his arrest. He chose to be a fugitive, so the court refused to listen to his claims. Years after the verdict had become final, he was arrested on the outstanding warrant, and was released only after serving over thirteen months in federal custody for refusing to disclose where he had hidden the money he derived from Sex.Com. When you have read the story, I suspect you'll agree that Cohen never reckoned all he stood to lose from his encounter with Gary. As it happened, notwithstanding Cohen's gift for taking the measure of men, Gary and I fell outside the ambit of his experience. We were warriors.

Our world, far from being a tidy one in which we can trust the law and authorities for protection, is a ground of endless contention. Whether we fight with words and proof, or with weapons of destruction, there will always be tragic outcomes, unfair successes, and outrageous results. Might never makes right, and victory cannot cleanse the taint of injustice. For right to have a fighting chance, it must be at least as smart and hopefully tougher than the forces posed against it.

Most trial lawyers have heard they should study Sun Tzu's *The Art of War*, Clausewitz's *On War*, and Machiavelli's *The Prince*. It is good advice. Trial lawyers have inherited a role derived both from the medieval tradition of trial by combat, and the 18th-Century tradition of deductive reasoning. The duty of loyalty to the client harks back to the early days, when a man in trouble sought a champion rather than a scholar. Most clients still judge their lawyer's worth primarily by his commitment and zeal. It is a fair standard by which to judge, because it measures their courage, without which right and justice are substanceless words.

To courage, the advocate must add skill gained from study and practice. Finally, there is that essential ingredient — resources to pursue the battle. Then, perhaps we can have a fair contest, one fair enough that we would all lay down our weapons to play, secure that our fortunes are better determined by the application of rules and argument than on the all-destroying fields of war. To inspire those who wish to fight for right, to help train warriors old and young, and to share my love of the lore and legend of strategy, I have written this book. May your weapons always be sharp in the service of the good.

CHAPTER ONE

PIZZA IN OJAI

WHEN I FIRST MET GARY KREMEN, IT WAS A BEAUTIFUL DAY. I had been delighted to receive a phone call from my old friend Robin Kaufer, with whom I graduated from UCLA Law School in 1986. Since then, she'd earned an advanced degree in tax law and become an IRS lawyer. Not exactly what I expected from our days at UCLA, riding motorcycles, worshipping The Ramones, and holding poetry readings in the law school courtyard, but she's still got her kinks. Robin said she was coming through town with a friend on the way to a party in Santa Monica, and since her friends were usually smart and made good conversation, I was anticipating their arrival.

It was the summer of 1999. I was living with my wife and two of our three kids, Joshua and Ana, in a two-bedroom apartment in Carpinteria, California, a beachside community a few miles south of Santa Barbara. We had recently arrived after six years in Oregon, and I was looking to set up a criminal defense practice in Ventura County. Local legal gossip told me the prosecutor was overzealous, filed lots of cases, and was doing everything possible to help defense attorneys earn a living. Sounded good to me.

I opened an office in Ojai, a little town about 20 miles inland from Carpinteria, and a nice motorcycle ride from our apartment. The office was tiny, but had high-speed Internet and a Ventura County phone number, so I figured I was ready for business. I was re-contacting old L.A. buddies to see what I could stir up, working on a couple of Oregon cases, and living on savings while things picked up. My son was working at Starbucks, my wife was working as a legal secretary, and my daughter was working as a page at the Santa Barbara Library. I was doing laid-back things like meeting my wife for lunch with homemade sandwiches, picking up my daughter after work, and occasionally doing research on the Oregon cases.

I did my research in the old library at the Santa Barbara Courthouse. Outside the courthouse, a plaque commemorates the arrival in 1776 of Francisco DeAnza, the Spanish explorer who pioneered the overland

1

route from Sonora to Spain's coastal settlements. I was pleasantly surprised when I saw the plaque, because while DeAnza is a noted historical figure of the American Southwest, since childhood I'd thought of him as the man in the portrait on my Aunt Pearl's living room wall, with the big feather in his military hat. My aunt commissioned the picture because he is a direct ancestor on my mother's side. My mother and aunt were named Ainsa. DeAnza married into the Ainsa family as the fortuitous result of his search for relatives of his same name.

The Santa Barbara courthouse is a jewel, a large two-story building with white stucco walls and clay-tiled hallways. Broad spiral staircases at the corners of the building open onto the lawns of an expansive courtyard where weddings are often held. In courtrooms, immense murals record the progress of the California settlers, beginning with the gold-helmeted Spaniards wading ashore from their vessels anchored in the bay. In the large courtrooms the air is scented with leather and fresh sea air, which circulates freely through the building. I sometimes sat looking at the bold figures of conquistadors in leather armor, bearing muskets and crosses, planting vines and mining gold, and felt the thought stirring: What lands might I conquer?

Robin called from her cell phone on a Saturday morning, and I spun down to a parking lot in downtown Carpinteria to meet her and the mystery friend. The first thing I noticed was the car. It wasn't Robin's car. She wouldn't drive something like that. Her style was more the classic tangerine Porsche 914 she'd babied for years. This car was an old, beat-up Honda, with body work that looked like it had been done in the parking lot at the beach by a guy with a bucket, a can of bondo and a pack of sandpaper. The stereo had been ripped out, leaving a couple of wires protruding. The interior was the essence of grungy. And the owner was Gary Kremen.

Impish is the only word to describe him in those days. His constant mannerisms were emitting outrageous remarks punctuated by a playfully malevolent smile and questioning eyes. His grinning face, shining with mischievous glee, surmounted a nebbishy bulk that he nevertheless whisked about with considerable energy. I found it impossible not to like him.

Since it really wouldn't be out of the way, we agreed to take a day trip to Ojai so they could see my office. Tiny as it was, I was proud of it, and mention of the high-speed Internet connection piqued Gary's interest.

It's a nice drive from Carpinteria to Ojai. You leave the fog behind, rising into the hills to the mirrored expanse of Lake Casitas, a large drinking water reservoir in which swimming is not allowed (but boating is). Then you descend into the warm Ojai valley, which sports such attractions as wall-to-wall orange groves, a few nice restaurants, cheap office space, a new-age community, and a famously pink sunset.

We had lunch together, my wife Tara, my daughter Ana, Robin, Gary and I. Between bites of Hawaiian-style pizza, Gary spoke the fateful words: "I was the first person to register Sex.Com." He had been first to register it, he said, but a convicted thief by the name of Stephen Michael Cohen had stolen it using a forged letter. Cohen, Gary said, had done forty-six months in Federal Prison for fraud and other crimes, and had stolen the name shortly after his release in 1995. The story sounded screwy, but I make it a policy not to say that to a prospective client. Gary said he was disappointed with his lawyers, because they weren't doing a good job. He was particularly annoyed that they weren't interested in playing up Cohen's criminal past, which seemed to him like a trump card. He hadn't chosen his own lawyers, because the litigation was being financed by other people, but now he had money, and wanted control of the strategy. He wanted lawyers who would listen to him, and most importantly, win the case.

The wheels started turning instantly in my mind. This was 1999, and the dot-com skyrocket was gaining altitude. I was excited about the legal issues. Back in 1995, my Ashland office landlord, Lance Pugh, had put a bug in my ear about the Internet. Lance is a red-headed, fast-talking, forward-thinking, big-idea kind of person. He was one of my first business clients as a sole practitioner; indeed, I paid Lance half my rent in legal services. So he would routinely barge into my office, waving a copy of the Wall Street Journal, and start holding forth about how the Internet was going to change everyone's business life, and I needed to get on the bandwagon now! Sounded like a great idea, but finding Internet clients in Southern Oregon wasn't easy. Now here I was, talking to a real Bay Area dot-commer.

Gary was sitting there across from me at the table, grinning. Was he setting the hook, or was I? I looked him dead in the eye and said, "This is the case I've been waiting for." I didn't know how right I was.

CHAPTER TWO

THE HARDER THEY COME

SEX.COM PREYED ON MY IMAGINATION. As I read the LA Times at the Starbucks down the street from my apartment, it was all dot-com news. Barry Diller was paying homage to the new magnates, admitting that he admired their ability to painlessly raise the billions that he couldn't pull in with all his media assets. Opportunity was knocking loudly, and I was eager to see its face.

Down at the Santa Barbara library, I did a little research. The legal issues were open. There were no court precedents about the nature of domain names—were they property or not? What happened if you stole one? I started reading the news more carefully for domain name stories, and every one was about how valuable they were—selling for hundreds of thousands, even millions of dollars. And Sex.Com was the world's most valuable domain name. A guy could become somebody with a case like that.

A case like Sex.Com doesn't often come to a sole practitioner, but here was an opening. Gary was offbeat. I was offbeat. He was a bit of a loner, and so was I. His big money lawyers were letting him down—so try a street fighter on for size. Gary knows how to convey the impression of wealth. The junky car and sloppy clothes were part of the impression. I thought he could pay for the work, and even if he couldn't pay for all of it, there was always taking a share of the name. I waited for Gary to call back after our meeting, but he didn't.

A couple of weeks later I phoned Gary at his office on Montgomery Street in San Francisco, just a block downhill from that section of Broadway where the bars have names like "Centerfolds" and "The Garden of Eden." He said he'd been meaning to call me. I said I'd be passing through on my way to Oregon to cover a criminal case, so we made a date to get together. When I arrived, about a week later, he showed me around his office in the afternoon, and then we went to pick up Robin, who was getting off work. Together we enjoyed refreshments at a fish and brew place on an industrial wharf, the sort of gritty amenities Gary likes.

After drinking a few beers, we headed over to Gary's apartment, a nice walk-up on Fulton Street in Haight-Ashbury. Gary was sharing the apartment with an Asian accountant/tech-nerd/pizza gofer named Bob Deschl, and Ella, a hefty African-American woman social worker. Bob and Ella were nice, and sometimes we'd all eat take-out together in the living room. But on this day, they cleared out of the living room and left Gary, Robin and me to discuss business. Robin helped us do this by sitting very quietly on the floor by the coffee table, being her tiny pleasant self, while Gary ruled the room from a seat on the couch, surrounded by a pile of Wall Street Journals and Barron's financial news, which he read at breakneck speed, one page after another, while tossing off difficult questions with practiced ease.

After he threw me a question, his eyes would dart back to the print, and he would start flipping pages. When I returned an answer, his eyes would pop back up, stabbing like headlights on bright, and he would instantly ask another question that he had formulated while apparently reading the paper. It was like playing tennis close to the net with a guy who had an evil slam that he was constantly directing toward your backhand. We were playing a game in which it was necessary for me to rack up points, or this thing was going nowhere. The good thing about Gary is he pretty much has his scoreboard right out where you can see it. He lets you know when he likes what you're saying. He gives feedback and pushes for the next right answer. If you said good things, he would question the positive assessment by asking about downsides, weak points, and pitfalls. Happy talk would not make this man happy.

What made Gary happy were the little things. Months later he said the thing that impressed him the most was the pocket copy of Sun Tzu's *The Art of War* that I always kept in my briefcase. He also liked the fact that I had a chrome-handled lock knife with a slender four-inch blade that I used to perform minor cutting tasks. Besides playing with knives, my other sports are fencing and archery. He also liked these things.

That I was an Oregon lawyer also had appeal for Gary, because Cohen's lawyer was based in Oregon, and had played a difficult opening hand with remarkable skill. When Gary's lawyers started work on the case, they predicted easy victory. Apparently Cohen hadn't heard he was supposed to lose. Bob Dorband of Duboff, Dorband, Cushing & King, a Portland intellectual property firm, had been scoring devastating hits against Gary's case. I had read the paperwork, and there was an Oregon slant to Dorband's approach. His papers were spare, to the point, and armed with aggressive confidence.

Dorband had put Gary on the run by taking a daring tack, calling Gary himself a con man who was trying to steal Sex.Com. Gary was a come-lately who wanted a chunk of the Internet sex action, a pornographer wannabe looking to take what Cohen had earned with honest sweat. The accusation stung Gary painfully, and I rallied him to repudiate this lie. I called Dorband's lawyering "smallpox blankets and firewater," harking back to the days when lawyers, miners and railroads used phony deeds and bio-warfare to steal native land. How the West was really won. It was sneaky and dirty. Like the old rail barons, Cohen had produced a phony deed to steal Sex.Com. Gary needed a skilled civil lawyer with criminal experience and the ability to take the case all the way to trial. Califor-nia civil lawyers have little familiarity with criminal conduct, but as a prosecutor in rural Oregon, I had convicted many people of forgery and theft. These California never-tried-a-case lawyers didn't have the stuff to get down and go for the knees like I would. Gary needed to hire some-one with Oregon frontier savvy. Muleskinner wisdom. Someone like me. Have gun, will travel.

Gary liked my attitude. He also liked the fact that I was willing to sleep on his couch from the first night. I logged many other nights on that couch, generally five-hour stretches between two and seven, spent under a bare blanket with my head on an armchair pillow. In all fairness, Gary often offered to swap me for his bed, but that offer never seemed too appealing. Better an early dawn through the uncurtained street-side windows than a sojourn in the place where Gary formulated his dreams and nightmares. When dawn broke over Fulton Street the next morn-ing, we had forged a bond. After coffee from the latte shop on Fulton we agreed I would return soon.

I returned a few days later, on my way back from Oregon, and he introduced me to one of his lawyers, Sheri Falco. She was working at his Montgomery Street office, and provided me with a copy of her file. This file wasn't complete, I soon discovered. It lacked the court documents showing that Katie Diemer, local counsel in San Jose, had missed a cru-cial deadline, putting the case a hair's breadth away from final dismissal, and was now trying to get out of the case. Sheri was also trying to get out of the case, because Gary's litigation financiers had actually sued her, she said, although she didn't have a copy of the lawsuit. Gary wanted to be sure that I wasn't going to back away from the case if I were sued, and I assured him that first of all I would avoid the missteps that had led to the current representation problems, and second, since any such suit would be meritless, it would not affect my commitment to the case. Subsequently, when Cohen sued me, I lived up to this promise.

After another late night session of questioning and case strategy, Gary popped his proposal. Fifteen percent of Sex.Com in exchange for full-time work on the case. I explained to him that fifteen percent sounded great, but full -time was not an option, and I had to be paid hourly for my work. Considering the minimum I could take and still keep afloat with this monster case, I suggested fifteen percent plus $100 per hour and expenses. Gary took it under advisement and made an appointment for us to have a breakfast meeting the next day with his personal attorney, Steve Sherman.

The next morning at breakfast Steve was polite, but did not welcome my appearance on the scene. He had been presiding over the demise of the case for some time now, and had plans for the future. As I later learned, he had monitored the breakdown in communications that lead to Katie Diemer's inaction on the case. He knew that the breakdown in relations between Gary and the two pornography financiers lay at the root of the problem. He was ready to hand the seat that Katie wanted to vacate to some lawyer friends of his, and expected to broker the relations between Gary and new counsel. My appearance wasn't likely to put any money in his pocket, or the pockets of his friends. So why would he like me?

Steve is an equivocator. He just can't say "yes!" To him every cup is potentially a sieve, and he thinks lawyering means pointing out the many routes to failure. He did not want Gary to hire me, but had no answers for Gary's problems. So, squinting and shaking his head to communicate incomprehension, he suggested to Gary that it seemed unlikely a person in my position could contribute anything to the case. From Ojai? That was a long way from the courthouse. From Oregon? What was that about? Oh, Robin Kaufer was my UCLA chum. Ah, that explained it.

I began my assault on Steve's authority by trotting out my credentials. Top 25% at UCLA Law, 1986; worked for the mega-firm Morgan, Lewis & Bockius for my first two years; then did trademark litigation for Louis-

Vuitton at the L.A. office of the New York city firm of Reboul, McMurray, Hewitt, Maynard & Kristol. My last three years in L.A., I did plaintiff trial work at Mazursky, Schwartz & Angelo, a personal injury and insurance bad faith powerhouse with three famous partners who all had multi-million dollar verdicts to their credit. Admitted in both California and Oregon, I'd tried around sixty cases, chalking up wins in both states. I'd worked as a Deputy DA in Oregon, and was the first appointed member on the local Federal criminal defense panel. My civil caseload was all business litigation, and I was very excited about the Internet as an emerging area of practice.

Steve's resistance was a godsend. Gary could see Steve couldn't see the gameboard or the pieces, and worse yet, lacked the will to fight. I un-holstered my best sardonic attitude to attack Sherman's naysaying. This was just a matter of modeling Gary's style of putting the other guy on the defensive with pointed questions. Gary loved it. Sherman staggered.

Questioned later under oath whether this had been a "breakfast meeting," Sherman had this answer: "I ate breakfast." True as to me: I stuck to coffee, but in those days Gary rarely let a full plate get away from a table, so I'm sure he ate my food. Who cared about eating, anyway? I was hungry for business, and was pretty sure I had sewed up an arrange-ment with Gary. Later that day, at the Montgomery Street office, he gave me a three-thousand dollar check to investigate the case, and tell him how I would win it.

CHAPTER THREE

THE STARLIGHT SPECIAL

ARRIVING BACK AT MY OJAI OFFICE, my ordeal began. Gary tested my mettle by forcing me to run a gauntlet of five to fifteen emails a day, with follow up telephone calls to discuss each matter. My reply skills won his approval and soon I was on my way to San Francisco for a third time, riding the Starlight Special, the slowest train in the United States. It runs up the coast of California and is clearly intended as a tourist ride. The trip gave me a chance to read Gary's deposition.

Depositions, as everyone undoubtedly knows by now, are where the witness is put under oath, in a lawyer's office, and questioned ad nauseum in order to extract concessions. In Gary's case, the second day of depositions had been abruptly terminated by his attorney after Gary committed several verbal missteps. I understood why Gary did not want to resume his deposition.

On the good side, it was clear Steve Cohen had stolen Sex.Com. What Gary testified to, and turned out to be the gospel truth, was the following:

- He was an Internet pioneer, with a degree in engineering from Northwestern and an MBA from Stanford.

- On May 9, 1994, using the Internet and certified mail, he registered the domain name Sex.com in the name of "Online Classifieds, Inc.," a business name Gary was using at the time, without ever incorporating. Gary paid zero dollars for the privilege of registering the name.

- His business plans never got farther than one page of doodles, and he never created a website to use Sex.Com. He may have sent email a couple of times through Sex.Com, just to test and see if it was working.

- Shortly after October 17, 1995, Kremen discovered that the registration to Sex.Com was no longer his, when a friend told him that the WhoIs database did not indicate that he was the owner.

- Gary checked the WhoIs himself, and discovered the fateful news. Sex.Com was now registered to Sporting Houses Management Corporation, a Nevada corporation, whose registered agent was Stephen Michael Cohen.

- Further inquiries to the domain name registrar, Network Solutions, Inc., ("NSI") led to further unpleasant discoveries.

- NSI sent Gary's lawyer a copy of a letter on Online Classifieds, Inc. stationary, authorizing NSI to transfer the domain name to someone named Steve Cohen. But it was not the real company stationery, which had a custom logo and a different typestyle.

- Strangest of all, the letter was signed by "Sharon Dimmick, President of Online Classifieds, Inc.," one of Gary's former roommates, who had never been employed by Online Classifieds, Inc. in any capacity. Further, Dimmick's first name was misspelled. She spelled it "Sharyn."

Riding in the Starlight Express, which is so named because you coast into San Francisco at about 25 mph, sipping on the sun setting over the ocean waves as the hours drift away, I felt optimistic. But I also felt a twinge of fear. Assuming Gary's story to be true, Cohen was one of the most brazen people in the world. He was a forger, a liar, and as Gary had repeatedly emphasized to me, a convicted federal felon with a degree in bankruptcy fraud and attorney impersonation. I'd already seen Bob Dorband's paperwork, and it was formidable. I had a fight on my hands, and not with any ordinary foe.

ONLINE CLASSIFIEDS, INC.
(FOR YOUR ONLINE AD'S)
242 COLE STREET
SAN FRANCISCO, CA 94117

October 15, 1995

Stephen Cohen
1261 North Lakeview Drive
Suite J-825
Anaheim, CA 92807

                    Re: SEX.COM

Dear Mr. Cohen:

Per our numerous conversations, we understand that you have been using sex.com on your French Connections BBS since 1979 and now you want to use sex.com as a domain name on the internet. Our corporation is the owner of sex.com as it relates to the internet.

At one time, we employed Gary Kremen who was hired for the express purpose of setting up our system. We allowed Mr. Kremen to be our administrative and technical contact with the internet, because of his vast experience with computers and their connections to the internet.

Subsequently, we were forced to dismiss Mr. Kremen. At no time, was Mr. Kremen ever a stockholder, officer, nor a director of our corporation and as such, Mr. Kremen has no rights, titles or interest in our domain name. Further, the internet shows that sex.com is listed in our corporation and not in Mr. Kremen's personal name. In fact, Mr. Kremen is the president of a different and unrelated corporation called Electric Classifieds, which is located at 340 Brandon Street in San Francisco, California. Further, Mr. Kremen's corporation owns match.com which is listed with the internet registration.

We never got around to changing our administrative contact with the internet registration and now our Board of directors has decided to abandon the domain name sex.com.

Because we do not have a direct connection to the internet, we request that you notify the internet registration on our behalf, to delete our domain name sex.com. Further, we have no objections to your use of the domain name sex.com and this letter shall serve as our authorization to the internet registration to transfer sex.com to your corporation.

Sincerely,

Sharon Dimmick
Sharon Dimmick, President

11

CHAPTER FOUR

WITH FRIENDS LIKE THESE...

IN ADDITION TO SHERI FALCO, GARY HAD TWO BIG-TIME LAWYERS working on his case — Katie Diemer of Campeau & Thomas, a San Jose firm, and Joel Dichter of New York City. You would think three lawyers would be enough, but Gary had a problem. None of them were doing a damn thing.

The case had been filed in June, 1998, with legal fees being paid by two Internet pornography magnates, Seth Warshavsky and Ron Levy. Warshavsky, now a fugitive, was famous for putting Pamela Lee Anderson's sexual adventures before the eyes of millions, and Ron Levy is the owner of CyberErotica, a large Internet porn site. Gary had agreed that if Seth and Ron paid the cost of suing Cohen, that all three would jointly own the domain name after victory. Seth and Ron had outbid famous porn loudmouth Serge Birbrair for this privilege. The agreement became well-known in the porn industry as a result of postings on the infamous LukeFord.com website. Ford wrote that Gary was a "big dummy," a quote from Gary's own video testimony, which Ford viewed thanks to Cohen. Gary had called himself a "big dummy" when asked whether he was known by any other names besides "Gary Kremen." Gary turned a simple question about aliases into an opportunity for self-deprecating humor. Which Luke turned into an admission of stupidity. It takes a journalist. Everyone in "the industry" read Ford's website in those days, so everyone knew about the agreement. The problem was, said Gary, Levy and Warshavsky hadn't been paying the bills, and the lawyers weren't doing any work.

The case had started out well enough. Sheri Falco got a signed affidavit from Sharyn Dimmick stating under oath that she had nothing to do with Online Classified's letter to NSI, and hadn't signed it. Sheri also confirmed with Dimmick what Gary had said about their "relationship." There never was one. Kremen had rented a room in Dimmick's rent-controlled apartment at 252 Cole Street, the two had never gotten along, and Gary had moved out. Indeed, as later investigation would show, Dimmick was not even living at 252 Cole Street on October 15, 1995, the date of the forged letter.

Then Joel Dichter decided to do a strange thing. Apparently he believed that because the Sex.Com registration was in the name of Online Classifieds, Inc., the company should be a plaintiff in the lawsuit. One problem only—there was no such company, because Gary had never incorporated.

So, before filing the lawsuit, Dichter created Online Classifieds, Inc., a Delaware corporation, because there was already an Online Classifieds, Inc. registered in California. I wouldn't necessarily disapprove of that strategy, if you would just do one additional thing—have Gary assign his ownership of Sex.Com to Online Classifieds, Inc. It's nothing new for an individual to acquire property for the benefit of a corporation that they intend to create, and then later to give the property to the corporation after it is formed. This is called "assigning the rights," and it would have made the new Online Classifieds, Inc. the owner of Sex.Com by either of two directions—owning it directly based upon the registration, or owning it through Gary Kremen based upon the assignment. Dichter didn't do this.

On July 10, 1998, Gary's lawyers filed his original complaint, naming Online Classifieds, Inc., a Delaware corporation as a co-plaintiff, along with Gary Kremen. Cohen was on the mistake like a hawk. He knew how to search corporate databases. He knew Online Classifieds, had not been incorporated anywhere at the time of the original registration. He got the Delaware incorporation documents to prove it.

Cohen's lawyer, Bob Dorband, filed a motion to dismiss Online Classifieds, Inc. from the lawsuit on the grounds that it didn't even exist when Gary registered Sex.Com. Gary had no assignment to present in response to this argument; accordingly, Judge Ware ruled that Online Classifieds, Inc. was not the "real party in interest," and had "no standing" to sue Cohen. And Dichter stood there looking like Wile E. Coyote from the Roadrunner cartoons—still holding his exploded stick of dynamite, while Cohen disappeared around the bend with a final "Beep-Beep!"

The Online Classified, Inc. issue created more problems later, at Gary's deposition. According to the correspondence I've read, Gary failed to meet with his lawyer to prepare for his deposition on several occasions. Therefore, no one had explained to him the strategy that had led to the creation of Online Classifieds, Inc., or if they had, he couldn't remember it. Since Online Classifieds, Inc. had been dismissed from the lawsuit on the grounds that it had no standing, it was essential to stick with the "no assignment" story. Nevertheless, on the second day of his deposition Gary testified that he had in fact assigned the rights to Sex. Com to Online Classifieds, Inc., a Delaware corporation. By this blunder, Gary put himself on a spot that the judge had already declared a dead zone. I'm sure at that moment Dorband literally thought, "Checkmate."

What Gary was thinking at that moment is one of life's unanswered mysteries. As a lawyer once said in a luncheon during my early years: "If your client is just not getting it in deposition, and the answers are killing you, as a last resort you can always take your cigarette lighter and discreetly set his chair on fire." I'm sure that when Gary testified he had assigned Sex.Com to Online Classifieds, Inc., Katie Diemer would have been willing to soak him with lighter fluid and ignite him with her Bic, if necessary. As it was, she hustled him out of the room, got him back in long enough to say he didn't understand the meaning of "assignment," and adjourned the deposition in a flurry of acrimony. I bequeath to Katie my golden cigarette lighter, for in this, she did well.

After that encounter, Katie was shell-shocked. When we talked on the telephone, she had little confidence in the case. Her early correspondence with Dichter had expressed great confidence she would achieve a swift victory, but a series of reversals had attended her efforts. Judge Ware had dismissed Online Classifieds, Inc., and additionally, had dismissed Gary's claims for fraud, racketeering and unfair competition. The forged letter wasn't a fraud, Judge Ware ruled, because Cohen hadn't used it to deceive *Gary*. Even though Cohen was a convicted felon, and what Gary had alleged was a theft, this was not "racketeering" within the meaning of the statute. Finally, the theft of the domain name wasn't an act of "unfair business competition" because it hadn't caused any injury to "consumers." These were important claims. Katie's head must have been spinning.

Past experience told me that Katie was trying to convince herself that the client's lawsuit was worthless, and thus if the case were dismissed, it would cause no real loss to Gary. This is a common syndrome among attorneys who are tiring of a difficult case, since the law provides that even if a lawyer commits malpractice, the client must still prove that competent representation would have put money in their pocket. Katie was clearly trying to convince herself that even if Gary had hired Daniel Webster, Clarence Darrow, Gerry Spence and Johnny Cochran, he would never have recovered Sex.Com.

The waiting room in hell is papered with documents that lawyers forgot to file. Most commonly seen among them is the fabled "Opposition to Motion to Dismiss." On November 12, 1998, Cohen filed a Motion to Dismiss Gary's second amended complaint. When it landed on Katie Diemer's desk, she went missing. She never filed an opposition. Not filing opposition to a motion to dismiss is roughly the same thing as walking to the center of the ring, hands down, eyes closed, waiting for the knockout punch. When I finally got my hands on the motion to dismiss, and learned what Katie hadn't done, I pointed out to Gary that he was about to be knocked out. Gary started pounding the table, demanding to know why an opposition had not been filed. As a result, Katie asked the judge for more time to file an opposition to the motion to dismiss.

I have seen some good excuses for not filing papers on time, but Katie Diemer's absolutely takes the cake. Her motion for more time to respond to Cohen's motion to dismiss said that she had negotiated an extension of time with Bob Dorband, or thought she had, but couldn't remember for sure because she had had a hockey accident, and had memory problems. Judge Ware, a kindly and understanding jurist who overlooks the foibles of attorneys as part of his general procedure, granted the extension. That gave Katie until July 12, 1999 to file an opposition to that dreaded motion to dismiss the second amended complaint. Through that brief window of time, daylight shone for me.

CHAPTER FIVE

WHAT MORAL HIGH GROUND?

At THAT BREAKFAST MEETING WITH STEVE SHERMAN, one of my pointed questions was whether we had seized the "moral high ground" in the case. Steve seemed perplexed. His face twisted into a mask of near disgust. "What moral high ground?" said Steve, "This is pornography!" He seemed revolted by the perverse nature of the question. I learned something there. Gary's lawyers were weak because they were apologizing for the case. They were ashamed of their product. They didn't want to be seen in public with Sex.Com. I pointed out to Steve, in California-speak, that theft was immoral: "Like, uh, Thou Shalt Not Steal?" Steve rolled his eyes.

But besides the fact that Cohen was a thief, there was a far more valuable moral high ground to seize. In 1999, Gary was not, and had never been, a pornographer. It was entirely unfair for Gary to be tarred with the porno-brush simply because Cohen had chosen to make Sex.Com the cornerstone of international online sex sales. When I met him, Gary was a bit ashamed of the case. He preferred to make money in regular business. He was a business consultant and a new technology engineer. He'd been written up in Forbes magazine and other publications as a tech visionary. He wanted to sit down with venture capitalists and corporate attorneys to craft billion-dollar deals. He didn't want to have to explain that on one day in May, 1994, his dirty little mind had told him to register Sex.Com. More important, he didn't want to talk about how he was willing to fight to regain control of the name, presumably to get his hands on all that porn revenue.

Cohen, of course, had no compunction about being the king of sleaze. Covered in slime, he extended the warm hand of greeting to Gary—"Come," he seemed to invite, "join me in the mud to fight for the Queen of Sleaze." Cohen was confident that Gary would eventually slink away, like a john whose wallet is stolen by a prostitute. And this, I learned, is the great achievement of a good confidence man—his victims go quietly to avoid humiliation. We had to escape the stigma that attached to sex itself, which made Gary and Cohen look, as I told Steve and Gary, like

16

"two junkies fighting over a dime bag." Your average judge or juror might throw up his hands and just say, "Who cares? It'll kill you both!" Gary had to get out of the business of slandering himself by the very act of pursuing the lawsuit.

Having read Gary's deposition carefully, I knew there was no testimony about how Gary would have developed the site if Cohen hadn't stolen the name. During two days of depositions Cohen and NSI's lawyers never asked Gary what he would have done with the site. I assume this was because they thought just like Steve Sherman—of course Gary would have turned the site into a porn portal. There were no documents indicating that Gary intended to create a porn site. Attached as an exhibit to Gary's deposition there was just one scribbled page of a "business plan" in Gary's typical scrawl, with references to "sex workers" and other vague terms on it. I read those deposition transcripts carefully, and in the end I was comfortable—my plan could proceed without risk of contradiction.

We were free to announce to the world what was obviously the case, but everyone had overlooked—that Gary Kremen, the Stanford MBA and Internet visionary, the originator of "Match.Com," the world's largest matchmaking site, would have developed Sex.Com as a "public health, woman-friendly site" à la "Dr. Ruth" or "Dr.Koop.Com." And when that fetched a belly laugh, we hit 'em with the backup punch—*don't laugh*: it would have made good business sense, because instead of harvesting a few million porn-dollars, Gary would have developed a public company and harvested hundreds of millions of dollars. In mid-1999, this argument was believable. Hell, I believed it. And Gary loved wearing his new white hat.

CHAPTER SIX

THE IMPORTANCE OF BEING FIRST IN LINE

THE CORNERSTONE OF GARY'S CLAIM TO OWNERSHIP OF SEX.COM was a simple principle known to every schoolchild—he was first in line. This principle is universally used to distribute benefits in a civilized society, and NSI had used it to distribute domains. If being first in line meant nothing, or if it could be overridden by theft, we were on the way to anarchy. Well aware of its importance, judges have boiled it down to a pithy aphorism—"First in time, first in right." The principle had often been applied to real estate and water rights, as in *Yuba River Power Company*, where the California Supreme Court held that the first person to register a water right owned the right, over and against a claim jumper who dug a ditch upstream from the original claimant's point of diversion. *Yuba River* was an old case, though, dating back to the early days of California law, and no court anywhere had applied its holding to the registration of Internet domains, so the argument was far from certain to prevail. Still, as principles go, it was among the most solid, and I was determined to stake the case on it. Our entire system of resource allocations was built on it, so whenever anyone asked me why Gary should win the case, I had my answer ready—he was first in line.

Katie Diemer had filed three complaints, and seen all three dismissed. She had adequately articulated Gary's status as the first to register, but that alone was insufficient. We had to argue that by being "first in time," Gary had become "first in right," to hold the registration of Sex. Com. A magic word was required, and that magic word was "property." Being first in line had given Gary property rights in Sex.Com, something that Katie's complaints had never specifically alleged, even though the newspapers were daily announcing domains selling for large amounts of money. Wallstreet.Com had sold for $1 Million, and Business.Com for $7.5 Million.

This part of the argument was well supported by California law, that defines property as "everything capable of being owned." Sex.Com was obviously capable of being owned, and the owner had the power to con-

18

trol the most popular webpage on the Net. The way I saw it, Sex.Com was a property magnet, drawing in other pieces of property in the form of credit card subscriptions to Internet pornography, bringing in $24.95/month. Sex.Com was a node, an in-drawing spiral galaxy of credit transactions generating a white hole of cash that was gushing into Cohen's pockets. In June 1999, Cohen put out a press release that stated:

> "Sex.Com boasts over 9-Million members who pay $24.95 per month for access to the world's largest sex-related Internet site, which receives more than 146-Million unique 'hits' daily. Advertisers on the 1,000-page-deep porn site pay up to 1.5 Million monthly to display their banners. For premium ad space, there is a waiting list of over one year."

You do the math. That's a lot of money for a country boy. The way I saw it, all of those credit card transactions were Gary's property. It's an old principle in property law that property owners hold not just the rights to the property itself, but all "appurtenant" rights. In other words, you don't just own the cow, you have a right to the milk. So if property is wrongfully taken, the owners should receive "restitution" of everything that was lost—not just the cow, but all of the milk the thief got from her while they were deprived of possession. Why? Because any other rule would encourage people to steal, by allowing them to keep all the benefits produced during the time they held the property unlawfully.

This theory of restitution had not been emphasized in the prior complaints. However, it was very clear that under the California Unfair Business Practices Act, the court could order restitution of money wrongfully obtained.

Restitution was essential to Gary's case, because it would have been impossible to show that Gary would have made anywhere near the money that Cohen made from operating Sex.Com. Cohen, after all, was a criminal, familiar with the adult industry and its profit potential. He knew the players, didn't take crap from anyone, and made money with the ruthless effectiveness of a con man who wouldn't know regret if it ran over him in the street. Cohen allowed some of the hardest core pornography to be shown on Sex.Com without even a cursory check to determine whether the user was an adult.

The theory of restitution says that if you let the people keep the profit they make from using stolen property, it will encourage people to steal, because they will get the value of the property for as long as they are able to hold on to it. To explain this better, I had a story. When I was a kid living in Valencia, Spain one summer, some guys stole the bus that ran from town to the beach. They operated the bus all day long, and collected all the fares. At the end of the day they were arrested. Do you think the judge just gave the bus back to the bus company and let the thieves keep the fares they collected? Of course not. The bus company owned the bus and the fares.

Pushing the property angle improved our claim against NSI. If Sex. Com was property, and Gary was the owner by virtue of being the first to register the domain name, then NSI should have some obligation to Gary to protect his property from being transferred to another person without his permission. Just as there had been a land rush on the American frontier, there had been a land rush in cyberspace. Gary had been an early prospector, who identified a valuable claim and staked it. NSI had been hired by the government to serve as the land office in cyberspace. When Gary recorded his registration, NSI assumed a duty to dispose of that property only according to his wishes, because he had sole authority over it as the owner.

These rules of law go back a long ways. It is well established that if you leave personal property with someone to take care of, such as a horse or a saddle, they have a duty to take care of it for you. This makes you the "bailor," and the person receiving your property the "bailee." When someone performs a bailment for pay, that is called a "bailment for consideration," and if the bailee mistakenly gives the property to the wrong person, they are responsible for conversion of the property. Liability for conversion is pretty much absolute. According to California case law, a parking lot attendant that gave a parked car back to a passenger to drive was responsible for conversion when the passenger crashed the car. It was no defense for the parking lot that the attendant was perhaps reasonable in releasing the car to the passenger. The terms of the bailment were that it should only be released to the person who deposited the car and had the ticket. The passenger did not have the ticket.

Significantly, in our case, neither did Cohen. NSI had granted Cohen authority that only Gary had. Gary created the domain name by thinking it up, deposited it with NSI for safekeeping by registering it, and as the administrative contact, was the only person with a right to change the registration.

Nevertheless, Katie had not pled a claim for conversion against NSI. Perhaps she thought that in order to be liable for conversion, NSI had to show some intent to convert the property, or some desire to join with Cohen's wrongful intent. Lawyers unfamiliar with the law of conversion are apt to make this mistake, but I had tried a case in Portland a few years earlier in which my clients were charged with conversion, and I knew it to be a claim that is deadly in its simplicity. The absence of wrongful intent is no defense if the property was someone else's, and it was taken without authority.

NSI had been well aware of the dangers that lay down the path if they ever admitted that domain names were property. NSI having been in the Internet business a lot longer than I, had firmly taken the position that domain names are not property. In a series of judicial decisions, NSI had gotten judges to agree that domain names were more like toll-free telephone numbers, which could also be arranged to read "1-800-Sue-Them." Users of 800-numbers had lost the battle to establish 800 numbers as property long ago, and NSI had been pushing the analogy ever since. NSI suffered a brief setback when a Virginia judge found that domain names could be seized by creditors to satisfy a money judgment. However, a year later the Virginia Supreme Court reversed the decision, finding a domain name to be more like a telephone number than an item of personal property. Strangely enough, in mid-2000, NSI began appropriating and auctioning off the domain names of registrants who had failed to pay their registration fees. This seemed an awful lot like seizing property to satisfy a debt, but who am I to judge?

Indeed, it would be for Judge Ware to decide, and I was not excited by the prospect of going toe-to-toe with NSI over the property issue. Even as news stories heated up the environment with stories about domain names selling for five and six figures, I was acutely aware that the temperature in the courthouse was a few degrees lower.

I hit the books hard for days on end, digging through case law for rulings that would help us out. I found a few. In addition to *Yuba River* establishing a property interest in being the first to register a water right, there was *Kalitta Flying Services*, that determined engineering drawings were property subject to conversion. And there was *Thrifty-Tel v. Bezenek*, a case the judges grappled with the interface of technology and law in a case that could only come out of California.

Thrifty-Tel was a phone company that sued two kids who had tried to gain free long-distance access by staging a brute force attack—firing huge numbers of random passwords–at Thrifty-Tel's computer. The clumsy hack slowed the long distance system down considerably, which Thrifty-Tel alleged as damages in a suit for trespass. On appeal, a verdict for Thrifty-Tell on conversion was upheld, and the court explained that the cyberattack was a "trespass to chattels," for which damages could be awarded. The kids had trespassed because each random number was a physical thing, an electron packet, trespassing on Thrifty-Tel's computer. Since the computer was an item of personal property, not a parcel of real estate, what had happened was actually a "trespass to chattels." The last time I heard about chattels was in the *Taming of the Shrew* by Shakespeare, when the husband tells his unruly wife that she is but a chattel. A more concrete example of trespass to chattels would be someone borrowing and returning a delivery-man's bicycle. But here was the California appellate court, exhuming this ancient cause of action out of dusty books that no one had opened in a long time.

The court had gone back to the future to find a cybertort to fit the need of the day. Further research showed that trespass to chattels had turned out to be a handy cybertort. Intel deployed it successfully to prevent a disgruntled former employee from spamming Intel workers with negative information about the company. Judge Whyte in the San Jose courthouse had ruled in Intel's favor in that case.

I agreed with the court's conclusion in *Thrifty-Tel v. Bezenek* that random numbers are really packets of electrons, and that bombarding someone's computer system is a physical invasion. I questioned Gary about how the Internet worked, forcing him to provide facts about the engineering and architecture of the system. Again and again I looked at the maps of the domain name servers, the long lines making a net over the globe, imagining the flows of communication as concrete data packets moving through telephone wires, fiber optic cables, Cisco routers, Sun servers, and into the offices, dens and garages of the world. I saw the faces of all those net-heads out there, basking in the monitor's glow as they journeyed through cyberspace, the artificial world that we had created.

I've been reading science fiction since I was a kid, and still have my original paperback copy of William Gibson's *Neuromancer*, where the word "cyberspace" first appeared in print. I knew that what happened to Sex.Com in this lawsuit was going to make a mark on the face of the Internet. Given the way that porn had taken to the Net, Sex.Com was obviously the world's most valuable Internet domain name. Since value is a characteristic of property, the more valuable something is, arguably, the more likely it is to become property. Being the most valuable domain, Sex.Com presented the best-case scenario for a judicial finding that domain names are in fact property. The eyes of the world would be upon this case. Indeed, they already were.

The case had garnered major tech-media attention when Wired.Com published Craig Bicknell's *The Sordid Saga of Sex.Com* just before Gary and I met. The article was favorable to Gary's position, while expressing appropriate skepticism for what looked like a long shot. We wanted to maintain that buzz, and a good way to get more publicity about a lawsuit is to send copies of the complaint to reporters. So you want the complaint to be interesting, lively, informative, hell, well-written! Under California law, anything you say in a complaint is absolutely privileged, which means it cannot be the basis for a defamation lawsuit, even if absolutely false. So your complaint can be the basis of a news article about all the claims you have alleged. The complaint told the story of the origin of the Internet itself, Cohen's criminality, his use of the forged letter to steal Sex.Com, and the fabulous wealth that was now flowing his way as the result of the theft. Following the lead established by *Thrifty-Tel v. Beznick*, I concretized everything. I described all of the electronic credit card transactions that were happening via Sex.Com as "data packets" that were appurtenant property of Sex.Com. I emphasized the relationship, as it were, between the milk and the cow.

I charged NSI with conversion on two grounds: first, that NSI was the bailee of Sex.Com for the benefit of Kremen, the bailor. Second, I alleged that NSI and Cohen had conspired to convert the Sex.Com domain name. This second allegation had a reasonable basis in fact, because Cohen had been quoted as saying that he had a "girlfriend at NSI," who could get him any domain name he wanted. Gary had heard this from Lee Fuller, an adult website operator who had a cubicle next to Cohen's at Midcom Corporation in 1995, when Cohen faxed the forged letter to NSI.

To strengthen our claims against Cohen, I built up the California Unfair Business Practices claim. This claim arises under California Business & Professions Code § 17200, a mainstay of California business tort law. This is a very broad statute that basically makes it unlawful to do anything unlawful. I'm not kidding. If you can find anything else unlawful that a defendant did, in a business context, you can probably also make a claim under California Business & Professions Code § 17200. And under that law, the court can grant you all kinds of fantastic relief. The court can order the disgorgement of unlawful profits. The court can grant attorney's fees, and punitive damages. The only thing the court can't give you is a jury trial on that claim. But that's a small price to pay for all the other benefits.

Unfortunately, Cohen had scored an effective hit against the Unfair Business Practices claim, when he convinced Judge Ware that Gary had to allege some sort of injury to "consumers" in order to state an Unfair Business Practices claim. This was simply incorrect, but Katie had failed to counter it in her opposition to the motion to dismiss, and the judge had gone along with Dorband's argument, dismissing the claim. I didn't want to fly straight back through the opposition of the court's prior ruling, and thus decided I had to allege some consumer injury resulting from Cohen's operation of Sex.Com. So, I took a look at the Sex.Com site, clicked on the banners found there, and learned what I needed to know. Like other porn operators, the advertisers on Cohen's site were engaging in mousetrapping, which causes a single click on the banner to trigger a sneaky bit of coding that commandeers your browser and funnels you into an endless loop of advertising banners from which there is no exit except to shut off your computer. After a mousetrapping session, your hard-drive needs a shower, and it is usually a good idea to delete all the temporary Internet files and reboot. You should run one of those pop-up purging programs, so that no innocent member of your family will be exposed to graphic sexual content. That sounded like consumer injury to me. Since it was common knowledge that the pornography site operators would often elicit and resell information such as birthdates, email addresses and credit information, I alleged this as a source of consumer injury. Finally, I alleged that Cohen was inflating advertising rates at Sex.Com by circulating inflated traffic figures via press releases. This qualified as consumer injury, because pornography sites are consumers of advertising.

I also gave the breach of contract claim against NSI an injection of steroids. This claim looked anemic, because the only documents that you could call a contract were the email registration from Gary and his certified mailing of the printout. Gary hadn't paid to register Sex.Com, because registration was free. Any lawyer would look at it and say, "where's the consideration?" When talking contracts, consideration doesn't mean good manners, but rather Gary's payment of something having value. If you don't have to pay for your contractual rights, you don't get any. Consideration can be as little as "a peppercorn," but it must be there. In Gary's case, I'd found a peppercorn of value. Although Gary hadn't paid for the privilege of registering Sex.Com, he had surrendered personal information—his name, phone number, email and home address. He thus became one of the ever-increasing database of domain name registrants that NSI's initial public offering prospectus touted as a source of continuing value. Free registrations came swiftly to an end in mid-1995, and the registrants' payment of fees became part of a swelling juggernaut of financial benefit that converted NSI into a stock market darling on the strength of registration revenue alone.

When you write a complaint alleging unusual facts that don't fit the mold of past cases, you have to engage in imaginative pleading. To get past the complaint stage, you must recite the legal formula and confidently assert the things you hope to prove. It takes a lot of legal research and careful writing. In the four days before the filing, I spent about fourteen hours a day at the USF law library, leaning over my laptop, smelting down ideas and forging them into arguments. Pounding facts and law together, I felt like Vulcan hammering in his forge, tempering and sharpening his weapons. An argument is a pointy thing, and the point always goes toward your enemy. The sharpness of the point is comforting to him who holds the spear.

The third amended complaint ran to 43 pages. As it developed, I shared the progress with Gary. We talked over the cell phone during the day, and back at his apartment we'd go over revisions in the evening. You can only convince a client that you are sincere by actually doing the job, and I was doing it. My only problem was that my 43 page opus kept needing further revisions. The time to get the final filing together was fast approaching. And computers can always tell when you're nervous, can't they?

CHAPTER SEVEN

COMING IN UNDER THE RADAR

Now, ALL OF THE TIME THAT I HAD BEEN WORKING on this third amended complaint, and thinking all these high falutin' legal thoughts, I had not been Gary's attorney of record in the case. Katie Diemer, Sheri Falco, and Joel Dichter remained in position. Strictly speaking, Gary Kremen wasn't supposed to be filing anything but an opposition to Cohen's pending motion to dismiss. Judge Ware had told Katie Diemer that if she wanted to file a third amended complaint, she would have to give him a copy of it so he could look at it, according to the "local rule," and approve it for filing.

When faced with a motion to dismiss that has a serious likelihood of final success, you really need to come up with a good amended complaint. It's less work than writing an extensive argument, and as a practical matter, motions to dismiss are often granted "in part," so you end up having to "re-plead" your complaint anyway. So why not just write it and make the other lawyer's arguments irrelevant? Besides, I didn't want to defend Katie's complaint, which didn't tell much of a story and omitted all mention of my precious "data packets" of property. So I focused all my energies on submitting the "proposed" third amended complaint to Judge Ware. Of course, I still needed to file at least a nominal opposition to the motion to dismiss, and also an "association of counsel," to establish my official role as "counsel of record," before attempting to file any papers at all. I had allotted a small amount of time to prepare those in a pro forma fashion after I got done drafting the Third Amended Complaint.

So there I was, in Gary's living room, working on my laptop, and printing out legal documents on a cheap HP inkjet printer. I got the association of counsel cranked out, but as I was trying to hack out the opposition to the motion to dismiss, my poor old laptop was breathing really hard. Characters were taking seconds to appear on the screen, and finally it just froze up, swallowing the document into the void. Bob Deschl, Gary's pizza delivery man and computer jack of all trades, tried heroically to resuscitate it, but it was no use. I had cut it too close, and it was time for me to jump in my car, fight my way through traffic from San Francisco to San Jose, and file what I had prepared. And I had to leave early to pick up my daughter, who was arriving at the San Jose train station that same afternoon.

I also wanted to drop by and leave copies of everything with Katie Diemer, whose office was just a few blocks from the federal courthouse, and mooch a few photocopies off her while I was at it, since I hadn't had time to make any. Now this was an interesting situation. I hadn't talked to Katie in weeks. She'd been ordered by the court to file an opposition on or before July 12, 1999. Something in my bones told me she was just sitting on her butt, doing nothing. If that was the case, I wanted to catch her at it, and it wouldn't be bad to have a witness. Since Ana's train was arriving at 2:30 p.m., she could be that witness. It seemed like the timing would all work out, since the courthouse closed at 4:00 p.m.

I picked up Ana, right on schedule, and headed over to Katie's office, a big gold cube on Santa Clara, the main drag in San Jose. The receptionist and the secretary were very nice, and sat us down in the conference room. We thought Katie was going to come walking in any minute, but then a funny thing happened. She called me on my cell phone. So there I am, sitting in Katie's conference room, talking with her on my cell phone while she is sitting in her office. Finally, after a few minutes I tell her, "I'm sitting here in your conference room." She sounded like I had just put my hands in a place where they shouldn't be. Her voice went up an octave, "You're in my office?!" I explained to her that yes, I was, and that I was going to file some documents in the case. After a few more minutes of talking, Katie declared that it was silly for us to be talking like this, and I invited her to come down and meet me in her conference room.

When things like this happen, you're always glad there's someone around to talk to about it later. You can check your impressions against theirs, and in this case, it was fun to get Ana's impressions of Katie Diemer, which confirmed my own. Katie presented as a tall, rather imposing woman in a dark, tightly contained suit that was not entirely unflattering. A frizzy explosion of flaxen hair reaching to below the shoulders. A slightly puffy face with a severe expression covering over what seemed to be a lot of nervousness.

I gave her the documents and let her know what I was doing. Clearly, it wasn't the way you usually do things. When a client replaces his lawyers, you almost always do it by filing an agreement in writing between the client, the outgoing lawyer, and the incoming lawyer, called a "substitution of attorney." But in this case Katie had told Judge Ware that she was "unable to act" because of a "conflict of interest" existing between Gary Kremen and other people whose names she did not mention. These were of course Ron Levy and Seth Warshavsky, and she told the judge that she would tell him whatever more he needed to know in a secret, *"in camera"* hearing that Cohen's lawyers would not be allowed to attend. Judge Ware hadn't accepted Katie's offer to discuss the grisly details of the conflict of interest, however, instead ordering her to file an opposition. Which Katie was not doing. She was going to stand on her claim that she "could not act" and watch the case die. Gary was therefore justified in doing whatever was needed to break the logjam, including hiring a stealth-attorney to flip a filing over the transom at the last possible moment. So I had no apologies for my presence.

Katie admitted she had no opposition to the motion to dismiss prepared. Only I, and the papers spread out on the conference table before me, could prevent Gary from losing Sex.Com forever, from having the gem slip through his fingers and down into the gutter of the legal system, from which it could never be retrieved.

But Katie wasn't giving up. Did I know, she asked, who was running the litigation? Did I know about Seth Warshavsky and his company IEG? Did I know about the firm of Newman & Newman in Seattle, which represented Mr. Warshavsky? What I knew, I responded, was that none of these people was doing anything to keep the case from being dismissed, and I had to act. She told me that she had called Mr. Newman, and he was going to call back in just a few minutes. She asked me to please wait. It was 3:40 p.m., twenty minutes before the gates of hell were going to open up and swallow Gary's claim to Sex.Com. I told her I had to go. She told me that it was only ten minutes to the courthouse, and I should really wait to talk to Mr. Newman. I told her I couldn't. I got my copies from the secretary and headed over to the courthouse.

Once there, I was comforted by the sound of the clerk's stamping machine putting the beautiful purple ink on my paperwork, "Received for Filing, July 12, 1999." My baby was safe.

As we left the courthouse, it was closing. As we drove down the streets of San Jose a few minutes later, my cell phone rang. I had the pleasure of speaking with Derek Newman. Like Katie Diemer, he asked, "Do you know who is running this litigation?" My answer was simple, "I've always presumed it was Gary Kremen, the plaintiff." Derek responded that wasn't the whole story, and I said I understood that. But I wanted to end this interference, so I said "If you're telling me that Gary Kremen is not the plaintiff in this action, and that he is merely masquerading as the plaintiff pursuant to some sort of agreement in which an undisclosed entity is the real party in interest, then I want to know it right now, so I can advise the court of it, because I will not be a party to any kind of deception of the court." Our conversation ended a few moments later.

I had done it. I had wrested control of the case from the other attorneys. I had gotten past Steve Sherman's nay-saying, Gary's vacillating, and Katie Diemer's obstructionism. I enjoyed a warm glow of triumph.

It would have been great to split town right then, but I had to finish up that opposition to the motion to dismiss that I'd lost in my laptop crash. Ana and I spent the night in a Best Western, and the next morning, as early as I was able to stir myself, I started finishing up the opposition to the motion to dismiss. But since it was one day late, I also had to write a motion under Rule 6(b). I call these "motions to deem timely filed," because "deem" is a magical word that reminds the judge that when he says so, a late filing becomes timely. But the writing project took too long, and as going out for breakfast turned into checking out at noon, Ana's mood got grumpy. At age seventeen, hunger can attack ferociously, and as we left San Jose in the two-p.m. heat, I was apologizing for the litigation lifestyle and promising a great sushi dinner in Walnut Creek by way of atonement.

With the last of my paperwork filed, Ana and I were free to head for Oregon. It's a lovely feeling when you've done your work, and you can finally rest. Filing a complaint is an act of war. You have to work yourself up to it, and you know it's only the beginning of a lot of trouble that you're heading straight into for the hope of victory. I guess that's why you send armies forth with flags, banners, trumpets and beautiful maidens waving. After getting close to the action in Katie's office, Ana was jazzed on the intrigue that enveloped the case, so she was cheering me on eagerly.

As we poked along through the Silicon Valley traffic jam, we compared notes and listened to heavy metal teen angst tunes off the "American Werewolf in Paris" soundtrack, enjoying the sounds of rage and destruction, then switching over to the sweet sounds of Frank Black as we neared Walnut Creek. There, at Tokyo Lobby, our favorite sushi bar, we unwound with the natives, enjoying excellent sushi, multiple color TVs, and impeccably polite service from the very Japanese waitresses, in short, a heroic repast. Afterwards, we got lattes from the Starbucks across the street and resumed our course for Oregon. By midnight, we were back in the cool mountains, seeing the bright stars.

CHAPTER EIGHT

FORTUNE SMILES

THERE'S A USEFUL SAYING TO USE WITH CLIENTS when nothing is happening, but you believe that they will get justice some day in the distant future: "The wheels of the law grind slow, but they grind exceedingly fine." Perhaps it was Tulkinghorn, the old lawyer who ended up being murdered in Bleak House, who uttered this Dickensian phrase. In any event, you'll note that it's a long time from July 12, 1999, when the motion to file a third amended complaint was actually handed to the clerk in San Jose, and October 4, 1999, when Judge Ware finally ruled on the motion. During that time, I reversed course on my move to Southern California, and moved back to Oregon.

I had decided Sex.Com was the most important piece of legal business I was likely to stumble across, that Ventura County wasn't as hoppin' as I thought, and what the hell, if Bob Dorband lived in Oregon, it would all make sense in some weird way. After all, if Cohen had an Oregon lawyer, that must be a good thing, so Gary could have one, too. I got a space at 800 West 8th Street, upstairs from my old friend Peter Carini, a Southern Oregon criminal defense lawyer with New York style and a stellar trial record. The building was right across from the courthouse, and was owned by Lee Werdell and John Hanson, another couple of trial lawyers in the Oregon tradition. Typical Oregon legal maxims would be: Lay traps! Bushwhack! Win! Smile! Oregon trial lawyers can be inspiring companions.

If you want to wake up every morning and know that someone is going to be studying everything that you have done in order to find fault with it and accuse you of screwing up, you should definitely become a trial lawyer. This experience will become your daily fare. I don't know if other people will admit it, but I still experience fear when I see envelopes printed with my adversary's letterhead on them, or when I see alien paper coming through the fax machine. It's nasty. You know they don't mean you any good, they want to rip your heart out, decorate their den with your entrails, soak your grave with cheap whiskey, and dance all over it in hobnailed boots.

For a sole practitioner, there are additional problems. You have neither the prestige of being with a large firm nor their deep pockets. Some lawyers figure they can probably scare you away from the meat if they just growl loud enough. So the first stage when lawyers encounter each other is a little bit like the opening scene in *2001, A Space Odyssey*, where two types of apes face off at the watering hole, and the facial expressions get really nasty.

Bob Dorband has mastered watering hole etiquette. In person he is unflappable, pleasant and cool. On paper, his fangs show and drip. Frankly, he scared the bejeezus out of me with his first letter. Dorband's letter alleged a species of wrong that you have to be a lawyer to appreciate—he claimed that local rules required me to file a motion for reconsideration of the court's prior dismissal of the RICO claim before moving for leave to amend the complaint. My attempt to end-run the local rules, he claimed, was subject to monetary sanctions under Rule 11 of the Federal Rules of Civil Procedure. Today it's easy to laugh at Dorband's toxic pettifoggery, but back then I chose the safer expedient of sending him a conciliatory letter with a taste of steel, assuring him I was right on every issue, and had never been sanctioned so much as $1 in 13 years of practice, a record I intended to preserve.

My show of courtesy was strategic. I wanted to minimize the energy spent exchanging nasty letters, because arguing with other lawyers isn't the point of litigation. The point is to get favorable court decisions, one after the other, all the way to final victory.

The first favorable decision came on October 4, 1999. I drove to San Francisco and crashed at Gary's. The next morning Gary and I went to court in his car—yeah, the same old beater I had first seen in Carpinteria, still no stereo, still no paint job. We headed upstairs to Judge Ware's 4th floor courtroom. It's a nice courtroom, not too big, with a gallery that probably accommodates 60 people. We walked in, and the place was jammed. The gallery was stuffed, the jury box also filled. The judge had put us at the end of the calendar, so we would be the last attorneys to make oral argument. In a complex case, this is a signal that the judge wants to give the argument plenty of time, presumably because he's interested.

Being last to argue also gives you plenty of time to size up the judge. Does he listen? Does he question? Does he allow argument or cut it off?

I was immediately charmed. Judge Ware is a handsome and congenial man, with warm African features of mahogany color. His voice is gentle and respectful. He rarely barks, almost never contorts his features, and treats everyone with respect.

When Dorband and I rose to argue the case, the judge let us know who the spectators were. They were two classes of students he was teaching at the local law schools. He had distributed copies of our court papers to them as part of their study, and they were attending to get a little education in courtroom procedure. After we concluded with our arguments, the judge informed us, we would "go off the record," and the law students would be allowed to ask questions.

The formal argument was polite, and proceeded much as I had expected. Federal judges, when presented with a properly prepared motion to amend a complaint, are supposed to "interpret the rules liberally," so that "substantial justice can be done on the merits." In other words, plaintiffs shouldn't be cut off at the knees before they have an opportunity to present evidence to support their claim.

But Dorband had a good point. He had already won a motion to dismiss several important claims. Motions to dismiss are intended to "narrow the issues" to be explored in formal discovery, and to "simplify the case" before trial. This means that you should proceed from more claims to less, as the issues get eliminated. A plaintiff, some judges reason, shouldn't come into court with one theory of law, and when faced with motions to dismiss, respond with a sort of hydra defense, sprouting two claims for each one that is cut off. The judge had dismissed the racketeering claim, and Katie Diemer had acquiesced in that ruling, filing no racketeering claim in the second amended complaint; nevertheless, here we were alleging racketeering again. And there were other fun claims thrown in there, too. The new claim for conversion and conspiracy to convert against NSI. A claim for "slander of title" on the theory that Gary held title to Sex.Com and Cohen had slandered his title by claiming to be the true owner.

Throughout the argument, Dorband was fiercely eloquent, arguing for his "narrow the pleadings" approach, and suggesting directly and indirectly that Kremen was the real shyster here. Judge Ware took it all in stride. He questioned me gently, with a touch of humor, about why I had filed the racketeering claim again, after Diemer had allowed it to lapse.

Was I asking him to ignore precedent and permit the reallegation? I conceded that he would have to go against precedent, but that it was justified. He seemed pleased with my candor, granting the motion, except as to the racketeering claim.

Afterwards, the students asked a few questions. That was a touchy situation. How could we be off the record? Sure, the court stenographer wasn't writing this down, but the judge was hearing it all. And some of them had pointed questions. One young lady started talking about the statute of limitations, and I didn't feel at all comfortable with that. The novelty of the experience was disorienting. Dorband took refuge in talking about "hypothetical" facts, and the questioning ended quickly.

Fortune had smiled. The judge had delivered my baby. She was breathing, her eyes were bright, her cheeks were rosy. The fight for Sex. Com was on in earnest.

But that didn't mean Gary was happy. He felt cheated because Judge Ware had again rejected the racketeering claim. Gary couldn't understand how the "Racketeer Influenced and Corrupt Organizations Act," aka "Civil RICO" didn't apply to Cohen. He didn't understand that few judges approve of Civil RICO claims. This law was criminal in its origins, draconian in its provisions, and in the eyes of conservative scribes, threatened to turn every securities salesman into a mobster.

On the way back to the office, Gary started a fight, demanding that I sue someone or other that I really didn't want to sue. He fired me. He hired me back. We arrived in San Francisco at his office, and although I had briefly ceased to be his lawyer, by the time we got inside, he regretted his brief intemperance, and things were back to normal.

Of course, normal with Gary Kremen is not normal at all. Things were looking great for him, but not so great for me. He owed me over $11,000 at that point, and $1,500 of that was out-of-pocket costs. I had sent him a simple agreement to sign, but he kept saying he wanted to come up with a more formal, lengthy agreement. He had something in mind of the sort he had entered into with Warshavsky and Levy, involving the creation of a new corporation that would receive the Sex.Com ownership interest once the litigation was successful. But I told Gary that wouldn't fly. It didn't look like that had worked out so well for Warshavsky and Levy, so I had a simple solution—a present grant of my 15%. Like I own 15% now. We had talked and re-talked this in the preceding months. We were obviously at a high water mark for the attorney-client relationship, and if this boat was going to float, it would have to be now. As Shakespeare said, "There is a tide in the affairs of men..."

CHAPTER NINE

DOWN THE RABBIT HOLE

ALTHOUGH LEWIS CARROLL WAS A MATHEMATICIAN, LAWYERS LOVE HIS WRITINGS. Alice's world of absurd characters and paradoxical declarations perfectly mirrors the arbitrary realm of "The Law." In Wonderland, as in law, things are often so just because they are. Also in law, logic is subordinate to authority. For Alice, things were not always so strange. Once she was a normal girl in a normal world. It all changed when she fell down the rabbit hole. My life changed when I fell into that dot that divides Sex.Com precisely in twain. In chaos theory, they talk about "strange attractors," vortices of force that generate order and disorder in equal shares. Like a force of myth or legend, Sex.Com distorts reality, makes all things believable and nothing incredible. Just to go after it was to join in a fabulous quest. Or so I thought.

It's the intoxication of advocacy. When you are fully charged up, totally committed to the advocate's role in an important case, the energy changes. The atmosphere will almost start to shimmer. You are speeding ahead, plying a sword that is both immensely heavy and totally maneuverable. You feel the enemy on the other side, as he parries your blow, and your opposed wills clash like ringing steel. The blades dance, you thrust, evade, lure his edge and seek the opportunity to strike. It's a game you play for a living, and it feeds your body and soul. You identify with your victories, and each victory contains the energy you need to move on to the next one. Along the way, you make a living, but the victories themselves are worth far more than the money you're paid.

And that's my problem. I enjoy it so much I'll practically do it for free. I've spent too much time treating cases like motorcycles that you can kick-start and tear ass all over the dirt in. I've come to see clients and witnesses as fuel to burn, weapons to deploy, and obstacles to be destroyed. Sex.Com was like a big, fire-breathing road rocket with 100,000 cc's ready to blast off like a George Lucas creation hitting hyper-drive with the Empire in hot pursuit. God, I wanted to ride that thing, but it was dead stock still. In October 1999, Gary had no gas money. The time left to take discovery was ticking down, and Gary wasn't doing much but getting behind on his legal bill, so two things had to happen. He had to find some money, a lot of it, and I had to find a way to make it until he did.

We came up with an agreement that hung on a big if. I would keep working on the case if he promised to pay me $55,000 when he got a few million bucks out of a stock IPO that he was sure would be happening within the next few months.

You can imagine what your wife says when you come home with one of these agreements. She's like, "An IPO?" And you're like, "Yeah, you can make a lot of money on them." You reassure her that you're not going to put another 500 hours into this case and have nothing but an unfulfilled promise to show for it. She squints her eyes and shakes her head with a tight smile on her pretty lips. I have a small collection of worthless agreements to show for lots of work done free, so this is a bit of a sore point with her.

But I had to go on. I was down the rabbit hole, where things just get "curiouser and curiouser." It seemed curious enough to a lot of people when, just five months after I had moved to Carpinteria and put an Ojai address on my stationery, I was back in Medford, Oregon, renting office space with my old friend Peter Carini across from the courthouse. "So what about Ojai?" they would ask. The answer was always the same. I had a big case that I was working on now, and I needed to focus on it and keep costs down.

Peter thought I was crazy. He'd saunter into my office in his tailor-made suit, snugly buttoned over a custom shirt and matching tie, ask me about the case and act interested. But when his true feelings came out, he just shook his head and snorted. The whole thing was going to come to nothing, and it was sad because I was pouring my soul into it. Of course, he wouldn't say this straight out, instead expressing disappointment that I wouldn't throw in with him full-time in the criminal defense biz. Peter is the undisputed king of Southern Oregon DUI, with sights set on the statewide crown. With me handling drug cases, we would've been unstoppable. His disappointment was visible.

The office was a fun place. My daughter Maria, who had stayed in Oregon when the rest of us moved to California, was Peter's secretary, so I got to spend time with her. I had an upstairs space with good sun from big windows to the north and west, and a nice view of the parking lot and the blue Oregon horizon. I could drink beer on the landing and look at the backside of the old courthouse. It got good sun from big windows to the north and west. I brought in my huge oak library table desk, set up the computer and my new three-in-one HP 3100 faxer, scanner, printer, a beast that is still in service to this day, and now, surely, I was ready for anything.

It was good to be around people, too, because even though they take up your time, they give you ideas. Also, the marveling tone of a couple of secretaries like Kim and Teresa can really make you feel smart, which feeds your desire to go engage in more exploits. Lee Werdell was a serious trial lawyer who had an associate named Sue Whatley, who was not good at getting up in the morning but liked to work late. We became good friends, and I started to give her small projects on the case. John Hanson loved to wander into my office and ask questions with this wide-eyed look, while poking through my mail. He was generous with his praise, telling me I was farsighted and this was all going to come in really big for me. He complained a bit about my excessive use of the fax paper, so I bought my own fax machine.

My office quickly took on the look of a paper nightmare. I had four Bekins boxes of documents from Katie Diemer's copy of the file, an endless stream of works in progress, storms of paper coming from Dorband and Dolkas. I attached a satellite to the roof of the building for faster Internet access. Gary wanted to give me an even bigger dish that he planned on getting from Hughes Engineering as part of a consulting deal. Fortunately, I was able to simply transition to DSL. It was too much work, for too little money. But the New Economy was hitting on all cylinders. IPOs were blasting off everyday, like volleys of spaceships lighting up the sky, heading for new planets. I had a piece of that new world. I was reading Wired, surfing the Net, and talkin' tech like nobody's fool. I was filing papers, writing, talking and emailing like a son of a gun.

And then it happened. Gary became a millionaire. A company called Interwoven went public on October 8, 1999. Gary was in a position to cash in nearly immediately. Unlike many of the other stockholders, his holdings were not under any sale restriction, and thus could be sold immediately. That was great, because after an IPO, a lot of stocks spike up in value, but by the time the restrictions are lifted, they've taken a slide. Selling sooner is often better. But the transfer agents, the people who actually give you your stock, so you can turn it into money, weren't cooperating. They didn't like the idea that anyone wasn't under sale restriction.

So I shook the money tree, calling the lawyers for the transfer agents, implying threat as politely as I could, while Gary played the crazy client. He would call up the transfer agents and threaten lawsuits. Then I would pick up the other end and apologize for my client's untoward behavior, but emphasize that his frustration was understandable, given that his stock had no restriction and he should be allowed to sell it immediately. Dot-commers got away with murder in those days, so it was kind of like cleaning up after a bratty kid—all smiles and apologies.

After about a week of heckling the transfer agents, the money broke loose for Gary, but as became our usual pattern, I then had to break my share loose from him. Gary wanted to pay me, but he also wanted me to promise to sue more people. I had some serious concerns about adding more defendants in the case. We had already sued a bank in the British Virgin Islands, and a bank officer, Andrew Keuls, but I had never served them with the lawsuit, so they had never appeared. I didn't want more defendants appearing. Too many defendants make a case completely unmanageable, as more and more lawyers show up to beat up on the plaintiff's lawyer. I couldn't afford this risk, and drew the line. It would not be a good idea to seek to amend the complaint to allege more claims against new defendants. Gary almost fired me again, threatening right up to the line. I knew that if he fired me, I'd never get paid for the work I'd already done, which amounted to several hundred hours. It was like tying a rope to restrain an oil tanker that was gently drifting away. Gary was a millionaire now, and could have any lawyer he wanted. But we talked it through. The rope held. He wire transferred $55,000 to my account. Peter couldn't believe it.

I could hear the jet fuel flowing into that big red road rocket with the 100,000 cc engine as I settled into the cockpit. I was surrounded by the armored embrace of an Internet war chariot. Scanning the instrument panel, all my weapons were available at a touch. The visor slowly lowered over my eyes, and through it I could see the beautiful designs of war, and in the corner of my vision, a clock pulsing down the months, weeks, days and minutes left to win the game. My hands rested firm on the controls as I and the whole machine gently became weightless.

It's happening now. Judge Ware is clearing me for takeoff, thumbs up, wearing an aviator cap. Near the starting line, I see a young girl. Is it Alice, poised to drop her hanky, announcing the start of the contest? Do I hear Baby Sex.Com crying out for me to save her? Is that dragon Steve Cohen, oozing smoke, holding her captive? Is that Black Knight Bob Dorband? What's that racket? Down at the end of the runway, frantically gesturing with her crown askew and her sceptre held high—The Red Queen! No, it's Gary screaming "Off with their heads! Off with their heads!" I've already hauled back on the throttle. I hurtle past Gary, past the dragon and Baby Sex.Com, then past Judge Ware's smiling face as big as the sun as I clear the runway, watching the blue get bigger in front of me—heading for the open sky.

CHAPTER TEN

GARY'S DEPOSITION, PART TWO

GARY HAD TO FINISH HIS DEPOSITION. I had been holding out on this, despite repeated demands from Cohen's and NSI's lawyers. At the October 4th hearing, when Dorband said that Gary was refusing to finish his deposition, Judge Ware showed one of his notable traits—a willingness to order people to do things despite no motion being on calendar, and with no notice to the party about to be ordered to do something, that the issue would be coming up. Immediately upon hearing that Gary's deposition hadn't been concluded, Judge Ware ordered it to proceed within 30 days. Maybe that's one of the reasons why Gary was feeling crabby on the way back from the hearing.

Depositions adjourned under hasty circumstances often lead to problems. Having read the first and second days of Gary's deposition transcripts carefully, I had established to my satisfaction that he never said anything to contradict the "Dr. Ruth" strategy. Gary's sketchy, one-page doodle of a business plan had been briefly identified in his first two days of deposition, and referred to casually. It made no mention of Dr. Koop, Dr. Ruth, or a "kinder, gentler Sex.Com," as *Wired Magazine* referred to it years later in April, 2001. By the time we showed up at Gary's deposition, Dorband and Dolkas were aware of this new twist in the moral high ground, because it had been specifically alleged in the third amended complaint.

I bet they were kicking themselves that they hadn't "gotten Gary in cement" on this issue during the first two days of deposition, when it would have been easy. They had been operating on the supposition that if Gary had ever gotten around to it, he would have operated a pornography site. It didn't seem to have occurred to anyone that Gary, not being a pornographer, might have done something different with it, based on his fundamental inclination. That inclination was evident in his other ventures, like Match.Com, that Gary was creating while Cohen was building Sex.Com into a pornography website. Match.Com expressed Gary's own desire to get a date, and ultimately became the world's most successful dating site. Match.Com was acquired by Cendant Corporation for $50

41

million. Not that Gary got any of that money–he had already been forced out of the company by that time.

Gary and his friend Kevin Kunzelman would often remark that they had played their positions in Match badly. But few people knew of this wrinkle in the story and Gary would never reveal it, finding it politic to be perceived rich even when he wasn't. Cohen learned the truth about Match, and would deride Gary for it: "He didn't make any money out of that!" But what good did it do? Most tech-groupies believed otherwise. And unlike pornography, dating was part of a wholesome, American lifestyle. Match.com prided itself on being a site where people actually met and married. Match gave credence to the "wholesome Sex.Com" scenario.

Gary handled his third day of deposition well, maintaining the truth of what was alleged in the third amended complaint, that if he had developed the Sex.Com website, he would have done so differently, and in a manner to serve the public interest. I was relieved that there was no nasty cross-examination on this issue. It was more a disbelieving silence. If I had been cross-examining Gary on this topic, I would have been much tougher on him, examining the one-page business plan in greater detail, and challenging him to indicate where it reflected his kinder, gentler intentions. But such questioning was not done. Neither Dorband nor Dolkas attempted to nail Gary down about when he had originated the Dr. Ruth approach, whether that had been before or after he prepared his one-page business plan, whom he had disclosed this plan to, and what objective evidence there was to show that he ever had such an intention.

Gary's claim was barely questioned, on the assumption, I presume, that it was so preposterous no one would believe it. What Dorband and Dolkas didn't think was that the story would be circulated so widely in the press, and be credited by a judge. As the months went by, this story proved to have legs. Some people poked fun at the notion, but Judge Janice Stewart of Portland discussed the Dr. Ruth theory in her thirteen-page opinion halting the RICO lawsuit Cohen later filed against Kremen and myself. The fact is, Gary carried off his white-hat schtick with understated élan.

The fourth day of Gary's depo was another story. Gary had pushed himself to the limit the night before, and was exhausted. Sitting in front of Dorband and Dolkas, with the videotape running, Gary was goggle-eyed and bleary, his thinning black hair looked sticky, his sweatshirt more worn than usual. Dorband led off with a roundhouse. I'm sure he realized he should have asked the question long before, but there's never a bad time to ask someone, "Are you taking any drugs that might impair your memory?" I don't flinch. No worries. I'm thinking Gary will answer "no," of course, because he could remember an IP address or the last email you sent him regardless of his condition.

Gary answered, "Maybe." Worries. This is called "opening the door" to areas of inquiry that should be kept shut. Dorband continued his questioning. I felt like a security system vainly bleeping "intruder" to an unresponsive occupant. I wanted to stop everything, but the video was running. Dorband asked the nature of the drugs involved, and Gary described an assortment of tranquilizers. Then Dorband asked the identity of Gary's psychiatrist. I hesitated before failing to object. The name popped out of Gary's mouth, and immediately I was kicking myself. I objected to all questioning about diagnosis, treatments or complaints, and instructed Gary not to answer them, but it was too late to prevent the inevitable: a subpoena from Dorband to the good doctor for Gary's medical records.

When the doctor received Dorband's subpoena, I successfully moved the court for an order to quash it, thus protecting Gary's psychological records from disclosure. After the danger was past, Gary had the chutz-pah to claim his "maybe" answer was *good* for him, because he didn't say his medications *did* cause memory problems, just that they *might*. He thought this was good, because it would give him wiggle room to adjust his prior testimony. Unfortunately, there would be no wiggle room left, or any matter left to the imagination, if the records were out in the open. And the judge could easily have required the doctor to produce them. We had dodged a bullet, and now Gary was trying to out-lawyer me. At least the ordeal was over.

CHAPTER ELEVEN

THE FRENCH CONNECTION

WHILE GARY WAS DEVELOPING HIS DATING AND CLASSIFIEDS WEB-
SITES, Cohen was executing a well-planned strategy to make his theft secure by acquiring a trademark in Sex.Com from the U.S. Patent & Trademark Office (the "USPTO"). On May 20, 1996, seven months after Cohen
sent the forged letter, one of his lawyers, Leonard Duboff of Portland,
filed USPTO Service Mark Application #751-6638. Although many people
scoffed at the notion of trademarking "Sex," on the grounds that it was
"merely descriptive of the product," Duboff almost did it. The key to his
near-success was Cohen's willingness to swear in his official trademark
declaration that, based on his prior use of the mark in commerce, Sex.
Com had become "distinctive," despite its descriptive character. Based
on Cohen's declaration, the USPTO examining attorney concluded that
Sex.Com was a valid trademark, and ordered it "published for opposition" in the Trademark Gazette. Gary then learned of the application, and
Sheri Falco filed an opposition.

When I took over the case, I sent the USPTO a copy of the third
amended complaint, which caused the USPTO to suspend proceedings.
Still, the mere fact that the USPTO had approved Sex.Com for publica-
tion was troubling, because one thing was becoming increasingly clear
in the legal world – trademark ownership trumps the mere registration
of the domain name. If Cohen could establish that Gary had registered
the domain name in violation of Cohen's pre-existing trademark, then
Gary would be a cybersquatter, with no rights to the name at all. Cohen's
cross-complaint against Gary alleged a cybersquatting claim under the
new anti-cybersquatting law. So Cohen's "trademark defense" was very
much a live issue.

We got the complete Sex.Com trademark application file from the
USPTO. Cohen's application included documents that claimed to show he
had used Sex.Com as part of an online business called the French Connection BBS. The file contains a series of documents that tell a believable story
of events that never happened. Without anyone to contradict those facts,
it's not surprising the USPTO examining attorney was deceived.

The USPTO awards trademarks only to those who show that they generate revenue from use of the trademark, so Cohen had to do the numbers for his imaginary business activity. Looking over his shoulder on March 19, 1997, we would have seen him seated at his computer, typing this:

I, STEPHEN M. COHEN, declare that:

1. I am the owner of the website http://www.sex.com and am making this declaration in the belief that the trademark "SEX.COM" has become distinctive of the services of my website by reason of my substantial and continued use in commerce of the mark for at least seventeen (17) years immediately before the date of this statement. Prior to use of the mark on my website, it was used on my electronic bulletin board.

2. The mark SEX.COM is recognized in the trade and by consumers of my services indicating my services.

3. Income from services performed under the SEX.COM mark since its introduction has been as follows:

1979	$4,872
1980	$11,370
1981	$13,770
1982	$15,320
1983	$14,780
1984	$15,270
1985	$18,550
1986	$21,990
1987	$41,020
1988	$57,720
1989	$68,010
1990	$72,233
1991	$88,670
1992	$62,450
1993	$84,950
1994	$97,010
1995	$186,440

As an inspired piece of imaginative writing, this apparently dry statement of numerical income would not seem to rank high; however, upon further consideration, the subtleties appear. No one can fail to notice that business has improved steadily over the years without any notable alteration in the trend except for a brief stumble, from $88,670 to $62,450 in 1992, when Cohen suffered minor business interruption due to his induction into Club Fed. Nor could anyone miss the run of double numbers that seems to put the whole column in motion. Each number is a helpless conscript in Cohen's war against reality. Take $72,233, a royal number if ever there was one, who appeared, like a state dignitary on the wrong floor of an apartment building, in the decade-marking year 1990. Compare Cohen's highjacking of this regal figure with his induction of the hard-working $15,270, who rang in solid returns for 1984. Finally, in 1995, the year he stole Sex.Com, like the sun separating the clouds, his numbers break into six figures, a sign of much better days to come. History is thus manufactured by those bold enough to seize it while others are napping.

When I started practicing as a lawyer in L.A., trademark law wasn't cool. Anything to do with the USPTO was considered deadly dull, to be avoided by a smart associate at all costs. Patent and trademark lawyers were considered nerds, and the only sexy intellectual properties were music, movies and software. Nevertheless, after two years in the L.A. litigation department of the venerable Morgan, Lewis & Bockius, I was lured by substantially higher pay to a New York firm that did the trademark enforcement work for Louis Vuitton, the famous luxury goods manufacturer.

Our receptionist at the firm, the lovely African goddess Donna Grimes, loved to say every syllable of the firm name: "Hello, Reboul, MacMurray, Hewitt, Maynard *and* Kristol," she would brightly recite every time she answered the phone. The job was politically incorrect. I spent much of my time filing lawsuits against people who sold luggage that looks exactly like Louis Vuitton, complete with the intersecting "LV" logo, but is actually counterfeit, manufactured in Korean linoleum factories. These lawsuits were necessary to avoid the damaging effects on the brand that result when a Beverly Hills matron mistakenly grabs the cleaning lady's purse off the counter on her way to meet with her charity group, and ends up trying to pay for lunch at an exclusive eatery with a handful of bus tokens. Thus, I worked hard to get the fake stuff out of the garment district chop shops and South Central LA swapmeets in order to keep prices for the real stuff high at Neiman Marcus, Saks 5th Avenue and other trendy outlets.

I called this job "keeping the world safe for luxury goods," and learned the usual MO for the trademark enforcement lawyer, which is a sort of rinky-dink imitation of undercover narcotics work. Certainly it has a similar effect, keeping prices high by suppressing the sale of contraband. I often refer to the DEA as the Office of Narcotics Price Maintenance. Like the DEA, we hired trademark narcs and set up buy-and-bust operations. First we hired private investigators to "make buys" of the infringing merchandise, then we would use these paid informants to swear out an application for a search and seizure order, which would be secretly issued by an obliging federal judge. With a crew of off-duty LAPD and a stack of paperwork about three inches thick, we would head over to the infringer's place of business, then and there to take the phony luggage into custody, leaving sad-faced Koreans with a stack of legal documents and nothing left to sell. This was called a good day.

One day I had too much of a good thing. The night before I'd seized a bunch of luggage from a gal named Melissa, who was selling through Tupperware-type house parties. She was a nice blonde gal with about six years of partying on her thin Mayflower features. She had good quality fake LV. Because of the controlled setting, I went alone with only one cop, a cool-handed off-duty LAPD homicide detective. Our narc, Jodi, ushered us into Melissa's living room and we saw all the tan and brown leather LV logos. The homicide dick is standing behind me as I move forward with a stack of papers. Melissa smiles her "Hello, gentlemen" smile, but it freezes on her face, and she follows up with "What's goin' on?" She looks incredulous. Jodi's having a hard time, but she stays professional. I give Melissa the paperwork and explain why we have to take the stuff. I put the fake LV in the back of my car, street-value around $10,000 dollars.

The next morning I went downtown to do another, much bigger raid. I drove my car, a turquoise-blue late-seventies Dodge Swinger with a white vinyl top, to a loading dock near Santee Alley in the L.A. garment district. There, by pre-arrangement, I met my crew—a half-dozen off-duty cops, my boss Andy Tashman, and the disgruntled Mexican worker who was tired of making $25/day working for the big LV pusher. This guy, who told me the job was a step up from selling Mexican popsicles for $8 a day, had signed an affidavit fingering five different locations. I left my Swinger with Melissa's luggage in the back seat. That day we seized about $200,000 worth of luggage from three locations, packing it into big trucks for transport.

When I got back to my car, though, I not only had three parking tickets, I had an empty back seat. A Swinger is a two-door style, and the two doors are easy to pop with a slim-jim. Someone had done it. No evidence against Melissa. I had to report to the judge the status of the lost evidence, so I buried the information in a declaration that I handed to Melissa when she showed up at the post-seizure hearing. Any lawyer seeing the loss of the evidence, would've hit the sirens and the overhead lights, and had me up against the wall. My case against Melissa would've evaporated. It might be difficult to prove Melissa's LV was counterfeit, now that I'd lost it. But Larry Lydick, Senior Judge, never mentioned the disappearance of the evidence at the court hearing, choosing instead to lecture Melissa about the error of her ways. I felt like the abyss had yawned open, then shut, swallowing only Melissa.

I left Reboul after barely a year doing this kind of work. At the Christmas party in New York City that year, a partner asked me how I was enjoying "the Vuitton work." With a chipper smile I responded without hesitation, "Oh, it's great. I love making Korean women cry." The partner laughed wryly, and several other lawyers raised their champagne glasses and murmured assent to second my candor. Still, I've often said we learn the most from the worst jobs, and what I'd learned at Reboul proved useful early on in the Sex.Com case, when Gary and I performed a search of all the computerized docketing records of the United States Federal Court system, looking for any cases in which a Stephen Michael Cohen had been a party.

Our search turned up a large number of lawsuits involving Cohen, including one called *Ashton-Tate v. Stephen Michael Cohen, John Cook and the French Connection*. Indeed, Cohen had identified this case in his Rule 26 disclosures, but without providing the case number. I knew it was a trademark and copyright enforcement lawsuit filed by the SPA, the Software Protection Association, to seize computers that were being used to sell pirated software. As it happened, while at Reboul, I also worked for the SPA. So I subpoenaed the records from Howard, Rice, the big Bay Area lawfirm that had represented the SPA. A paralegal was able to retrieve a box of documents including a videotape. For a few hundred bucks, she sent me the lot.

The box contained printouts of what appeared on the computer screen when you dialed up the French Connection back in 1989. These were made by the SPA investigators, who signed declarations filed with the court, describing the business operations of the French Connection. Private investigator Richard Klaus's declaration said he'd met Cohen, who took him to the address of Midcom in Orange County, showed him a million dollars worth of computers, and told him they were running the French Connection. The Klaus declaration also stated that the French Connection charged a $15/month membership fee, for which the user obtained access to a large database of pirated software. The French Connection had no sexual content. It was a supermarket for stolen software, including some of the big moneymakers of the day, like Lotus 1-2-3, WordStar and Word Perfect. Best of all, the videotape showed Richard Klaus dialing up the French Connection on a personal computer, revealing how the system worked. It did not, at any point, open a portal into a world of online porn.

The box also contained a news story from an Orange County newspaper, detailing how Cohen had been charged by the City of Tustin with running a house of prostitution. Some of the jury believed him when he said no, it was a private swing club, because he was acquitted. Although the French Connection in the eighties was never what Cohen later claimed it was, but rather what Klaus's videotape shows, Cohen reimagined events, blurring the line between the Tustin swinger-club activity and the French Connection, to gin up a plausible story for claiming that Sex.Com was his based on prior use. Cohen's claim that he began using Sex.Com five years before domain names were invented in 1984 was not a gaffe, but part of the big-lie strategy. The way Dorband explained it, ".com" was a file ending, like ".doc" or ".exe," and Sex.Com was a "service" that earned money and became distinctive. I think I got more benefit from the SPA's suit against the French Connection than the SPA did. Cohen gave the SPA lawyers the runaround for months, dodging service of process, pretending to be a lawyer named "Frank Butler" for purposes of delay, and promising to settle, but never signing the settlement papers. The file was ultimately closed for lack of action. Although originally filed under seal by the SPA, by 1999 the seal had been lifted, so I looked forward to showing the documents to Cohen at his deposition.

To nail it all down, I wanted to find Richard Klaus. My private investigator, Paul Nyland of Beverly Hills, traced Klaus to a pair of P.O. Boxes in

Chloride and Bullhead City, Arizona. I sent him two Express Mail letters, one to each mailbox, but he never answered. I was disappointed, since I wanted to go to Chloride, having never been there. I often wondered who Klaus was hiding from.

CHAPTER TWELVE

AN INTRODUCTION TO FEDERAL DISCOVERY PRACTICE WITH FULL MILITARY METAPHORS

DISCOVERY UNDER THE FEDERAL RULES OF CIVIL PROCEDURE could be described in a number of ways. It might be described as a labyrinthine castle in which many young attorneys become lost, billing countless hours and still unable to find the essential facts of their case. On the other hand, it might be described as a massive siege machine, which if deployed with implacable determination and sufficient attorney time, can breach the walls of many a sturdy citadel.

First, we have the general disclosure provisions of Rule 26. This rule lays down the guidelines for discovery, and tells the lawyers what they can expect the court to require the other side to produce in the course of litigation. All parties to the litigation are required to disclose, right at the outset, the documents and witnesses they intend to use to prove their case.

From a strategic point of view, Rule 26 disclosures might be likened to getting your enemy's map of the battlefield. However, since this is a forced disclosure, you can expect it to be rather sketchy, more of an exercise in trying to avoid telling the other guy anything he doesn't already know than the open-handed business of "laying your cards on the table," which young attorneys sometimes think is the right way to go. Indeed, some law school teachers will even tell you this sort of thing: "Tell the other guy about your case. Let him poke holes in it. Then you know where to shore things up. Maybe you'll learn something from him or her in the process."

The only problem with this idea is that if you don't know the strong and weak points of your case in advance, or what the other guy already knows, you are likely going to hurt yourself by making uninformed disclosures. Additionally, you should make the other guy show you his case before you even consider disclosing yours. Finally, since deception is one of the major skills to apply in the art of war, even the truths you disclose should serve to mislead your opponent in some way. For example, you can win points for candor by "revealing" things the other guy already knows. You then act surprised when he discloses that he already knows these things, flattering him for his perceptivity and astuteness. This type of exchange works wonders for relationships and costs your client nothing but maybe the price of a few drinks.

Within the context of the general discovery rules, if the compelled disclosures are a map, then the artillery is the Rule 34 document demand. Like artillery, if you target it well, you can score a direct hit and request damning documents that the other side is powerless to hold back. Carelessly drafted document demands can be attacked on grounds of vagueness, burdensomeness, and a host of other defects. Requests for "every document," may produce far less than one hoped. Indeed, no matter how good the artillery gunners are, you're going to have to send in infantry units to follow up. Additionally, document demands are like artillery in that they are slow to reload and retarget. Generally a request for documents will remain unanswered for at least 30 days, and thus, as the time allowed for discovery begins to run out, the delaying tactics to avoid producing necessary documents become more and more crucial, and your demands for production must necessarily become more forceful.

Another favored discovery tool for experienced litigators is the famous "request for admission." Doing requests for admissions is a lot like playing "battleship." In litigation, if somebody admits something, on the record and under oath, it relieves the other party of any duty to prove the fact that has been admitted. I like requests for admissions because of their psychological effect. Like document demands, they require a response within 30 days, but they have a much nastier consequence for non-compliance. If your lawyer fails to respond to a document demand, he gets either a nice phone call or a nasty letter from the other guy, asking him when he is going to get the damn documents. If your lawyer forgets to respond to requests for admissions, they are "deemed admitted." So the lawyer can't ignore them. And since requests for admissions require the client's response under oath, the lawyer has to get together with his client to discuss the requests long before the time to send responses. In my experience, this makes lawyers do what they hate the most: call the client, send him the requests for admissions, and engage in a detailed discussion of the facts of the case.

The last type of annoying paper you can send your adversary is an interrogatory, a written question that his client has to answer under oath. Depending on who is sending the interrogatories, they can operate as well-targeted sniper bullets pinning the adversary down to a fixed position, or forcing him to seek refuge in a cover story. On the other hand, some people dispatch a set of interrogatories like an invasion of lice that do little more than irritate the enemy soldiers. Many insurance defense firms, for example, send out vague interrogatories that are dangerous only if you don't provide a response of some sort.

My philosophy of responding to interrogatories is to answer in a manner both verbally extensive and factually spare. But sometimes I like to answer with such brevity as to be arch: "Irrelevant. You know the answer already." Discovery judge Patricia Trumbull described my answer as "smart-alecky" when I answered Cohen's question asking "who" knew some facts with the blunt response, "You know who." Hey, they did know who. I understand what Judge Trumbull meant, though . . . more ink, less attitude, Mr. Carreon. Let's try, "Such facts are already within the knowledge of the propounding party."

After paper discovery, we come to the true cruise missile/attack fighter/helicopter gunship of litigation, the deposition. A deposition is always a costly process. For the lawyer, it usually means a full day of work, not counting travel. For the client, it means, at a minimum, paying for the court reporter, the lawyer's time, travel, witness fees, costs of videotaping, and the cost of producing the transcript.

A cruise missile type deposition is where there is one witness out there who knows a key fact or set of facts. You know they know it, and so does the other guy. It's just a matter of getting it on the record before trial so that you're sure the witness is going to say what you think he will, you won't be screwed if you can't manage to get him to the trial itself, and you can finally stop arguing with the other guy about what this witness is going to say. It's expensive, but if you target it accurately, it hits the target, and when the deposition is over you have secured that position on the map.

A jet-fighter deposition is where you are relatively sure that there are a large number of issues to be nailed down with a witness, because they were in a good position to know things that you now want to establish in your case. A good example would be a nurse in a medical malpractice case, or a mid-level banking employee in a bank fraud case. Merely because of where they stood, they had to observe necessary things, but they will likely be difficult to ferret out and nail down. So for the jet-fighter type mission, you pack a lunch, as detailed a map as you can, a list of targets, questions, and as much ammunition, I mean paperwork, as you can possibly carry. Your hope is that when you see your target you will know it, and you will find the right weapon to take it out. These types of depositions often take a full day, as you keep flying over the terrain, trying to pick up clues and respond by establishing your version of events, or the opposite of the other guy's version, whichever is appropriate.

Finally, we have the helicopter gunship deposition. This is where you know that you're dealing with a hardened adversary's emplacement. We're talking about top level tobacco executives, malpracticing surgeons, and defendants like Cohen, who have all the advantages of wealth, inertia and cynicism. A helicopter gunship deposition continues until the witness is exhausted, all of the documents have been discussed twice, every crucial question has been asked at least three times and objected to twice, and the court reporter has started to talk about her babysitter.

Most litigators with five years experience have been through all of these types of depositions, and are familiar with them. Cohen introduced me to a new type of deposition, however. This is the decoy deposition. Like a decoy duck, the decoy deposition has no substance beyond appearance. A decoy duck may float, look and perhaps even quack like a duck, but it is fake. The same is true of decoy depositions.

CHAPTER THIRTEEN

AN ARMADA OF DECOYS

I RECENTLY HEARD A NEWS REPORT ABOUT AMNESTY INTERNATIONAL trying to restrict the sale of torture devices. I heard about stun belts, tasers, compliance batons, self-tightening handcuffs, and other nasty devices. Fortunately, aside from being handcuffed briefly by the LAPD after a motorcycle accident in which I was injured and my motorcycle damaged, I have never been subjected to any of those devices. Aside from being kicked in the ass for years during military school, and having the aforesaid LAPD try to break my arms just before they handcuffed me, I have rarely been the victim of intentional efforts to cause me suffering.

No, in order to bring the experience of torture into my own life it has been necessary to purchase a fax machine. Why a fax machine, you ask? Because using a fax machine, that I had to pay for, my legal adversaries are able to instantaneously beam into my office scores of pages of accusations, challenges, arguments, and other terrifying things. The other guy can spend months pulling together information, gathering it into an attack refined through hours of dedicated effort. And the whole thing pops into your office in ten minutes, neatly typed, meticulously argued, carefully proofread, arrogantly signed.

Every lawyer's favorite time to send a fax stuffed with powerful toxins and terrifying portents is 4:48 p.m., Friday afternoon. That way they can screw up your whole weekend. Most fax machines ring before they begin to fuck up your life. Then, like a loyal servant who has become a mouthpiece for the enemy, they begin to spit out just what you did not want to see, packaged for your consumption by the last person you wanted to hear from, the other guy.

So it was that, on the evening of November 12, 1999, the fax machine began to disgorge its ill-omened load of paper, faxed directly from Duboff, Dorband, Cushing & King. What popped out was a flotilla of decoy depositions. Without the slightest preliminary discussion, Cohen had announced his intention to take nine different depositions at locations around the globe so far separated that I doubted any two were in the same time zone. The names of the people were unusual, like Thanin

Sacchasiri. His deposition, the first of the nine, was set for December 3, 1999, in Bangkok. Then there was Eliyahue Roussos, whose deposition was scheduled for December 16th, in Tel Aviv, in the morning. During the afternoon of the 16th, Dorband planned to depose Ami Dvash in Haifa, presumably a short but dusty cab-ride and a couple of roadblocks away through what was not then an actual war zone. I was vexed that three depositions were scheduled in Moscow, which seemed too much like a great place for me to last be heard of. On the bright side, the junket was scheduled to conclude on December 22nd in Athens, so I could probably celebrate Christmas in flight on the way back to Oregon.

I gathered up and reviewed the pages that had piled up in the tray of the fax machine and spilled over onto the floor like toxic waste. After assembling the pages I got the drift pretty quickly. Cohen wanted to give me "diesel therapy." This is a term that federal prisoners use to describe the kind of treatment you sometimes get from the Bureau of Prisons if you're a naughty prisoner, or if you're just unlucky. The United States Marshal Service has a fantastic fleet of trucks and buses in which they move prisoners all over the country. Sometimes prisoners spend more time on the road than they do in jail. The process is tiring, soul-wearying, and guaranteed to wear down the spirit of the most hardened prisoner. Being in jail is bad, but being imprisoned in transit is even worse. Cohen wanted to chain me to his deposition schedule and soak up Gary's entire litigation budget before he got a chance to pursue any of his own discovery. Making things worse, all of these depositions were during *my time* that I'd already scheduled for Cohen's deposition. Finally, these depositions were happening during the holiday season right before Y2K, when airports, hotels and the skies themselves would be jammed with vacationing civilians. I could smell the jet fuel already.

Never had I heard of anyone abusing the discovery process so blatantly. Around the same time as the decoy depositions, Cohen also served subpoenas on Gary's doctor, three of his former attorneys, and five former business associates. All were to take place during the same one-month time period. Gary was willing to throw me at the task. He was a millionaire now, and if necessary, he would match Cohen penny for penny. However, I would rather have hung by my thumbs for a designated period of time than pursue this useless "discovery."

I imagined the nine decoy depositions as intercontinental ballistic missiles, arcing across the globe from their various launching pads, converging on my desk. I had to bunker in to survive the attack, and began building a hardened emplacement, which in Federal discovery comes in the form of a "motion for protective order," under Rule 26. Of course the motion would be granted, because Cohen's tactic was transparently outrageous, but it would be a lot of work to write it. I would win, but I wasn't going to get a whole lot of sleep until the motion was filed.

CHAPTER FOURTEEN

THE EXTRA-LEGAL PARALEGAL

I ARRIVED WITH MY WIFE AND DAUGHTER IN SAN FRANCISCO a few days before Thanksgiving 1999. It was raining at the airport, where we parked on the roof. We wheeled their luggage into the international terminal while dodging the falling drops. In 26 years, my wife Tara and I had been separated rarely for more than a few days, and now she was leaving with my 18-year old daughter for Kathmandu, Nepal. Ana would be spending several months in a Tibetan language and Buddhist studies program. They were excited and looking forward to the adventure. I was looking forward to spending all my time on Sex.Com. Like the gravity pull of a black hole, Sex.Com had started to rip apart the stitches of my life. As Ana and Tara drifted past the event horizon, I was confident I would see them on the other side. For the moment, Dorband's decoy depositions were the largest objects on my view screen, and I desperately needed to get my shield up.

After spending a decent interval at the airport, mourning the departure of my loved ones and having a drink, I headed into the city to meet with Gary and a guy named Mark Irvine. Gary was thrilled to have me all to himself, and he'd even hired Mark, a paralegal, to help me prepare the motion. Part tenant's rights advocate, part pro-se litigator, Mark was tall, blonde-haired, apparently sincere, a veteran with a liberal prescription for pain killers and the noisiest laptop computer I have ever heard. Gary had used him in his unsuccessful fight to retain the Fulton Street apartment from which he had been evicted recently.

Mark introduced me to the Hastings Law School Library in downtown San Francisco. He thought it was a wonderful place, and I liked the printer setup for laptop computers. We labored there together for a couple of days cranking out the motion for protective order. Mark surfed the Internet to find out approximately how much it would cost and how many hours I would have to spend on airplanes to cover all of these depositions. The totals were impressive. My motion informed the judge that I would have to fly 222 hours, and Gary would have to spend around $17,000 on airfare. After adding in the cost of paying me at my reduced hourly rate, the total cost to Gary of defending the decoy depositions would be over $70,000.

In addition to arguing that the decoy depositions were intended to obstruct Gary's efforts to obtain discovery against Cohen, and to waste attorney time and money, we filled the judge in on a few other details. Many foreign nations do not take kindly to the American deposition procedure. Some countries consider that people who take depositions in their country are undertaking unlawful judicial acts without authorization. (Perhaps some governments think Americans conduct depositions like the locals conduct their own "judicial investigations," but I think this assumption is unwarranted, as there have been no Amnesty International accusations against the American civil justice system.) In any event, you can get thrown in jail for conducting a deposition in the wrong country. Since a number of these depositions were scheduled in countries with completely undemocratic legal systems, such as Moscow and Greece, I thought I'd push the "risk, danger, burden" angle for all it was worth. It was my life, after all.

We also pointed out to the judge that Cohen was obviously trying to get deposition testimony from people who would refuse to appear at trial. Even a Federal District Court subpoena has no power outside U.S. territorial limits. "Extraterritorial witnesses" cannot be compelled to appear at trial. However, their depositions can be submitted on the grounds that they are "unavailable," i.e., outside of the jurisdictional power of the subpoena. Thus, Cohen figured he could notice the depositions, get the testimony, use it at trial, and never have to present these witnesses before a jury. If I failed to attend the depositions, they could go forward without cross-examination, and an uncross-examined deposition, admissible at trial, is a ticking bomb you have not even had the opportunity to try and disarm.

To up the risks and increase the pressure, Dorband used a tactic he was often to repeat. He insisted that I get all my motions for protective order filed by November 24, 1999, or he was going to book all of his plane reservations in anticipation of proceeding with the trip. Thus, I was under the gun to produce the motion for protective order within that time frame. Two full days were required to prepare the motion, writing, researching, adding exhibits, and finalizing all the paper. What's ironic and painful about writing a motion for protective order is that, in order to get the protective order, you need to show it would be "burdensome and oppressive" to go forward with the discovery. Meanwhile, the whole time you are writing the motion for protective order, you are burdened and oppressed.

When the work was done, everything prepared, filed and sent off, Mark Irvine and I had sushi together. He was affable and intelligent. I thanked him several times for his hard work on the project, and anticipated that we would work together in the future. Unfortunately, a few weeks later, he and Gary had a major falling out. He ultimately sued Gary for stealing his shirt and some prescription medications. But the big claim he asserted was that Gary had induced him not to go to law school in exchange for the promise to pay for his law school education if he would work on the Sex.Com case instead. This allegation sounded so crazy and absurd that it was hard to believe when I saw it in Irvine's complaint. In retrospect, however, anything seems possible.

After a brief effort to mediate the decaying relations between Mark and Gary, I gave up. But Gary wasn't through with him. After defeating Mark's lawsuit with an onslaught of legal firepower wielded by the redoubtable Steve Sherman, Gary pursued a jihad to ban Irvine from the legal system as a "vexatious litigant." To me, this seemed like taking a cane from a blind man, since Irvine didn't do much else but sue people. For Gary, it was like target practice for a budding Billy the Kid. He was growing up, and the world would hear about him.

CHAPTER FIFTEEN

WE'RE NOT GOING TO BANGKOK (OR ATHENS, MOSCOW, HAIFA, ETC.)

IN THE UNITED STATES FEDERAL DISTRICT COURTS, some judges are appointed by the President, confirmed by Congress, and serve for life. We call them "Article III judges" because their offices were established by Article III of the U.S. Constitution. Article III judges are not required to adjudicate the discovery squabbles that inevitably erupt in litigation. Federal Magistrate judges, who are not appointed by the President or confirmed by Congress, referee the verbal jousting matches between attorneys squabbling over what documents shall be produced, what witnesses shall be deposed, and what interrogatories shall be answered. The Magistrate assigned to hear discovery motions in our case was Patricia Trumbull.

On January 11, 2000, we had our first discovery hearing with Judge Trumbull. I had five motions on calendar that day, which is like serving the Judge five Big Macs at once. One is fine, two is too many, but for god's sake, five! Still, it was the only thing we could do—Cohen had barged into the discovery arena, demanded to use all the time deposing his witnesses around the world, wanted my client's medical records because Gary said his medications caused memory problems, and wanted the records of two of his former trial lawyers—Katie Diemer and Sheri Falco—and one of his corporate lawyers—Aaron Alter. When we filed our motions on November 24th, they effectively blocked all the depositions from going forward until the Judge made her decision, and although we would have liked the decision earlier, she was taking her time.

I didn't think I was going to have a difficult battle on the motion for protective order to prevent the extraterritorial depositions. I thought Judge Trumbull would immediately perceive the entire stratagem for what it was, and grant a protective order. I was surprised when she led off with a mini-lecture about how this courthouse was very familiar with disputes involving international discovery, and there was nothing unusual about them. The suggestion was that, should it be necessary to take international discovery in a large-stakes Internet case, the parties would simply have to ante-up to meet the demands of litigation.

Why could I simply not attend the depositions by telephone, Judge Trumbull wanted to know? I had an answer ready: Because the whole case was about fraud, because the Sex.Com domain name had been stolen by use of a forged letter, because Cohen had been convicted of bankruptcy fraud and impersonating attorneys in the past, and because, most importantly, we could not trust Cohen to present witnesses who really were who he claimed they were. As I pointed out to the judge, "there could be anyone on the other end of the telephone."

The judge had another question. "What good will it do you to be there?"

I told her I could "ask them for their driver's license, and compare it with the person who was sitting in front of me." This argument was successful. At the end of the hearing, the judge granted a protective order, telling Cohen's attorney that he could proceed with the depositions wherever he wanted, but full videoconferencing had to be arranged for Kremen's attorney at Cohen's expense. In effect, the judge called Cohen's bluff. Immediately after the hearing, Dorband told me that if he had to pay for videoconferencing, he'd just skip the depositions, and submit signed declarations instead.

So there we were, no trip to Bangkok, or elsewhere. And as for Gary's medical records, we won that protective order too. Gary's former lawyers, Judge Trumbull said, would have to submit to deposition, but as it happened, Dorband never followed up on them.

Thus, at great cost of time and energy, we were able to obtain a commonsense result. Courthouses are wonderful places to waste time in furious activity. On January 11th, that furious activity resolved itself into precisely the result I wanted: nothing. Cohen got no documents, no depositions, no medical records, and I got no diesel therapy. Sometimes just not getting smashed is a big win.

The subtler, but more important win occurred on the battlefield of Judge Trumbull's mind. It is hard to convince a judge that your adversary is acting in bad faith. Judges presume that discovery devices are generally used for legitimate purposes, and that when a dispute kicks up it's probably the fault of both parties. Winning with Judge Trumbull meant convincing her that I was wearing the white hat.

In written court filings, of the sort I sent to Judge Trumbull, I always led with Cohen's criminal fraud convictions, and referred to "the forged letter" and the "stolen domain name." Good trial lawyers control the language of a case by producing accurate sound bites that sell a concept in a short phrase. If a guy cheats people, call him a con-man! If no one disputes that the letter is a forgery, call it a forged letter! If property was taken from an unwilling donor without compensation, call it a theft! The subject of the case was blatant theft by deception, so I was justified in using direct language. Cohen's act of theft was unconscionable, and righting the wrong was self-evidently just. This was not ordinary commercial litigation — it was a civil prosecution.

For years Cohen was able to cynically deploy the legal system against Gary and many others, using the profits from Sex.Com, a fire hose of cash, to present a very aggressive defense, while cloaking his ruthless tactics behind a plea for fairness: "Sure, I'm an ex-conman, but I've paid my debt to society. Pornography is just a business, and I'm just a businessman." To me it was a transparent tactic. I still had to sell that to the judges. At that hearing, Judge Trumbull began to see the first glimmerings of my vision, and a portion of her mind changed from Cohen territory to Kremen territory.

CHAPTER SIXTEEN

MAKING LEMONADE

We're all familiar with the saying, "When life gives you lemons, make lemonade." When my fax machine sprang to life, and started spewing out a lawsuit against Gary Kremen, alleging multiple tortuous acts, and seeking $9 million in damages, this was clearly an incoming shipment of lemons. This lawsuit was procedurally presented as a "counterclaim" by "counter-plaintiffs" Cohen, YNATA and Sandman Internacional. A counterclaim is no different in its effect upon the "counter-defendant" than a regular lawsuit, and gives the "counter-plaintiff" full rights of discovery and other procedural devices for wreaking havoc. As it was still spewing out of the fax machine, I called Gary and told him that Cohen was cross-claiming against him for $9 million for Defamation, Unfair Competition, and Cybersquatting. Then I had a question: "Gary, do you have insurance for your business activities?" Yes, he thought he did. I told him to fax me his policy immediately.

Gary may have had trouble finding some documents, but he had his State Farm insurance policies to me within hours. It looked very good. He had one policy for $1 million in coverage, and another for $300,000. They both covered slander, that is, defamation. I called Gary back with the happy news. We would be making lemonade, and State Farm was buying the sugar!

Of course, as the old adage goes, "there's many a slip twixt the cup and the lip," and State Farm might have very different ideas about springing for our lemonade party, but I knew once Gary understood the principles of insurance bad faith law, his burning sense of urgency would get us either a defense or a hell of a lawsuit against State Farm. Because insurance companies don't always like to defend you when a guy like Cohen, worth maybe hundreds of millions, sues you because you called him a thief. Or they might not defend you very aggressively. The key to getting a good, vigorous defense, worth hundreds of thousands of dollars, is knowing the law of insurance bad faith.

I learned about insurance bad faith first from Steve Schiffrin, a much-published author on freedom of speech and the First Amendment who now teaches at Cornell Law School. Steve was brilliant, way too brilliant in fact to be fully appreciated by a classroom of 75 new law students lucky enough to learn basic tort law from a bona fide fucking genius. Steve was what you'd call pudgy, with thinning, sandy hair, and the complexion of a guy who rarely–if ever–goes to the beach. He was sweetly sarcastic, and enjoyed dealing legal propositions with a broad outward sweeping movement of his right arm, hand extended, palm upward, with a satisfied pursing of his lips, and eyebrows contracting to make the point.

Steve introduced us to insurance bad faith law as the place where the law of torts—which deals with legal wrongs between strangers—collides with the law of contracts, which deals with legal disputes between contracting parties. You often get more in damages for tort cases, where you recover the entire loss, including things like pain, suffering, and emotional distress, than in contract lawsuits, where damages are usually limited to the face amount of the contract.

Steve introduced us to the case of *Crisci v. Security Insurance*. In that case, an elderly Italian widow named Rosina Crisci owned a rental with a second floor walkup, which was insured by Security Insurance for $10,000. She also had a very hefty female tenant. One day the stairs broke and the hefty lady fell straight through, leaving her hanging in midair, which caused physical injury and a "severe psychosis." She had no prior history of mental problems. The hefty lady's lawyers sued the landlady, and Security Insurance appointed lawyers to defend Mrs. Crisci. The lawyers who Security hired scoffed at all of the plaintiff's settlement demands, which started at $400,000, but dropped to $10,000, and even lower, to $9,000. Even though Security's expert physicians predicted a verdict in excess of $100,000, the company offered only $3,000 for the physical injuries, refusing to pay "one cent" for the psychological injuries. Mrs. Crisci offered to kick in $2,500 if Security would pay the $6,500 difference between that and the final $9,000 demand, but Security rebuffed this opportunity as well.

The hefty lady went to trial and got the $100,000 trial verdict Security's doctors had warned about. Her lawyers collected $10,000 from Security, the full amount of the insurance coverage, and then reached a settlement with poor Mrs. Crisci, who lost everything. As the California Supreme Court put it, Mrs. Crisci, "an immigrant widow of 70, became indigent. She worked as a babysitter, and her grandchildren paid her rent. The change in her physical condition was accompanied by a decline in physical health, hysteria and suicide attempts. She then brought this action."

Mrs. Crisci sued Security for "breach of the covenant of good faith and fair dealing." This "covenant" imposes a duty on the contracting parties to "do everything necessary to achieve the purposes of the contract, and nothing to defeat those contractual purposes." The California Supreme Court held that the covenant of good faith and fair dealing was especially important when it comes to an insurance contract, because it is a contract for personal security and peace of mind. Thus, the court found that by rejecting a settlement demand within policy limits ($10,000 or less) when it was reasonably clear Mrs. Crisci would lose far more at trial, Security violated the covenant of good faith and fair dealing. Therefore, Security was subject to "extra-contractual damages," that is, (gasp) the full $100,000 Mrs. Crisci got hit for at trial, plus Mrs. Crisci's emotional distress, plus some punitive damages. This is now called "opening the policy," and is justified on the grounds that it is the only way to teach insurance companies to not take risks with their insured's interests, thinking "well, worst comes to worst, we just pay the policy limits." Instead, they must settle every case as if they were going to have to pay the whole adverse verdict, for only then are they acting fairly.

During my first year at UCLA Law School, I completely missed the significance of Steve Schiffrin's lecture on the *Crisci* case. But it became my daily bread at Mazursky, Schwartz & Angelo, where I worked on large claims, like Gary Lehto's, who was rendered paraplegic when his car was rear ended by a car driven by a career drunk and owned by his drunken dad. Allstate screwed that case up when it refused to settle for the $25,000 policy unless Lehto gave a release to *both* father and son. Mr. Lehto's final verdict was for $3.5 Million. An insurance company must treat these "over-limits" cases with the greatest solicitude, because if an insurance adjuster refuses to settle a multi-million dollar case for $25,000, Mrs. Crisci's descendants may well have their way with the insurer's assets.

At MS&A, we wanted them to refuse to settle. Sometimes we'd get a case on referral from other, no-name plaintiff lawyers who had been rebuffed by the insurers. When the adjusters saw MS&A on the case, their whole attitude would change. They would become eager to pay what had been out of the question before. My standard tough-guy response to these last-minute converts was, "In the future, always settle with a schmuck if you can. You missed your chance this time."

Gary's insurance policies for $300,000 and $1 Million were utterly dwarfed by the liability risk presented by Cohen's $9 Million claim. Thus, even if Cohen only nicked Gary for a sixth of his total $9 million damages demand, it would exceed the value of both policies combined. You can see how that excess potential makes the risk of refusing to defend Gary one that State Farm would consider carefully. If Cohen got a $9 million verdict against Gary, because State Farm refused to defend him, Gary could sue State Farm for the loss, or even sell Cohen his right to sue State Farm. With this kind of leverage, the insurer must step up to the plate and defend.

The insurer then has one more decision to make—whether or not to "reserve its rights." By "reserving its rights" the insurance company says to its insured, "Okay, I'll pay for your lawyer to defend this claim, but it may not really be covered under your policy, so I'm not promising to pay the verdict if you get hit, although I'll defend you until then." If an insurance carrier "reserves its rights," their insured is actually benefited in two ways. First, the carrier must then pay for a lawyer, chosen by the insured, to advise the insured how to deal with the insurance carrier. Second, the insured also gets to pick their own lawyer for the main defense, rather than having the insurance carrier pick one of their "panel counsel." So reserving rights can get expensive for an insurer.

State Farm at first denied coverage altogether under the $1 Million policy, and agreed to defend under the $300,000 policy, while reserving its rights. Thus, I tried to arrange to have State Farm retain the best First Amendment and speech law firm I knew of, Irell & Manella in Century City, Los Angeles. Irell & Manella thinks of itself as a firm that combines stellar intellectual firepower with a take-no-prisoners litigation ethic, basically promising to take your adversary on a rocket ride to hell. Actually, they are famous for delivering on this boast, and billing in a manner commensurate with their achievements. I clerked there when I was at UCLA, so I put a call through to partner Morgan Chu, who I figured was probably still representing ABC on speech issues. He put me in touch with his associate, David Codell, a 1999 *magna cum laude* Harvard graduate and a gem. David was interested in the case, so I started trying to get them onboard as Gary's attorneys to defend against Cohen's cross-complaint.

The plan to hire Irell & Manella was looking good until Jose Guillermo, the State Farm adjuster who had been assigned to the case, realized who they were and how much they charged. Their billing rates were way out of line with State Farm's usual rates for insurance defense counsel. So State Farm withdrew its reservation of rights under the $300,000 policy. This decision was a no-brainer. Simple arithmetic. Better to be on the hook for $300,000 indemnity than pay for separate counsel, plus the cost of Irell & Manella's rocket fuel. State Farm was then able to select one of its own panel attorneys, rather than have me make the choice for them.

State Farm hired Richard Diestel for the job. Initially, Rich was not taken with the case. I don't think he had any intention of becoming involved in what he thought of as pornography law, and his involvement with defamation cases seemed neither deep nor extensive. However, it was my job to get him to spend abundantly from the great big bag of State Farm money, and Rich had an obligation to provide Gary with the best defense against Cohen's counter-claims that could be mustered. It would not be long before he felt the sting of Gary's emails, cell phone calls, and abrasive letters. He was in no way ready to start representing *Gary Kremen in Cohen v. Kremen*, but that had nothing to do with it. He was in the ring, Bob Dorband was in the other corner, and the bell had just rung. "Rich," I told him, "you are going to make a lot of money on this case."

CHAPTER SEVENTEEN

WHERE'S THE DOGBITE?

COHEN BOUGHT HIMSELF A LOAD OF TROUBLE when he alleged defamation against Kremen, claiming that Kremen had falsely called Cohen a thief by accusing him of "stealing Sex.Com" in an interview with *WiredNews.com Magazine* writer Craig Bicknell. The wonderful thing about having to defend a defamation claim, and having an insurance lawyer to help you do it, is that truth is a defense to defamation. Gary could win the defamation claim by proving that Cohen really had stolen Sex.Com. That's how it became Rich Diestel's job to prove that Gary Kremen was speaking the truth when he said Cohen had stolen the domain name. Cohen had created a two-front war. We now had two guns instead of one. Best of all, Diestel had an unlimited supply of ammunition and a directive to keep expending it until the threat of Cohen's counter-claim was extinguished.

Still, Rich was a little slow on the trigger. While he wouldn't ever really say it out-and-out, he must have been extremely uncomfortable with the case. His discomfort is perhaps best explained by a remark Rich made about how State Farm adjusters were reacting to the wave of Internet cases they were having to defend based on a simple homeowner's insurance policy. Lots of tech businesses having been launched from bedrooms and garages, these cases generated a type of case load for the insurance adjusters that they hadn't previously seen. According to Rich, when confronted with a case like Sex.Com, the adjusters were wont to ask, "Where's the dogbite?" Rich was describing his own reaction, as well.

Rich likes simple stories. Simple stories like, "my client's dog bit the neighbor's kid." The nice thing about a story like that is, it's easy to investigate. You can find out that the kid was always torturing the dog, that he isn't doing well in school, and that he stuttered even before he was bitten. You can get the kid's medical records, his school records, and the dog's veterinarian records. There is a limited universe of facts, a limited number of witnesses, and you can tell when your job is done.

By contrast, the Sex.Com story, being primarily the creation of Stephen M. Cohen, was replete with switchbacks and confusion, with more corporations than you could shake a stick at, with forged documents and prison records, and imaginary witnesses scattered over the globe. Cohen's skein of lies frustrated Rich, even as it obsessed Gary. Rich thought it would be difficult to win using a trial story that was difficult to comprehend, let alone explain.

Before you sell your case to the judge or jury, you have to at least be able to sell people like Rich, who have been paid to agree with you. To sell Rich, I had to master all of the available facts, and render them in a simple, convincing story: "Cohen is a crook, he stole Sex.Com, and he's hiding the money in a bunch of phony corporations." Once I was able to articulate that story, and support it with documents and testimony, Rich bought it. What he bought even more was the fact that Bob Dorband, Cohen's lawyer, was one of the trickiest rascals to ever walk up the courthouse steps. Bob tied Rich's tail in a knot so many times that it made Rich furious toward the end of the case. That was when the lemonade really started flowing. Once Diestel was pissed.

Rich got along well with witnesses. I won't say he got as much information out of a witness as I did, when we did depositions together, but I think witnesses generally tended to feel more comfortable with him. That was a good thing, because they would open up, and I could get more stuff. Rich was the kind of guy that you could stolidly share some hotel food with, while swapping the occasional war story, and cursing Dorband and Cohen. "That's fucking bullshit." That's the sort of thing that Rich Diestel would say. He said it more often and with increasing conviction as the case wore on.

Diestel's investigator, Phil Stuto, did some good work, too. He interviewed several of Cohen's ex wives, and found a dying witness by the name of Arnaldo Peralta, whose name Cohen had forged in order to obtain Mr. Peralta's "permission" to incorporate a California company with the name of Omnitec, since Mr. Peralta already operated a company with a confusingly similar name—Omni-Tech. Stuto was also the only person to get a trip to the Islands out of this case. He seized his opportunity, early in the case, and promptly got his ass to the British Virgin Islands to check out Cohen's phony corporations. He didn't learn anything, but then again, it was never clear why he was going in the first place.

Once discovery reopened, Diestel gave us additional moral high ground with Judge Trumbull. Many judges are more sympathetic to a plea for more discovery from a defendant who is being pressed with the threat of damages. Somehow it seems unfair to allow someone to be sued for damages and prevented from getting evidence to prove or disprove those claims. So Diestel, in his position as Gary's defender against a claim for $9 Million, had a strong interest in finding out just how Cohen had incurred those damages. As lost profits, presumably. To verify those, we needed to see financials. Since Cohen had no intention of producing any accurate financial documents, our strategy was first, to file motions to compel production of documents and attendance of witnesses, second, to attempt to enforce those orders, and third, to file new motions to compel compliance when Cohen inevitably failed to comply. A judge can only tolerate so much disrespect of her orders. With both Diestel and myself filing motion after motion, it wasn't long before we were regularly able to recount an increasingly familiar tale of woe to an increasingly sympathetic Judge Trumbull. We gained momentum as the judge resolved one discovery battle after another in our favor. As we banked each victory, we had the piles of paperwork, the airline tickets and deposition expenses, the sixteen hour days to show we'd paid for each order dearly. In litigation, there is no substitute for pushing ahead aggressively in discovery. Diestel shared that burden with me like no one else.

Throughout the case, it was good to have a dignified guy like Rich Diestel standing there, employed by the most legitimate entity in the world, an insurance company, denying everything, admitting nothing, and insisting that he's going to get a complete dismissal of all claims. That stuff really cuts some ice with judges and juries, even when it's a bad case. And when a guy like that is plainly in the right, he is unbeatable.

In this case, Diestel was blessed with luck. He didn't have to compromise one damned thing. He participated in the total defeat of Cohen's position in a case that will impart a flavor of the exotic to his entire career. You wonder what could ever make him want to go back to doing dogbites.

CHAPTER EIGHTEEN

RENT-A-NERD

Henry Ford once made a comment about experts. It happened when he sued a man for slander who had said he was ignorant. Trying to prove that Ford was in fact stupid, the lawyer pressed Ford about some obscure point of history or science. Ford shot back that he saw no reason to clutter his mind with that type of information when he had "a row of push buttons" on his desk, pushing any one of which would put innumerable experts in all areas of human knowledge at his fingertips. If that was ignorance, then, well, he was stupid. You can imagine he got the better of the argument with the jury. To possess experts at your command, apparently, is better than to know something yourself.

We needed an expert. Gary found one. Affectionately, I call her a nerd. Ellen Rony is never so comfortable as when she has her Apple notebook computer on her lap, sitting in her solarium, culling through a few hundred emails from the friends in her vast global community. She corresponds with the luminaries of the Internet universe. Even the fearsome Phil Sbarbaro, longtime lawyer for NSI, called her a friend. Well, of course that was before he'd threatened to cut off her toes, but what's a few digits between friends? No, Ellen might look like any other single mom with a dog in a suburb north of the Golden Gate Bridge, but the sleek profile of her pampered BMW suggested she had potential as a litigation weapon.

Ellen was the author of the Domain Name Handbook. Gary got a copy of the book for me, which comes with a CD-rom. Ellen was an Internet buff who had gotten so into chronicling the history of NSI that she actually had stuff saved off their old web pages that couldn't be found anywhere else. This made me aware of something I had been worrying about — the evanescence of the Internet record. The thought immediately casts an Orwellian shadow across the mind. Ellen Rony brought me face to face with the fact that the Internet had completely eliminated the need for the cutting and pasting department that was a necessary part of the Newthink/Newspeak system in the novel *1984*. In Orwell's novel the future was routinely rewritten, but the paperwork was immense. Entire newspapers had to be rewritten and reprinted, archived for history's sake, then revised again. I remember in reading the novel that the very cumbersomeness of the process comforted me, as I thought that it would be impossible to accomplish that kind of historical revisionism. The paper record was a bulwark against it. And here, the Internet had destroyed one more barrier to deception, dissimulation, and alteration of the historical record. Truly, if corporations control the Internet, history is in unsafe hands.

Ellen's book is not the sort of thing you would ordinarily find piling up next to my bed. Even if I want to study cyberspace, I'd rather read cyberpunk science fiction and see what rubs off that way. Ellen's book had some good facts in it. Mind you, none about Sex.Com. The only mention of Sex.Com in Ellen's book mistakenly states that it was originally registered by Cohen's company, Sporting Houses Management Corporation. However, Ellen could not be faulted. She took the information directly from NSI's website. According to Ellen, NSI should have listed Kremen as the original first-time registrant, with Sporting Houses Management coming later. For some reason, NSI deleted Kremen's registration so completely that all records of the original registration were obliterated. Orwellian, again.

After reading a few chapters of Ellen's book, I found some useful stuff. Particularly I liked her clear and simple statement that the term *dot-com* had been invented by John Postel in 1984. This was useful in debunking a defensive claim that Cohen had engineered using the trademark laws to validate his theft of Sex.Com. Cohen claimed he acquired a trademark in Sex.Com by "using it in commerce" since 1979 as part of a computer bulletin board operation. So citing Ellen's book enabled me to argue early and often that Cohen's claim was absurd, since "dot-coms hadn't even been invented in 1979."

Gary and I first met Ellen at a little restaurant on the water in Sausalito. Gary comes from the don't drink at lunchtime ethic, but with the bright afternoon sun shining off the water, the three of us enjoyed our drinks. I forget what Ellen had, but it was something fruity and festive. I presume I had a Bloody Mary, your standard alcohol breakfast. My modus operandi with Gary was to back him up in all his flamboyant assertions about having lots and lots of money, to look well fed and well tended, and ask a few good questions. We wanted to recruit Ellen for our team because, as I repeatedly told her, she was the only person who could lay claim to being a published authority about the history and operation of NSI.

As with many a person, we were able to forge an alliance with a legitimate mainstream authority because we had taken the moral high ground. We circulated the third amended complaint widely to journalists and industry people like Ellen. Right there in the document Gary declared he was not a pornographer, and his site would not have been what Sex.Com had become. Gary enjoyed pitching this concept to Ellen, and his charisma caught fire as he did so, making him genuinely charming. His site would have been a far more wholesome, high-minded affair. This had an important effect on Ellen, who has a young son, Alexander, and hadn't given much thought to pornography prior to our meeting. Gary's presentation put her mind at rest, allowing her to concentrate on her field of expertise—explaining exactly how Cohen had managed to get NSI to transfer the name, and why that was every bit as much NSI's fault as it was Cohen's. At first, Gary paid Ellen, but eventually, State Farm started picking up the tab, because after all, we couldn't prove the case without her.

CHAPTER NINETEEN

NSI, SORCERY, AND I

THE PRACTICE OF THE TRIAL ARTS CAN BE ANALOGIZED TO SORCERY, which allows us to see the marks left on the modern lawyer's psyche by the medieval mold in which it was forged. The witch trials were, first and foremost, trials. The prosecutors who conducted them were priests. All the participants in those charged events were involved in a web of supernatural projections, but the influence of rationality was also felt. Much of the same dynamic inspires modern courtroom action, hidden beneath a veneer of modernity.

The courts use special language to inspire solemnity and add weight to the process. Papers are not merely mailed or delivered, they are "served" on the opposing party. One doesn't simply start a lawsuit, one "commences the action." Once started, the proceedings continue until "judgment." Judges often refer to themselves in the third person, delivering rulings in the capacity of "the Court." In many courts, lawyers are expected to show an exaggerated politeness, a courtly style if you will. There is still room for the use of an apt Latin phrase in argument before a judge.

Seen as sorcery, the trial lawyer's filings with the court operate as spells to destroy the foe. For the lawyer as sorcerer, the defendant is a demon who must be "summoned" and thus brought within the "jurisdiction of the court" that can pass judgment upon him. Until the lawyer places a person under the court's jurisdiction, he relates to him just like anyone else. Once a lawyer establishes jurisdiction over someone, he may deal with that person using the power of the court. Using that power, a lawyer can dispossess a person of their property, detain and imprison them, end the bonds of matrimony, sentence to death and otherwise modify the earthly relations of the members of our society. The business has very little to do with kindness and much to do with compulsion.

In criminal prosecutions, the prosecutor establishes jurisdiction over the defendant by arresting him. The act of arrest establishes the court's authority. In civil cases, the formal service of the summons and complaint on the defendant establishes the court's jurisdiction. After ju-

risdiction is established, the defendant is held in a magic circle, and ig-
nores the court's directives at his or her peril. When thinking as a sorcerer,
all cases are magical contests, and all procedural devices are viewed as
spells. A motion to dismiss, for example, is a "terminating spell," as is a
motion for summary judgment.

If you go about summoning demons and putting them under the
court's jurisdiction, you quickly learn they don't like it. They try to break
out of the magic circle in which you've confined them. They curse at
you. The complaint is the first spell where you allege that the demon
committed certain wrongs that the court is bound to redress. This spell
must be constructed to meet formal requirements. The lawyers for the
demons (defendants) often first move to dismiss the complaint on pe-
dantic grounds, using legal erudition to argue that the complaint does
not recite the "elements of the claim" in the proper fashion, or that
it has been filed too late, or that this demon is immune to that spell.
The beginning of adequate plaintiff-side sorcery is building an excellent complaint that will hold even a nasty demon. A good complaint
anticipates some defenses that will be raised and heads off objections.
Thus, when the inevitable motions to dismiss arrive, the plaintiff sorcerer can defend the complaint with arguments thought out before the
complaint was even filed.

NSI didn't bother with motions to dismiss like the ones that Cohen
hurled at Gary's first four complaints. NSI did what classy defendants
do–it filed an answer to the complaint, saving its thunder for the Big
Kahuna, the Motion for Summary Judgment. When I first went to work
in the trenches of sorcery as a young apprentice, it was commonly said
that motions for summary judgment were rarely granted. This no longer
seems to be true. Years of tort reform rhetoric has made judges more willing to terminate cases and free civil demons who in the past would have
been required to stand trial. Particularly in the Federal courts, a Supreme
Court case called *Cellotex* gave federal judges a shot of testosterone that
made them more willing to dismiss lawsuits at summary judgment. NSI
is a big winner under this policy change. As of 1999 NSI had won virtually every lawsuit against it via summary judgment, which made about
eighty wins in a row. So I was not looking forward to receiving NSI's motion for summary judgment.

NSI filed its motion for summary judgment in mid-December, 1999.

NSI's take on the case was simple. NSI admitted that Gary had been the first to register the domain name. NSI admitted it had transferred the domain name to Cohen, in response to the October 15, 1995 forged letter that appeared to be from Online Classifieds, Inc. However, NSI claimed it "did not know anything about Ms. Dimmick's relation with plaintiff," and thus had no idea that the letter was forged. NSI also argued that Gary didn't have a contract with NSI, because Gary had paid nothing for Sex. Com, and "the domain name registration application is... devoid of any language indicating any expectation of a *quid pro quo*." NSI also argued that since domain names were "not property," Gary had no rights to the name arising separately from contract. Thus, argued NSI, Gary's problem was with Cohen, and NSI should just be dismissed from the case. As spells go, NSI's motion for summary judgment had very good prospects for getting the nod from the judge, the arbiter of our magical contest.

When the dark cloud of summary judgment looms, however, and things look bleak, the plaintiff sorcerer initiates a two-fold course of action: (1) Buy time, and (2) Build the record. Thus, the first and most important spell after filing complaints is the "time spell." One must deprive an opponent of the pleasure of making things happen on his or her schedule. And one must free oneself of the pressure of working on a deadline imposed by the other guy. If bad things are about to happen, your first battle cry is, "Not now!" Later you will have time to build the record, write your arguments, and organize your evidence.

As soon as I got the motion from NSI, I looked it over to learn what new, additional facts I didn't have that would enable me to defeat the motion. I then wrote Dave Dolkas, NSI's counsel of record, a letter asking him for an extension of time to oppose the motion while I gathered those facts through discovery. Naturally, he wouldn't give me the extra time, so I filed a motion under Rule 56(f), asking the judge to give me more time. I wrote a skeleton of what my bigger opposition would be, mainly emphasizing how much I needed to get these additional facts that I didn't yet have, and thus my need for *more time*. Under 56(f), the judge is basically always supposed to give you that time.

Usually, when you file a 56(f) motion, the judge will just reschedule the hearing on the motion for summary judgment so you can complete the discovery you claim will enable you to prepare the opposition. That had been my uniform experience up until this case. However, this time, something new happened. Judge Ware kept the hearing on NSI's motion scheduled for January 24, 2000, and scheduled my motion for more time to be heard at the same time. This meant that on January 24th, the judge could either give me more time or grant NSI's motion for summary judgment.

On January 24th, I stood in front of Judge Ware. He was very pleasant, but got right to the point—he didn't see how he could hold NSI liable if its people were duped by Cohen's forgery. Judge Ware likes to question the advocates. He asked me whether the letter was a forgery, and whether NSI was taken in by Cohen's deception. I answered that the letter was a forgery, and that NSI may have been taken in by it, but there was some evidence to indicate that NSI conspired with Cohen to aid in the theft of Sex.Com. Judge Ware asked what evidence that was. I felt like I was standing in front of locomotive that was just pausing briefly before running me over. Well, I told Judge Ware, there was a man named Lee Fuller in Riverside, California, who told me Cohen had told him "he had a girlfriend at NSI, and he could get any domain name he wanted." Judge Ware questioned further. Had I spoken to this Lee Fuller myself, directly? Yes, I confirmed, I had. I felt as if the locomotive shifted into neutral, although its engines were still throbbing, while I held it at bay with a slender reed. Because of that slender reed, Judge Ware said he would give me more time to conduct discovery into whether "the domain name Sex. Com was not transferred by Network Solutions in the normal course of business." Part one of the twofold strategy was complete—I had more time. Now for part two—building the record through discovery. Judge Ware could help there, too.

Remembering Judge Ware's willingness to order Gary to resume his hastily adjourned deposition, I asked Judge Ware to allow me to take the depositions of appropriate persons at NSI. Judge Ware questioned further. Who would I depose, and what would I ask? I would want to question the human resources manager of NSI, at least, I said. No, said the Judge, he wouldn't allow me to pry into the sex lives of people at NSI; however, if I wanted Cohen's deposition, Judge Ware volunteered, he would order that to take place. I could hardly believe this was happening. Dorband had been stonewalling on producing Cohen, but I hadn't filed a motion to compel him to appear at deposition, and here the judge was just offering it. Yes, I responded, I wanted to do that, and an order would be a big help. No problem, said the Judge. Where do you want to take the deposition? San Diego, I responded. Fine, said the Judge, and he ordered Cohen to appear for deposition "at the Edward J. Schwartz United States Courthouse on February 3, 2000 at 9:00 a.m. for a deposition" covering "any matters pertaining to this litigation."

Judge Ware gave us until February 14, 2000 to file an opposition to NSI's motion for summary judgment. That gave me just shy of three weeks to prepare for and depose Cohen, prepare an expert declaration from Ellen Rony, and build my record in opposition. When I left the courtroom, I could still feel that locomotive idling on the track, waiting to resume its advance.

CHAPTER TWENTY

TO THE COURT OF PUBLIC OPINION

I'VE MADE A FEW SPEECHES ON COURTHOUSE STEPS, and always been dissatisfied with the results. Reporters never seem to agree with me about what is important about the case. The best policy in dealing with the press is to formulate a sound bite that is witty enough to be quotable, and coherent enough that they can't cut out a part and distort it. In Southern Oregon, I tried to sound folksy, as well. When a reporter for a Medford television station asked for a quote about a victim's rights initiative, I said: "It's kind of like a TV dinner. Some parts of it look pretty good, and other parts you wouldn't feed to your dog, but when you read the ingredients, you don't want any of it." This was quoted accurately and completely by the TV news, the Portland paper, and the local paper.

Gary was eager to do a press release. He thought it would win the case if enough people realized that, as Gary put it, "the guy stole it!" He believed NSI would be impelled by public opinion to return Sex.Com. That seemed an unlikely result to me, but I didn't oppose doing a press release. The case was news, and I had a legitimate legal reason for wanting to provide notice to the public that Cohen didn't lawfully own Sex. Com—I didn't want him to be able to sell it to an "innocent buyer" who could then try to claim "bona fide purchaser" status, entitling the "BFP" to retain control of the name. Cohen was already making that argument with respect to the corporate alter-ego defendants, YNATA, Ocean Fund, and Sandman Internacional. The more people that knew Sex.Com was stolen, the less tenable it would be for Cohen to stage a BFP defense with new "innocent buyers."

I hired a friend to help me put together an email list of high-tech reporters, and together we wrote an email press release of several pages, detailing the essence of the case as we knew it. The release accused Cohen of stealing Sex.Com, and announced that he was a convicted felon who had served time in Federal Prison. Just a couple of days before Cohen's February 3rd deposition, I hit 'send' on my email and fired the press release off to a list of around thirty reporters. The reverberations of that act would be felt for some time.

CHAPTER TWENTY-ONE

STEPHEN MICHAEL COHEN

ON FEBRUARY 3, 2000, I WOKE UP IN MY FAVORITE HOTEL, the Hilton Torrey Pines, San Diego. Every time I go there, it is blessed with the same fresh smell of sea air, the sound of rolling waves gently sighing somewhere out beyond the balcony in the warm light. The rooms are homey and modern, in cool, well-matched colors. The air is fresh with the scent of huge eucalyptus trees. I was glad Gary had gotten to be a millionaire. The last time I stayed at the Torrey Pines was ten years before, when I tried my first case, so it had nostalgic associations. It was a good place to start a hard day. A Sikh drove me to Beth Ballerini's court reporting office on Kettner Boulevard, where the tough part began.

There was Dave Dolkas, with a goatee and a laptop, and Bob Dorband looking fresh-faced and unflappable in his shirt sleeves, settled in behind the conference table, ready to rock. Bob Dorband is a charming man, not very big, with a full head of white hair that appears not to have gone grey so much as to have been chosen in precisely the same color as Mozart's wig in the movie Amadeus. And while Dorband has never displayed Tom Hulz's trademark manic Mozart laugh, that high-pitched yip that cracked up whole audiences the world over, Bob Dorband's speech pattern does resemble the warm, convincing tone Mozart would use when he stretched the truth. Insidious, bedeviling, a tone to set your teeth on edge. Bob has a way of presenting his position so well that you feel foolish opposing him. Your own position starts slipping away like teflon under your fingers. He gives you argumentative vertigo.

And there, to my right as I walked in the door, at the head of the eight foot conference room table, sat a man with an incredibly ugly tie. The man with the very ugly tie also wore a very satisfied look. The look was one of those embryonic grins that seems about to gestate rapidly and cover the entire face with a giant smile of satisfaction. It was one of those looks that seemed to say, "C'mon, you're dying to know what I'm smiling about, so ask me." The smile was on the face of a good-sized Jewish man who overall looked humpty-dumptyish, although not grotesque, but more Bob Hoskinsy. And with a Bob Hoskinsy close-cropped haircut.

Hoskins could probably do this role perfectly. Just cut the English accent, flatten the tone so it drops back in the throat, and blur it over with an American accent somewhere between Jersey and Newport Beach. It is a voice that lays out just the facts, ma'am. It is a voice that says he is not here to screw around, that he is too big for that, and that we should just get this over with because it's a joke. The tie was red and black, pure strawberry red, India-ink black, with *pleats* in it. That tie was like the last thing a bug sees before it gets squashed flat by a flyswatter. I was not among friends.

Except Rich Diestel. And of course there's Beth Ballerini, the proof of God's mercy to the numerous San Diego attorneys who patronize her, no doubt because of her absolutely unfailing good cheer, casual blonde ambition, and total accuracy in preparing deposition transcripts. And meet the videographer, Jerry, a bit of a silver-haired guy who's seen it all, most recently from behind the lens of a large legal videotape unit with dials and a backup videotape, provided courtesy of State Farm Insurance. Gee, I guess we're all here, so we might as well start.

Right after Beth swears Cohen in, Dorband starts with a sort of soft left jab. "Charles, before we begin."

I respond, "Sure."

Dorband: "I'd like to bring up something that came to my attention yesterday, which was the filing of a press release apparently that came from your office. And are you acknowledging that there was a press release?"

Backing up, elbows forward, gloves high, I respond, "I'm not here to answer questions, Bob—What's your concern?"

Just getting wound up, Dorband starts with the body blows: "The timing of the press release was highly suspect. It happened the day before Mr. Cohen's deposition.... The fact that this press release was issued I think is highly unethical and improper and an attempt to disturb my client's ability to testify at the deposition today."

Ouch! Unethical. I hate that word. It always means that things have become intensely personal. For unethical conduct the Bar can yank your ticket, pull your card, take the "esquire" right off the end of your name. And there was no doubt that playing with the news media put you right into an area where ethics could be an issue. I'd come out of prior media encounters with no more mishap than being misquoted, misinterpreted and subtly maligned. I hadn't really thought it would be any different in this case, which was of course willfully stupid, because Cohen had already cross-claimed against Gary for defamation with respect to the Wired article. What was I thinking? Without realizing it, I was taking risks I'd never planned on, like a cabbie who gets caught up in a chase scene in some crazy movie, and ends up driving like Dale Earnhardt on his last lap, all because someone said, "Follow that car."

But I'm not thinking about ethics for long. At that point, it's a little bit after 9:00 a.m., I'm jack-full of Starbucks Americano, the judge told Cohen to be here, so he wouldn't dare try and walk, and I've got to make this work.

Dorband lays out his proposal: "We will proceed with the deposition. If there are questions of a personal nature that my client feels uncomfortable in answering, we will reserve our rights to answer those questions at a later date after the judge has been able to rule on whether we can trust that the information that is going to be given in this deposition and in this proceeding will be kept confidential."

Although Dorband didn't have the right to demand confidentiality for this presumptively public proceeding, my back was against the wall. I had to get Cohen's testimony, or all of the expense of flying to San Diego, and most of the advantage of having Judge Ware order the deposition to take place at all, would be lost. So I cut the deal. It would all go forward under wraps.

I felt like I was in a boxing ring. I am no boxer, being more of a tuck and roll Aikido type myself, but my dad was a professional boxer in his late teens and early twenties until a bout with TB forced him to hang up his gloves. His aggressive drive to compete in multiple weight-classes weakened his health. He told me he could lose or gain up to 20 pounds in a few weeks time. In the end, he said TB was a blessing. Good thing he caught it, or he'd have ended up like those other old Mexican boxers we'd run into on Sunday morning, shopping for tortillas and menudo in Phoenix. He'd point out a fellow with a loping stride and a slightly foolish grin and say, "Ring a bell next to that one and he'll put up his dukes, asking 'where's the fight?'" He loved the sport and skill of boxing, but regretted its human toll. From this perspective, he taught me his fundamental rules — keep your guard up, use lots of short jabs and very few big swings, and train for endurance so when you need to, you can outrun the other guy and the clock. Above all, avoid hits to the head. My dad sat in the back row during my first trial down in San Diego. On February 3, 2000, he was in a nursing home, silent among his 90 years of memories. I would fight this one for him.

The bell rang. I stepped forward from my corner, my father's cautious voice in my ear. Cohen sat smirking, his bulk a silent challenge. He wasn't here to box. He was a sumo wrestler with tentacles. He wanted to wrap one of those long sucker tentacles around me, lock me in stupid wordplay, make Beth's fingers type endless bullshit, and squeeze the life out of my expiring body. Out of breath, out of words, my lifeless corpse would float to the surface. I could see that fate looming before me, to be left like flotsam in the wake of a remorseless con man who was absolutely detached from any personal issues I could affect. Cohen was above the fray. Dorband was just security. I was a nuisance, being evicted from a place I didn't belong. Contempt rolled off Cohen like fog off the slopes of a mountain. Like a mountain, he shrugged at the insignificance of it all.

Cohen was what Francis Wellman calls "the perjured witness" in his book *The Art of Cross-Examination*. Wellman advises fast questioning to trip up the liar, because he "can't make up lies as fast as you can make up questions." To ask questions fast, you have to know what you're going to ask. You need a list of questions. But if you put together a questionnaire, you may not listen to the answers you're actually getting. If a smart witness understands that you're working off a questionnaire, and you fail to explore the details of areas before moving on, they realize they can keep things from you, and you won't notice it. They start to nod along with you, allowing you to believe what they want you to believe, knowing that once they get through an area, you are not likely to return to it. So a deposition is not conducted like an oral questionnaire. You must stay loose, and adapt your questions to the rhythm of the witness. One way is to hook your next question to their last answer. You do it like this:

CARREON: "Does he work with a firm?"

A. "Yes."

CARREON: "Which firm is that?"

A. "Hochman & Cohen."

At first, the witness has to go along with it to get your rhythm started. But the rhythm feels safe and harmless. Since the witness is on the other side of a push-me-pull-you setup, they feel somewhat in control. They relax, you can begin to take advantage of it, pulling harder here, pushing harder there, without engendering too much resistance. Pretty soon you are sawing through the facts, and with luck your adversary is going along with it, lulled by the fact that his client appears to be okay with it. That's how it's supposed to work.

With Cohen, of course, nothing works right. Take this typical piece of questioning about Ocean Fund International:

CARREON: "What ownership interest did you have in Ocean Fund International?"

COHEN: "Stock."

CARREON: "How much?"

COHEN: "I don't recall."

CARREON: "Were you the majority shareholder at any time?"

COHEN: "No."

CARREON: "Who was the majority shareholder?"

COHEN: "It's ambiguous."

CARREON: "It's ambiguous? What part of majority don't you understand?"

COHEN: "What part of time do you not understand?"

CARREON: "When Ocean Fund was created... the approximate date?"

COHEN: "I can't even do that. I think—I believe it was in the year 1996 or—7, but I'm not quite sure."

CARREON: "Did you have to sign any papers in order to participate in the creation of Ocean Fund International?"

COHEN: "I probably did."

CARREON: "And do you remember what the nature of those papers was?"

COHEN: "No, I do not."

Cohen used my speedy rhythm to short-change me on information. As I learned things, I had to backtrack and pick them up and restart my questioning. Ordinary witnesses usually try and make the truth plain for you. Their biggest problem is mixing what they know with what they believe. Usually they know a lot less than they think they do, but they are so confident of the truth of it that they'll just throw their whole story in front of you. You can pick out the pieces of hearsay, opinion and prejudice, leaving the diminished resultant facts for your use. An honest witness will fill you in on the who, where, what, why and when with a rounded, all-encompassing response, but I got none of that from Cohen. Check out his smooth denial here, where he claims to own no portion of several companies which are all owned by his offshore holding company YNATA:

CARREON: "Tell us what you know about what YNATA Corporation owns in terms of interests, financial interests in other corporations, please."

COHEN: "Other than the corporations that I have listed which were Omnitech International, First City Financial, Sandman Internacional, Oceantel, those are the companies that I am aware of."

CARREON: "Do you have any ownership in any of those companies?"

COHEN: "No."

If an average witness had once held stock in these companies and later sold it, he would say so straight out. But Steve made me dig it out of him:

CARREON: "Have you at any time held an ownership in any of those companies?"

COHEN: "Yes."

CARREON: "Which of those companies did you have an ownership interest in at some time."

COHEN: "All of them."

So now I just have to find out when he sold the stock, and then we'll work our way back to when he bought it. Witness my attempt:

CARREON: "When did you cease to own Ocean Fund stock?"

COHEN: "1999."

Great, I found out when he sold it. Now to just find out to who, and for how much.

CARREON: "Who did you sell it to?"

COHEN: "I sold it back to the corporation."

CARREON: "For how much?"

COHEN: "I'm not sure of the exact amount."

CARREON: "Can you please give me an estimate?"

COHEN: "No."

When faced with an inability to estimate, a lawyer tries to help by holding up a "yardstick":

CARREON: "Can you please come to the nearest $10,000?"

COHEN: "No."

CARREON: "Nearest $100,000?"

Dorband interjects: "You don't have to guess."

Cohen takes the hint: "I'm not going to guess."

CARREON: "I'm not asking you to guess. You can't come to the nearest $10,000 and you can't come to the nearest $100,000; is that correct?"

COHEN: "Yes."

CARREON: "That would require you to guess. Can you come to the nearest $500,000?"

COHEN: "Yes."

I'm thrilled. I've got the "when," the "who," and I'm about to get the "how much" to the nearest 1/2 million, (it's gonna be a big number), so the shell game is almost over. I point at the shell with satisfaction:

CARREON: "And can you please give me that number, your best estimate?"

COHEN: "No."

CARREON: "And why is that, sir?"

COHEN: "Because there's a confidentiality agreement between myself and the other parties."

Cohen grins as he lifts the shell, revealing nothing, and scoops up the winnings. It was like trying to hit an enemy in a nightmare. My punches felt weak and horribly ineffectual. If we'd been in trial, the judge would berate Cohen for his uncooperativeness, and the jury would dock him points for arrogance. But it was only a deposition, and lawyers are expected to extract facts in the face of resistance. When they fail in the effort, it can be pathetic. I remember hearing Oliver North humiliate special prosecutor Arthur Liman during the Iran-Contra hearings. North disarmed Liman simply by admitting he had lied under oath previously, while insisting that he was telling the truth under oath at the time. Usually, contentions like North's fall flat, indicting the witness as a perjurer and undermining all credibility. But North was a gifted liar, and his justification–that he'd lied to fulfill his patriotic duty–will go down in history as one of the most successful public shellackings a lawyer has ever received at the hands of a felon. Voice choking and eyes watering, North convinced a nation of gullible viewers that lying was virtue and admitting it now was proof of his bravery. The lie slipped from Liman's grasp, and further efforts to pin North down were, as they say, like trying to nail jello to a wall. Due to this performance, North was spotted as a promising Republican talent, and made his run for Congress.

Cohen's deft economy in dispensing the truth, and his ability to entomb each needle of fact within a bale of misleading hay, should qualify him for some kind of position in government. He had a perverse grasp of corporate law, and an amateurish willingness to exploit the complexities created by multiple, overlapping corporations. In Cohen's universe of puppet companies, nothing was what it seemed, every sleeve had a trick up it, and there was always another wrinkle to be explored.

Ultimately, Cohen's testimony about his shell corporations became unbelievably tangled and incomprehensible, simply because his deposition was taken so many times that his lies became absurdly complex. In the end, Francis Wellman was proven right, except it wasn't so much that Cohen couldn't make up answers as fast as we could make up questions, but rather that his ability to make up credible lies diminished as he told more of them. Even as the contradictions became more numerous and blatant during depositions that continued in July, August, September and November, Cohen would never admit to having lied. He would just shake his head patiently once again to explain precisely how we had misunderstood him. He moved, as we say in the vernacular, from dazzling us with brilliance to baffling us with bullshit.

Near the end of the case, Cohen's construct of lies became an absurd machine, a demented battle android half shot away by enemy fire, able to do little more than limp forward with hard-wired sincerity, entreating, "You do not understand... repeat... let me explain..." But on February 3, 2000, at around 10:30 in the morning, that battle droid was in fine form, and my punches were landing on solid armor.

CHAPTER TWENTY-TWO

"JUST WAIT, IT'S ONLY THE BEGINNING."

"JUST WAIT," SHE SAID, "it's only the beginning." The lady telling me this was no ordinary 40ish 5'4" San Diego blonde with a bob haircut. She was Betsy Hartwig, an Assistant Attorney General for the San Diego office of the California Department of Justice. She was the prosecutor who convicted Cohen of bankruptcy fraud and related crimes back in 1992. We were eating cold sandwiches and coleslaw from paper cups in a deli down the street from Beth Ballerini's office during the lunch break after Cohen's morning session.

I really wanted her to open another prosecution on Cohen, this time for the theft of Sex.Com. But the Constitution requires that crimes be tried in the vicinity in which they are committed, and the theft was perpetrated in the Orange County office of Midcom Corporation. So Besty didn't see how her office could get jurisdiction over it. In retrospect, I am sure she did not want to endure any more stress-induced lifespan shortening of the sort that occurs when you spend your time chasing Cohen.

I had obtained the transcripts of Cohen's criminal trial and had a law clerk summarize them for me before I met Betsy. The transcript proved that Cohen had impersonated lawyer Frank Butler, and using that false identity, had represented a couple of clients named Polvadore in a bankruptcy proceeding. During that representation, he misappropriated money from the debtor-in-possession fund. He also advised his clients to hide their Rolls Royce rather than turn it over to the trustee, and aided their commission of other little improprieties. An IRS agent testified that despite many hours invested in reviewing financial records, the government still couldn't figure out Cohen's entire scheme, but some substantial sums were missing. The jury convicted Cohen of Bankruptcy Fraud, Making False Statements and Obstruction of Justice. Judge Judith Keep refused to allow him release pending sentencing and on January 27, 1992, sentenced him to 46 months. Cohen called her "a cunt" on the record, and appealed his conviction. He won his appeal as to one count of the conviction, and was remanded for resentencing. However, Judge Keep imposed the same sentence as she had the first time.

Cohen didn't waste his time in prison, though. His fine mind was still appreciated by those who knew him. His friends Bonnie Hite and Jim Powell came to see him when they needed legal advice about getting out of a time-share condo deal. Cohen kept his legal skills sharp suing his wife and her lawyer in a RICO case, and filed some prisoner lawsuits against the Bureau of Prisons to get better treatment.

Cohen also made friends in prison with noted securities defrauder Marshall Zolp, the inventor of the famous self-chilling beer can. Never heard of it? That's because the feds put an end to Zolp's efforts to promote this non-existent, but highly-desired beverage container, after he scammed several million from investors. After he got out of prison, during a casual phone call Cohen introduced Zolp, who was still in prison, to Bonnie Hite, another of the Sporting Houses directors. When Zolp got out a few months later, he and Hite quickly married and moved to Portland, Oregon. The marriage ended in a few months, but Zolp and Cohen appear to have worked together to create a couple of companies, Sporting Houses Management, and Gighlieri Fine Arts. Perhaps best described as an "investment vehicle," Sporting Houses, which ended up holding the registration for Sex.Com, was originally organized to gather investments and fund development of an offshore pleasure island Cohen called Camp Wanaleia, pronounced "Wanna-lay-'ya." Jim Powell was also a Sporting Houses Director, and most meetings were held at Midcom, Barbara Cepinko's company in Orange County. Cohen got an address for Sporting Houses in Nevada, and the company gathered about $300,000 from investors. Bank records I got from a Las Vegas branch of Wells Fargo showed Cohen in total control of the cash, which all went to him or one of his companies, Omnitec. Needless to say, Camp Wanaleiya, which was going to employ hundreds of prostitutes of the highest calibre, making them available to the most discerning connoisseurs of sensual pleasure, went nowhere.

Gighlieri Fine Arts was built around the most evanescent asset I have ever glimpsed; the slender side of an option to buy all of Lorenzo Gighlieri's entire artistic ouevre. Gighlieri is perhaps the premier creator of tabletop bronzes for the golf and boardroom set. Picture classical forms, nicely rendered, smoothly polished, at home in a paneled den, next to some photos of young guys in old fashioned football uniforms. With a luxury car salesman as its CEO, this venture also evaporated. According to Bonnie, Zolp eventually got in trouble with his Probation officer for failing to report, and fled to Tiajuana, Mexico to live with Cohen. By the time I got on the scene in 1999, Zolp's email address was Zolp@Sex.com. His street address was in Tortola, British Virgin Islands.

Betsy took in this news with gentle interest. I probed to see if I could get her to prosecute Cohen for stealing Sex.Com. She said she was talking to a couple of investigators about checking into Cohen's current doings, but I got the feeling I was working on a long shot. I had little time to worry about it, because I had to get back to the afternoon session.

CHAPTER TWENTY-THREE

"SO FAR, SO GOOD"

IN THE FRENCH PUNK MOVIE, "HATE," one kid tells another a joke. A guy falls out the window of a high apartment building. As he's falling past each successive floor, he tells himself "So far, so good, so far, so good..." When I came back from lunch to resume Cohen's deposition, I felt like I had fallen off the roof of a 20-story building, and had just passed the 12th floor. Somewhere during the next 12 floors, preferably within the next four, I needed to reverse the force of my downward plunge.

Before lunch, I'd tried my usual approach of starting without documents, to avoid giving the witness a place to rest their eyes to avoid your probing stare. Questions answered in a vacuum, without dates and names and documentary references, are often more honest. But Cohen had given up nothing in two hours of wordplay, and the pavement was getting closer. I had to start using documents to slow my descent. I started with one that was bad for Gary, the Delaware incorporation papers for Online Classifieds, Inc., that Joel Dichter had formed when he was Gary's lawyer. Dorband had taken control of Dichter's strategy, but I figured it would help to get Cohen to admit that the incorporation was not fraudulent. I thrust the document at him suddenly, accompanied by a vague, sneering question. Dorband saw the danger of the tactic, which is meant to provoke the witness to speak carelessly in response. Dorband immediately began running interception.

CARREON: I have marked as Exhibit 1... a statement... a designation by foreign corporation. It appears to be signed by my client, Gary Kremen. Have you seen that before?

COHEN: Yes.

CARREON: What difference does that... document make to you?

DORBAND: Objection. Vague, ambiguous.

CARREON: Does it make any difference in this lawsuit?

DORBAND: Objection. Calls for a legal conclusion, also.

· 93

CARREON: To your knowledge.

DORBAND: If you have—it would be an impermissible opinion.

CARREON: Do you—

DORBAND: If you *have* an opinion.

COHEN: If I have an opinion?

CARREON: Yeah, do you have an opinion?

COHEN: My opinion is that the attorneys of Gary Kremen tried to perpetrate a fraud upon the court.

CARREON: How does that document prove it?

COHEN: This is where they tried to back-date the corporation Online Classifieds, back to the date of 1994.

CARREON: Where do you see that attempt to back-date?

COHEN: Taking the reading of the original complaint plus this document plus the other documents.

CARREON: Where do you see on that document any attempt to back-date anything?

DORBAND: I believe that mischaracterizes his testimony.

CARREON: Do you see anything on that document that shows an attempt by my client to back-date anything? Look right on that document, don't look any place. Don't look anyplace else.

COHEN: I'll stick with my last answer.

CARREON: And your last answer is what?

COHEN: Taking all the papers into consideration, that was of my opinion, not of a legal opinion.

CARREON: So you admit there's nothing on this document at all here which backdates anything?

DORBAND: Objection. Mischaracterizes his testimony.

    Okay, I'm falling a little more slowly now, and I'm ready to attack the main issue. I grabbed the corner of the most crucial document, the forged letter itself, and twirled it like a playing card toward Cohen while simultaneously asking him:

CARREON: Here's what I've marked as Exhibit 2. Where did you get that? From the tooth fairy?

Dorband iced me down:

DORBAND: Would you please give the witness the opportunity to read the document, please?

COHEN: Would you read it to me, please?

CARREON: I'll give it to your counsel.

COHEN: I'm sorry.

CARREON: Where did you get it? From the tooth fairy?

DORBAND: Objection, if you're going to continue to badger the witness like this we're going to terminate the witness—terminate the deposition.

While Bob may have wanted to kill his client on occasion, I don't think this was one of those moments. The little slip lightened the moment anyway. I started again:

CARREON: Where did you get that document?

COHEN: I got it from Vito Franco.

CARREON: How did he get it?

COHEN: He got it from Sharyn Dimmick.

CARREON: Where did he meet Sharyn Dimmick to get this?

COHEN: Her address in San Francisco.

CARREON: Does Mr. Franco have a criminal record?

COHEN: No, he does not. Or did not.

CARREON: Does he now?

COHEN: No.

CARREON: Now, where did you meet him?

COHEN: Where did I originally meet him?

CARREON: Yeah.

COHEN: Through a friend.

CARREON: And where?

COHEN: I think in Los Angeles is where I actually met him.

CARREON: When?

COHEN: It's been so many years. 20-some-odd years ago. 20, 25 years ago.

***

CARREON: When was the last time you saw Vito Franco?

COHEN: The last time I saw him?

CARREON: Yes sir.

COHEN: In November of 1999.

CARREON: What was that occasion?

COHEN: Sitting in a jacuzzi.

CARREON: Where was that?

COHEN: Tijuana, Mexico.

CARREON: Does he work there?

COHEN: At that time, yes.

CARREON: Well, does he work there now?

COHEN: No.

CARREON: He worked there then?

COHEN: Yes.

CARREON: With what?

COHEN: Sandman.

CARREON: What does he do?

COHEN: When?

CARREON: Well, what did he do back when — you know, during the work day before he sat in the jacuzzi?

COHEN: He was building out the brand-new offices for Sandman.

CARREON: What's his area of expertise?

COHEN: He — background on him?

CARREON: Yes, please.

COHEN: He is an ex-police officer. He was a movie producer.

CARREON: With which police agency?

COHEN: I'm not sure. I think it was somewhere in Hawaii. He was — that's before he moved to California. He is a movie producer, distinguished, and he was also — he also did building.

At this point, I was close to gold, but somehow got off track. When I reread the deposition, I'm not sure why. Maybe I was just afraid to move too fast. At any rate, for an intervening 70 pages of transcript we engaged in sparring matches, in which Cohen used poor recollection, diversion, the Fifth Amendment, and a private confidentiality agreement to evade, deflect and block meaningful questioning. I was about three floors from the pavement when I returned to the crucial line of questioning:

CARREON: All right. Let's go back to the Sharyn Dimmick document. So Vito Franco gave this document to you, Exhibit number 2?

COHEN: That is correct.

CARREON: What did he tell you about it when he gave it to you?

COHEN: She signed it.

CARREON: She signed it. Did you send him to get her to sign it?

COHEN: Yes.

CARREON: Why...did you send him to get her to sign it?

COHEN: She agreed to transfer the domain name. Vito and I drove up to San Francisco, and Vito got it and he handed it to me.

CARREON: Well let's put it this way. Did you ever see Sharyn Dimmick's name on any document that purported to show that she was somebody with respect to Online Classified, Inc.?

COHEN: Personally?

CARREON: Yeah.

COHEN: No.

CARREON: Did Vito Franco?

COHEN: I don't know.

CARREON: Was there any other person involved in the production of [the letter]? And I'm not referring to Sharyn Dimmick, you know. I made it pretty clear that I don't believe Sharyn Dimmick signed it. So besides yourself and Mr. Vito Franco was there anyone else that was involved in producing this document?

COHEN: No.

CARREON: Where was it typed?

COHEN: On the computer system that Vito had.

At this point, my heart stopped in its chest. I couldn't believe I was getting this admission. He typed it! As the questioning progressed, I began to feel like I was in a dream. I wanted to pinch myself, because I couldn't believe the beauty of the things I was hearing. I was afraid that Dorband was going to set Cohen's chair on fire, or that Cohen himself would realize he was hanging himself. My headlong plummet had completely ceased. I was beginning to float upward as if in a dream. The dream continued:

CARREON: Did Mr. Franco tell you that Online Classifieds, Inc. had its own stationery and it did not look like this?

COHEN: No.

CARREON: Did Mr. Vito Franco tell you that he had generated this stationery on his computer?

COHEN: Yes.

CARREON: Did Mr. Vito Franco tell you why Sharyn Dimmick wasn't able to type her own letter?

COHEN: No.

CARREON: You had never spoken to Ms. Dimmick yourself?

COHEN: Not to my knowledge.

CARREON: You have never spoken to anyone who represented themselves to be Ms. Dimmick?

COHEN: Not to my knowledge.

CARREON: You do not think it suspicious that Mr. Franco found it necessary to create the letterhead for the letter to be written on?

COHEN: No.

CARREON: You did not think it suspicious that a company that has someone called a president did not have its own stationery?

COHEN: No.

CARREON: Who drafted the text of the letter?

COHEN: The text of the letter?

CARREON: Yes sir.

COHEN: Vito.

CARREON: Did you help him?

COHEN: I may have.

CARREON: This is dated October 15, 1995. When was it prepared?

COHEN: I don't recall.

CARREON: Was it prepared close to that date? Long before?

COHEN: I don't remember when he actually talked to her before we drove up, so I don't know what date it was—that it was—I know that he had asked me some questions about what should we put into the letter, and I responded to that.

CARREON: Had he interviewed Ms. Dimmick?

COHEN: Yes.

By now, it was clear that from any ordinary viewpoint, the letter was a forgery. Only in Cohen's world do we rely on documents signed by people we haven't met, printed on our home computer, using letterhead created for that very purpose. Franco, the guy who got the letter signed, would obviously be an important witness. So I asked about him:

CARREON: He located Sharyn Dimmick by what method?

COHEN: I don't know how he located her. I honestly don't know.

CARREON: Mr. Franco is still an employee of Sandman Internacional?

COHEN: No.

CARREON: Is he his own freelance person?

COHEN: No.

CARREON: Who does he work for?

COHEN: He doesn't.

CARREON: He's just chilling, huh?

COHEN: You could say that.

CARREON: Well, he was in a jacuzzi. I figured. Okay. Where is he? How can I get in touch with Mr. Franco?

COHEN: He's in heaven.

CARREON: He's in heaven? He's in heaven?

COHEN: He's in heaven.

CARREON: Wait. Well, we know that you and I have got a little bit of paperwork to do before we get in. So where can I find him short of there?

COHEN: He passed away.

CARREON: He did?

COHEN: Yes. He just recently passed away.

CARREON: I see. Where are his records?

COHEN: I don't know.

CARREON: I'm not going to pass away, am I?

COHEN: I hope not.

I added that last question because it just seemed that anyone who had any relevant knowledge about this case ended up dead. Earlier, I had asked Cohen about the French Connection and the Ashton-Tate lawsuit against himself and John Cook. Since then, John Cook had died. Not only that, Cook's mother had died when she was served with the lawsuit papers by Ashton-Tate's lawyers. Right on the spot. Cohen also told two different courts on two different occasions that Frank Butler, the attorney, had a heart attack. Cohen even stored some of his financial records with his father, an accountant, also deceased. It was more than coincidence that people who had important things to say about Cohen's business dealings seemed to be unavailable. Cohen's witness list was comprised, in equal numbers, of expatriates, foreign nationals, and folks on whom the ticker had just run out. So I continued digging in the graveyard of Cohen's memories:

CARREON: When did he die?

COHEN: He died—he died when I was in Comdex in Las Vegas this last, I think it was October. He was supposed to call me—sat in the jacuzzi the night before when I called his house, because I was upset because he didn't call me, and then I found out that he had passed away.

CARREON: So you—he died in Tijuana? Where did he die in Tijuana?

COHEN: He was a very private individual and I didn't realize that he was as sick as he was, and Vito never told me—when I was incarcerated, Vito had suffered a heart attack that I wasn't aware of. And Vito used to go to the hospital, and I thought he was getting blood transfusions. And after he died I found out that they weren't blood transfusions, they were kidney dialysis, and he went into the hospital for his kidney dialysis in Los Angeles. I believe it was Cedars.

CARREON: Cedars-Sinai?

101

COHEN: Yeah. And he told them he didn't feel good, from what his kids told me, and he stood up and passed out and died.

CARREON: And that was in October of 1999?

COHEN: I believe so.

Well, Cohen might have believed so, but according to the responses to the subpoenas I sent to Cedars-Sinai, no such person had ever been a patient. But on February 3, 2000, I just dug for more details from Cohen about this invented person.

CARREON: What did he do for you?

COHEN: What did Vito do for me? Vito did all the work. Vito ran and worked in several of the companies back in that day and age.

CARREON: Did he do a lot of private investigating type stuff, hunting people up and—

COHEN: Yes. Yes.

Along with the forged letter, Cohen had submitted a second document with NSI to change the registration of Sex.Com into the name of Sporting Houses Management. In this document, filed online with NSI, Cohen pulled a classic "spoofing" trick. He filled out the form in Kremen's name, because as the administrative contact, Kremen had the authority to change the registration. But he changed Kremen's telephone number and email address to his own phone number and a distinctive email address: steve@liberty.com. The liberty.com name was owned by his friend Stephen Grande, married to Barbara Cepinko of Midcom. I wanted to get Cohen to admit that combining information like this had to be done for a fraudulent purpose, but he just wouldn't go there. Maybe he was beginning to realize he'd given me too much rope already.

CARREON: [I'm going to] ask you to take a look at that document and ask if you've ever seen it before and when you saw it?

COHEN: I produced this.

CARREON: You produced that document?

COHEN: Yes, I produced that document.

CARREON: So you typed Gary Kremen's name on there?

COHEN: That's correct.

CARREON: Why did you do that?

COHEN: Because the letter authorized me to do it.

CARREON: Now, why didn't you talk to Gary Kremen?

COHEN: What was the purpose in talking to Gary Kremen?

CARREON: You knew that Gary Kremen was the systems administrator. He was the only person authorized to transfer this domain name.

COHEN: Says who?

CARREON: He was the only person authorized to transfer it according to—

COHEN: According to who?

This last bit of denial didn't matter much, though. He had lifted the veil quite enough. Maybe he felt the fraud had been declared legitimate for so long that he no longer saw any risk in discussing how the letter came into existence. He admitted he had never met Sharyn Dimmick, even though the letter said they had talked many times. He had written the letter on his own computer using a word processing program. The only person who had ever "met" Sharyn Dimmick was an old, dead friend of his. When he announced the news of Vito's death, he chided me for showing no respect for the dead. I told him "Mr. Cohen, I refuse to feel sadness at the death of your witnesses."

At his deposition, Cohen didn't say that Vito had paid anything for the name, or Dimmick's signature. Later, before summary judgment, he shifted to the position that he had paid $1,000 for it, but that he had no receipt for the payment and such exchanges would merely be small amounts between himself and Vito, a friendship that couldn't be burdened with paltry matters like accounting for four-figure sums.

There it was, elegantly simple. The letter was a forgery, Cohen had no reason to believe that it was legitimate, and it was the operative cause for the transfer of Sex.Com. My entire downward momentum had reversed. I was weightless, floating upwards past the balconies. As I passed the rooftop, I kept rising higher. So far, so good.

CHAPTER TWENTY-FOUR

"I'LL LET THE PANZERS OUT AND I'LL CUT OFF YOUR TOES"

THE LAST WE SAW HIM, JUDGE WARE WAS SITTING ON THE BENCH in his black robe, with his face as handsome as an oiled mahogany carving, giving me a short reprieve to depose Cohen and see if I could prove that NSI had deliberately helped Cohen steal Sex.Com.

The first rule you have to learn about litigation and trying cases is this one, "nothing gets in except through the mouth of a witness." That's right, no witness, no evidence. You can have a stack of documents 500 feet high, and unless they are "official documents," like court records, they are all inadmissible hearsay until a witness testifies that they wrote them, or read them, or relied on them, or in some way did something that makes them admissible. So don't go to court with a note or a letter. Go to court with a witness with the letter in his hand.

I had a lot of NSI documents and a lot of reason to believe that NSI had been so sloppy in transferring the domain name that it went beyond mere negligence, and rose to the level of recklessness, perhaps even disclosing the intention to help a wrongdoer steal the domain name. But why would a Judge believe what I had to say about NSI? I was the lawyer for the people who were suing them. It was time to get some mileage out of my rent-a-nerd.

Ellen Rony is obsessively precise. This characteristic pays off with an expert, who is hired for only two reasons–to say the things you want them to say, and to stand up under cross-examination when the other guy tries to get them to admit that they're wrong, or didn't read all the relevant documents, or that some other experts disagree with them, or that they're not sure, or that all the money they are being paid to testify has affected their testimony. A precise person finds it easy to pleasantly disagree, which leads to greater clarity of opinion, rather than mere hairsplitting, as the other guy would have it. Precision also provides an excellent blind for a bald denial. Which is the little curtain behind which the clever expert withdraws when all else fails.

In addition to being precise, Ellen had another good quality. She really thought NSI had screwed up. Ever since she'd learned about the theft of Sex.Com, she'd been disturbed by NSI's behavior. She was particularly surprised that NSI seemed totally comfortable having a blatant thief own the domain name, because she was well-acquainted with Phil Sbarbaro, the "house counsel" for NSI who had rebuffed my attempts to settle the case on easy terms. "Phil," as she called him, had clearly impressed her, because she described him and his suits in that honey tone women unconsciously adopt when describing powerful men. From her description, which was admittedly brief, I imagined Phil to be in his mid-40's, the kind of lawyer who favors custom-tailored banker-type suits, has a rather close-cut salt and pepper hairstyle, smiles charmingly, extends his hand ingratiatingly, looks the speaker in the eye and responds to all attention like the captain of industry he is. To me, he was just one more obstacle to getting Sex.Com, so she could think whatever she wanted to about him. And little did he know it, but Phil was about to get his tit in a wringer.

Ellen and I got together over a weekend, discussed the way NSI had transferred the domain name, and put together a lengthy declaration, must have been 15 pages, where she swore under oath that the forged letter was the most obvious fraud imaginable, and should have raised red flags for NSI. The letter, she noted, contained several absurd statements, including the idea that a company called "Online Classifieds" wouldn't have an Internet connection, that "Sex.Com" would be given away for free by a company involved in the Internet business, and that somebody giving away a domain name would simply sign a letter approving the transfer, and let the other party handle it with NSI. She then analyzed, with reference to four specific criteria, exactly how NSI had failed to follow its own policies, in particular by failing to contact Gary Kremen before transferring the domain name to a new registrant.

Apparently, Ellen's declaration landed with a resounding thump on Sbarbaro's desk, bypassing his urbane superego, due to the shock of having Ellen Rony, the author of The Domain Name Handbook, that is to say, in Phil-Sbarbaro-speak that mousy little hobbyist who called herself a "scribe" and presumed to document the "history of the Internet" as if anyone owned the Internet besides NSI, that poor woman whose mind had been manipulated by Charles Carreon's words and Gary Kremen's money, in other words, that woman who, who... who the hell did she think she was?

I can see it now. He calls his associate Kevin Golden on the office intercom. Golden appears, with his Irish choirboy looks and his notepad. Sbarbaro is already dialing Ellen's number. He points Golden to a chair and hands him the declaration of Ellen Rony. Golden hasn't fully appreciated the significance of this. Or maybe he hasn't read it at all. Doesn't matter, the phone's ringing. Answering machine. He leaves a message, telling Ellen to call him. Intense conversation follows between Sbarbaro and Golden. Golden feels defensive because he was unaware of the problem being so serious. Sbarbaro is over-reacting. Golden hasn't often seen him like this. They keep talking until a while later when Ellen calls back.

Phil puts her on the speaker phone. He feels like Frank Sinatra, hearing that some mug has just ratted on his best friend. He's going to play it cool, but with plenty of steel. He starts out by telling her how disappointed he is, that he thought she was a better friend than that, that NSI has such an important influence on the Internet, and that what she has done bodes ill for future collaboration. All that easy access to NSI documentation and information that she's had, including the link to her website, all that is put in jeopardy by this ill-considered action. Do you know anything about this Charles Carreon? He's insane, he tells her, echoing the words of David Dolkas who told the court in alarm, "Carreon's conduct must be stopped."

And this is where you have to cheer for Ellen. She's thinking, "look, Phil, I'm not a god-damned pet canary that lives on crumbs. If you wanted to hire me as a consultant, you could have sent me a check a long time ago". But she doesn't say this, instead she tells him that she's sorry he's upset, but she thinks NSI made a huge mistake here, and they ought to fix it. She may have even said a good word about me.

Well, leaning back into his chair and smiling at Golden to show him how a guy handles this, he tells her that well, Ellen, hate to break it to you but you're not really an expert about NSI policies. He tells her he's going to have her "disqualified" as an expert, and have her declaration "stricken." Ouch, that's gotta hurt!

And that's not all. If her declaration isn't stricken, he'll have to take her deposition. (Gasp!) And when he does, he tells her, he's going to "let the Panzers out, and I'm going to cut off your toes." He's satisfied with himself when he makes this statement. He can feel her wince as her nether digits are removed. She's not Jewish, but nobody likes Panzers, the feared World War II tanks that Rommel drove to victory in North Africa, mounted with the dread 88 mm. cannon that could blow a Sherman tank wide open while facing no risk of harm to itself. Just a little bit of history out of respect for Phil, since he is an ex-military man and I bet he still has his dress whites pressed and ready to go.

Well, you can imagine that Ellen was on the phone to me pretty quick after that happened. Me, I was crazy, livid, and not the least because he said I was crazy. I'm sensitive about that stuff, and it really got my blood going. So what did I do? Like any lawyer who is already mad, and wants to get even, I hit the books. Pretty soon I had it in hand, the *Erickson* case from the Ninth Circuit Court of Appeals, which clearly holds that it is improper to attempt to influence or coerce the other side's expert witness, or even to communicate with them directly rather than through the office of the lawyer who retained them. Thus armed with certain foreknowledge of his wrongdoing, and wanting to see if he would stick his foot in it any further until it became unretractable, I sent Phil a short letter, rebuking him for threatening my expert with "Nazi imagery," and "threats of dismemberment."

Phil's response was most gratifying. He wrote back that he didn't need my permission to call his old friend Ellen Rony, and that he was entitled to tell her anything he wanted. He did not deny having used Nazi imagery or threats of dismemberment, which under the circumstances, being something that an ordinary person would certainly deny if it were untrue, constitutes a "tacit admission" under the Federal Rules of Evidence. Then, and only then, did I write him the letter telling him about the *Erickson* case. His next letter was full-speed in reverse. It was so delicious I should have framed it. He said he was sorry, said he routinely did that sort of thing when he was a federal prosecutor, and offered to pay the fees and costs resulting from this "ex-parte contact" with my expert witness, which he grudgingly conceded was apparently technically unethical. Gary still hasn't gotten a penny from Phil Sbarbaro for the assault on Ellen, but I am sure he will ultimately spend enormous sums in an unsuccessful effort to force Sbarbaro to fulfill this promise. Nor has this captain of industry shown the small speck of gentility necessary to send an apology to Ellen, who apparently, is no longer his friend.

CHAPTER TWENTY-FIVE

WE FOUGHT THE LAW
AND THE LAW WON

IN THE INTERNET BUSINESS, AT THE PEAK OF THE BOOM, NSI WAS CITY HALL, as in, "you can't fight City Hall." Reading the history of NSI's judicial victories is about as uplifting as re-reading the Dredd-Scott decision. (You'll recall that was the case where the United States Supreme Court held that a man was property, if he was a slave in his state of origin, even when he crossed over into a state where slavery was illegal.) The NSI cases evoke the same sense of the courts bending to the winds of powerful interests. By accepting NSI's version of the facts without exposing them to scrutiny, the courts helped NSI build fortresses of judicially-reinforced ignorance. From reading the opinions, it is apparent that the judiciary collaborated with NSI to allow the wool to be pulled over its eyes. How could this happen?

The history of NSI may give some clues. How did it get going? How did it gain so much power? What interests does it really represent? So now for the quick history of the Internet that will soon be learned in the cradle from the mouths of Internet Barbie and Virtual-War G.I. Joe.

In the beginning there was DARPA and ARPA, and their mission was to provide a redundant network for communication among defense and educational computer installations. By redundant we mean that even if one link in the system breaks down, the entire system continues to function. What is amazing is that these scientists managed to collaborate to create the system. Under the benevolent aegis of defense spending, unimpeded by the concerns of crass commercialism, the engineers designed communication protocols based on the UNIX computer language that enabled many different kinds of computers running different kinds of software to communicate over the phone lines.

In essence, the early Internet pioneers put universal communication functionality at the top of their priority list. The most important thing was for all of the computers to be able to talk to each other. Historically, the Internet was foreshadowed by the legend of the Tower of Babel. This early public works project was made possible only because human beings possessed a common language. According to Hebraic historians, utilizing this common language, the nations of the earth attempted to build a stairway to heaven. Jehovah became wroth with this demonstration of arrogance, and rather than burning the tower down as he might have on another day, struck on a more devious solution. Jehovah "confused their speech." He smote them with the curse of varying languages. The builders suddenly found themselves unable to communicate, and as a result, abandoned their plan to ascend to the heavens by means of a ladder.

Even if we can't talk to each other, the Internet pioneers decided, our machines can! But the common language developed by the engineers had a disadvantage—it was numerically-based, cryptic and engineer-like. Sure, an engineer can rattle off an IP address (that's "Internet Protocol" address) like his newborn's birthday, but the rest of us have trouble remembering our phone numbers. So if I wanted my computer to call your computer, I would have to input all of these digits.

Along comes John Postel, the patron saint of the Internet, who certainly *looked* like a Deadhead, and worked for the University of Southern California Information Sciences Institute. While doing contract work for the U.S. government, Postel came up with a clever idea. Since anything arbitrary can equal any other arbitrary thing in the world of mathematics, why not equate numerical IP addresses with arbitrary strings of letters? Since any string of letters can equate to any string of numbers, all you need is a database that interrelates the strings of letters with the strings of numbers and automatically routes messages to the appropriate computer. And thus was born the age of the Dot-Com.

All IP addresses, decreed St. Postel, would end with a three-letter suffix, like .Gov, .Net, .Org, and most importantly to our story, .Com. To the left of the Dot, the user could put anything they wanted, up to a limited number of spaces. (This space has grown so much now, that domain names can practically be a paragraph long.)

Domain names, you might expect, would be a natural-born hit, a marriage of necessity and style. It was sort of bohemian, if you think about it. Bohemians started naming their cars to personalize the smog-belching carriages that rule and enable our lives. Now we could personalize our computers, and with more than mere sentimental effect. Naming your car is something you stop doing when you get your first real job (although the trend resurges among soccer moms, whose Suburbans proudly bear names like "Great White Beast," inevitably chosen by the micro-Viking progeny of a true trophy blonde).

But a name for your computer is not just a sentimental tag attached to a mechanistic object. It is a grubstake in the new economy. It is a homestead on the information frontier. It is a doorway to a community of knowledge, information and entertainment that is so compelling in its current, high-speed incarnation, that broadband users, who get more information faster, spend 28% more time at their computers than dial-up users. Dial-up now has market penetration roughly equivalent to that of television in the late 1950's. Meanwhile, the demographic profile of the average Internet broadband user is identical to the demographic of the dial-up user five years ago. I couldn't have rattled off this stuff three years ago, and by the time you read it, the numbers will have changed. And yet it was all there in potential form in the early 1990's, a glimmer in John Postel's eye.

When Postel invented them in 1984, domain names were adopted only by a tiny group of engineers spread around the country. They started emailing each other about their typical geeky topics, one of which was the future structure of the Internet. For about ten years it was basically managed by volunteers. In 1994, Postel wrote an email to some friends who were also helping to run the system, laying out the plan for an agency to administer the registration of domain names. Postel and his friends created an entity known as IANA, the Internet Assigned Names and Numbers Authority.

IANA operates out of a building in Marina Del Rey, California, and hosts a website at IANA.org; however, it does not have any corporate or governmental existence that I've been able to discern from my research. In response to a lawsuit seeking to compel IANA to create a ".Web" top level domain name, Postel filed a declaration stating that IANA was merely a "function," performed under contract for a security agency of the United States Department of Defense. Apparently, at one time, IANA had control over all of the domain names. Later, IANA transferred responsibility for managing the four main top-level domain names (.Com, .Net, .Gov and .Org) to the International Corporation for Assigned Names and Numbers ("ICANN.")

Meanwhile, the cash for funding the registration program came to be administered through the National Science Foundation, which put the domain name registration function out for bid to data processing companies. The contract was just for a few million bucks, so in May 1993 it went to NSI, a small company in Herndon, Virginia.

The National Science Foundation paid NSI to register domain names for free. In December, 1994, seven months after Gary registered Sex.Com, the NSF recommended that users start paying to operate the system. In May, 1995, NSI was bought lock, stock and barrel for $4.8 Million, by SAIC, Science Applications International Corp., a privately held San Diego company with a Board of Directors peopled by defense establishment magnates, including former Secretaries of Defense Melvin Laird and William Perry, former NSA chief Bobby Inman, and former CIA Directors Robert Gates and John Deutch. On September 14, 1995, NSI announced it would start charging $5 per domain name registration.

The cash cow started producing immediately. Between September 1995 and March 1996, NSI took in $20 Million in registration fees. The arrow just headed straight up from there, like an X-15 pilot in the movie, *The Right Stuff*. Boy, did NSI have it. Fueled with the power of absolute monopoly over a desirable resource, NSI went from being a cheap date to a supermodel in two short years, turning into a stock market darling at the beginning of the tech-IPO craze. NSI proudly described its glowing success in a July 1997 stock prospectus:

"Net registrations within the TLDs maintained by the Company increased by 233% from approximately 246,000 domain names registered at March 31, 1996 to approximately 818,000 domain names registered at March 31, 1997. The Company believes that commercial enterprises and individual Internet users worldwide are increasingly recognizing the .com TLD as a desirable address for commercial presence on the Internet. *** [T]he Company believes that the potential for continued growth of domain name registrations by commercial entities and services related to those registrations is substantial. Net revenue from Internet domain name registration subscriptions accounted for 76.5% of the Company's net revenue for the three months ended March 31, 1997."

The day NSI went public, at the opening bell on September 26, 1997, the market was drooling, and the first trade closed at $25/share, 40% above the $18/share offering price. By the end of the day, NSI had a market cap of $382.5 Million, and SAIC had sold enough stock to harvest a $9 Million profit, while keeping a 28% interest in the company. A little champagne was consumed in San Diego that night. The fruit of the Internet, born in the soil of DARPA, the Defense Advanced Research Project Agency, fell quite close to the tree.

Eventually, administration of the government contract with NSI passed from the National Science Foundation to the United States Department of Commerce and ICANN. A period of conflict between Commerce and NSI took place during 1999, with NSI taking the position that it "owned" the right to register all .Com domain names in perpetuity. NSI also claimed it owned the entire database of five million .Com registrations that it had registered during the period of its government-created monopoly. In late 1999, NSI gave up its death grip on the .Com franchise and database when it agreed with ICANN to allow the creation of additional registrars who could compete in the registration of .Com and other domain names. However, above all of the registrars, NSI continued to hold the privileged position of being both a registry and a registrar.

There is only one domain name registry, and it is NSI. There are now many registrars, but they all must register their domain names with NSI, the world's only registry. For this service, NSI charges $6. Thus, if you register a domain name with any other registrar, $6 of what you pay goes to NSI. Meanwhile, NSI collects the $6 plus a premium that has steadily declined from around $30 for every name that it registers directly through its NSI.Com registration portal.

The agreement with ICANN in 1999 also provided that NSI would have to choose between being the registry and being a registrar by 2001. However, for those who read the papers closely, it was disclosed in 2001 that NSI had managed to renegotiate the agreement, allowing it to continue operating as both the registry and a registrar until 2005. Since being acquired in March 2000 by Verisign Corporation, NSI and its corporate parent are probably destined for a merger with Microsoft. (Anyone hear the opening strains of Terminator II?) For all of these reasons and more, I took to calling NSI the "stainless steel saint." Every lawyer knows that some companies are more fun to sue than others. NSI was no fun at all.

NSI's counsel of record, Dave Dolkas of Gray, Cary, Ware & Friedenrich, had the kind of self-assurance that told you this man had no question where his next meal was coming from. Dolkas was tall, dark, handsome, and well-accustomed to winning. He wore his good quality suits very nicely, maintained unflappable dignity in the face of punk tactics, and seemed to know exactly how little work he needed to do in order to get out of a case for NSI. He relied on precedent, legion in his favor, which he recited in a matter-of-fact, almost bored tone. Without getting excited, he would ask the simple question, "Why are we being sued here?" This tactic has worked so well both with the public and the courts, that Ellen Rony entitled her chapter on NSI in the Domain Name Handbook, "NSI: Caught in the Crossfire."

NSI was caught in the crossfire in a number of cases. That is the primary problem with the body of law that was created when NSI responded with a coordinated strategy to a series of helter-skelter lawsuits attempting to compel it to do all kinds of stuff. These cases were often litigated by plaintiffs who exercised little forethought and not much staying power, so NSI racked up a series of victories. In NSI's repertoire of favorable precedents that they plied before the courts like a string of get-out-of-jail-free cards, are many instances of bad facts making bad law. For example, back when they had the registrar monopoly, they were sued for refusing to dot-com the word "fuck." Guess when they won that case? When it became "moot," because other registrars had been created that were ready, willing, and able to register Fuck.Com or anything else you could think of. The meaning of that case, to Dolkas, would be that NSI always wins. To me, it says that if you stall the process long enough, you can thwart it. But which meaning would the court infer?

NSI's opening brief told Judge Ware that the entire process of registering a domain name, or transferring an existing domain name, was so automated that it was almost automatic. In essence they argued that Cohen's letter would have passed in front of a minimum wage employee recruited from a technical college in Alexandria, Virginia, who would have accepted such a transfer as a matter of course and performed the change of registration as directed therein by the original registrant, Online Classifieds, Inc.

NSI retreated from this position in later filings, when I pointed out that Cohen had faxed the letter directly to David Graves, an individual who was far from minimum wage in the NSI hierarchy. In fact, Graves was the person regularly designated to testify on NSI's behalf in litigation. Additionally, at Cohen's deposition that took place after NSI filed its initial moving papers for summary judgment, Cohen testified he had spoken directly with David Graves, who had essentially told him what to put into the forged letter:

CARREON: Did you have any communication over the phone with anyone at NSI?

COHEN: Yes.

CARREON: Who were those people? Pertaining to this transfer right here.

COHEN: There would only be one of the—Dave Gray (meaning David Graves).

CARREON: And what did you talk to Mr. Gray about?

COHEN: Mr. Gray asked me to send him a copy of the documentation I had for the transfer.

CARREON: And this was all you were able to send him, this Exhibit 2?

COHEN: That's correct. Unless there was a cover sheet, which I don't remember, and there may very well have been.

As a result of this additional revelation, I made a motion to Judge Ware requesting to take the deposition of David Graves. Judge Ware denied the motion two months after granting summary judgment. Other motions I made while NSI's motion for summary judgment was pending, like the one protesting Phil Sbarbaro's improper contact with Ellen Rony, were also ignored until after NSI was safely out of the case.

NSI's exit from the case became final on May 8, 2000, nearly six years to the day after Gary registered Sex.Com, on May 9, 1994. Judge Ware's order granting NSI's motion for summary judgment recorded the date in the first line of the factual recitation. Judge Ware concluded that Kremen had no contract with NSI, making no mention of my argument that, by agreeing to become one of the registrants of domain names, Kremen had contributed to the growth of a user base that had concrete value to NSI, which it exploited specifically in its IPO stock offering by boasting about the number of registrants in its database. Judge Ware also concluded that Kremen was not a "third party beneficiary," that is to say, someone entitled to make a claim under the contract between the National Science Foundation and NSI, pursuant to which NSI became the registrant of domain names in the first place. Since NSI was paid millions of dollars to register domain names by the NSF, it looked to me a lot like a situation

114

where the NSF had sort of crowed out, "drinks are on the house," allowing anybody and everybody who wanted to register a domain name to have one for free. So it would seem that, in order to maintain quality control, anybody could complain about the quality of his drink. For purposes of quality control, it makes more sense to give registrants like Kremen the power to sue NSI, since as a practical matter bureaucracies that grant contracts to companies like NSI rarely police them effectively. And in this case they certainly did not.

Then Judge Ware got around to the big important argument. Was it possible to nail NSI for conversion? Judge Ware said no, concluding that there is "very simply no evidence establishing that a domain name, including Sex.Com, is 'merged in or identified with' a document or other tangible object." He acknowledged that "California law does recognize 'conversion of intangibles *represented by documents*, such as bonds, notes, bills of exchange, stock certificates, and warehouse receipts.'" But he adopted NSI's argument that "a domain name is a form of intangible property which cannot serve as a basis for a conversion claim."

Wasn't the registration agreement at least as much of a "document" as a warehouse receipt? The registration agreement gave the administrative contact sole authority to control registration of the domain name just like a warehouse receipt entitles the holder to claim the warehoused goods. When Gary printed out the online registration agreement and mailed it to NSI via certified mail, he emphasized the importance of this document. And the online list of names and numbers known as the Domain Name Server Tables is an electronic document.

Electronic documents are old hat under the Federal Rules of Evidence, which recognize all systems of symbol recordation, from clay tablets to palmtop advertising, as legally entitled to the name of "document." Smoke signals are probably out. But the registration agreement and the DNS Tables are, respectively, the deed and the land office records of the world of cyber real-estate. If a claim check for a parking lot or a dry cleaner is good enough, surely an online, printable registration record satisfies the document requirement.

Perhaps to avoid dallying with this uncomfortable notion, Judge Ware's opinion then launched into a litany of justifications for keeping to a conservative course of action, noting that Kremen's claim "invites abandoning the traditional strictures of conversion to encompass forms of intangible property never contemplated in its formation." Well, I'll agree that when the first common law judge held the stable liable for conversion when the wrong fellow rode off on the wrong horse, he wasn't thinking about Internet domain names. But the basic obligation that the stable operator breached when he gave the horse to the wrong rider is the same one that NSI breached when it let Cohen steal Sex.Com. Judge Ware was really saying that a law that has long been good enough for the stable hand or the warehouseman is too harsh for NSI, an enormous corporation awash in Internet money thanks to a taxpayer funded monopoly. He said, "The Court finds it inherently unjust to place NSI in this untenable position by virtue of performing a purely ministerial function."

Judge Ware then gave an economic argument in favor of his decision: "Furthermore, the threat of litigation threatens to stifle the registration system by requiring further regulations by NSI and potential increases in fees." Where he got that information, I'll never know. There were no facts presented to support that conclusion. The Judge clearly had not paid any attention to NSI's fees, which had skyrocketed far beyond the basic charge originally authorized. NSI is currently the most costly provider of domain name registration services, adding on oodles and oodles of extras whenever possible above the basic $6 registration fee, which of course, it also collects. And in any event, the "security costs too much" concept just doesn't make any sense to me, when the essential service NSI provides is keeping accurate records of domain name ownership. That's the bare, central task. It's like saying we don't have enough money to train nurses how to draw blood with clean needles. That's what they are doing. They should do it perfectly every time.

Trying to avoid "creating the proverbial slippery slope," Judge Ware buttressed his decision with the language of judicial restraint: "The Court is compelled to uphold this distinction rather than contort the cause of action to encompass property never contemplated." But this was not true judicial restraint—in fact its very opposite. The trend of California law has always been to use the tort of conversion to deter the theft of property, whether tangible or intangible, so long as the property could be said to be "merged with a document." Only by ignoring the evidence and refusing to acknowledge that the registration agreement is a document of title, was Judge Ware able to avoid the effect of this rule.

When judges declare themselves powerless to act, you can bet they'll be passing the buck to our elected representatives, in lines like this: "The Court leaves it to the legislature to fashion an appropriate statutory scheme to protect dormant domain names unprotected by trademark law." But the reference to trademark law and "dormant" names is irrelevant to the case of Sex.Com. Even if Gary had activated a Sex.Com website on the Internet, that wouldn't have given him trademark rights. Indeed, Judge Ware so ruled six months later, when he denied Cohen's claim of trademark protection and granted Gary's motion for summary adjudication. And even if the website had been heavily-used, that wouldn't have given rise to a conversion claim, either, since the theft of "eyeballs," as dot-commers refer to web-surfer traffic, would only be the loss of business goodwill, which is clearly not subject to conversion. So what's all that about?

It's all about avoiding any analysis of my claim for *conspiracy* to convert. Remember that one? Where I alleged that Cohen and NSI had collaborated to help Cohen steal the name? Well, I had found some evidence of that, when Cohen testified that he personally talked to David Graves, who told him what needed to be put in the forged letter in order to arrange a transfer without contacting Kremen. I had that testimony, but of course I needed to question Graves. I noticed his deposition and filed a motion with Judge Ware to compel NSI to produce him. I told the Court in my motion that David Graves had received the fax directly from Cohen, and that Cohen had previously talked to Graves to find out what information he should put in the forged letter. I never got to take Dave's deposition, because Judge Ware's opinion neatly undercut the necessity of looking at whether Cohen and Graves conspired to convert the name. Indeed, even if they did, under Judge Ware's ruling, it wasn't important.

The judge's arguments in support of the ruling—avoiding imposing liability for a routine function, not increasing the costs of registration, and leaving the issue to the legislature—don't justify the denial of Gary's claim for conspiracy to convert. Liability for conspiring with Cohen would not result from the performance of a routine function. Theft is not routine. Holding NSI liable for agreeing to accept a forgery would not create any "slippery slope," at least in the way we usually consider these things. It would fairly impose liability for an out-and-out theft. Judge Ware's opinion for NSI is most notable for its failure to discuss electronic documents and the unexamined contents of the Cohen-Graves communications. However, that hardly makes it unique in the annals of legal history.

CHAPTER TWENTY-SIX

LAWSUIT!

My MENTOR ARNIE SCHWARTZ TOLD ME I WOULD NEVER BE A TRIAL LAWYER until I was arguing to the jury, and I knew they were laughing at me, and I kept arguing anyway. I've had that experience. But I say you're not a real lawyer until you've been unfairly sued for a large sum of money. I passed that milestone on February 15, 2000. It began with Bob Dorband taking control of my fax machine. It got that intense look it gets when it's been possessed by the adversary, and out it came, a complaint filed in Portland Federal Court entitled *Stephen M. Cohen v. Charles Carreon and Gary Kremen*. The last pages came out of the fax machine. When I got to the prayer for relief, where Cohen claimed $50 Million in damages, it *was* a relief. The amount was so outlandish. If you say you're going to kill me by shooting me with a .22, it's believable, and it's scary. If you say you're going to kill me by dropping the Empire State Building on my head, it's laughable. So I laughed.

I continued laughing as I read the allegations. Cohen alleged that Kremen and I had conspired, years before we ever met, to arrange the theft of the Sex.Com domain name. Then we had encouraged Cohen to steal it and develop the website to its present profitable state. Now, in the last stages of the plot, we were suing to acquire control of the fully developed asset.

I immediately knew the genesis of Cohen's thinking. Kremen's original business plan was a two-page document. The first page was just a scrawl of notes in Gary's awkward hand. The second page showed initials, among them "CC," next to some percentages. So Cohen concluded I was CC, had known Kremen since 1994, and as we say in Oregon, had been "lying in the weeds" for five years, waiting to bushwhack him. Or more likely, Dorband concluded there was enough evidence to claim the allegations were made in good faith, and planned to use the suit to drive a wedge between Gary and myself. If I wanted out, but just wasn't saying it, this lawsuit was my exit vehicle. I could claim a conflict of interest and kiss Kremen goodbye, with my legal dignity intact. And that would get rid of the first lawyer who had really tried to move the ball.

Because the story was bogus, I wasn't worried about liability, as long as I got my defense from the Oregon Professional Liability Fund (the "PLF"). The PLF insures me for legal malpractice, but Cohen's claim wasn't for malpractice. He was suing me for representing Gary Kremen, and for calling him a liar. He was alleging that I had "exceeded the bounds of zealous advocacy," and strayed into defamation. While truth is a defense to defamation, insurance defense lawyers always hate it when they ask you a question like, "Did you say he was a thief?" and you say, "Yes." Right away they think you were injudicious or something. I thought lawyers were supposed to call things by their true names. Liar, thief—if the shoe fits, make 'em wear it!

But throw me a frickin' bone here! I was deprived of some important elements of a proper legal education. Most lawyers learn how to behave from watching their lawyer dads, or while hanging out with their lawyer uncles. I learned from watching 70s TV shows like "Judd for the Defense," and "The Young Lawyers" (they had cool cars, sweet little blonde hippie chicks in trouble for clients, and sparred in court with conservative judges who nevertheless had a streak of fairness). If I had only once in my life been to a golf course, or a tennis court, or an athletic club frequented by lawyers and their families, I would have realized that a lawyer is not expected to be a fiery advocate in search of justice. A lawyer must cultivate a careful manner, and in all things, particularly public speech, refrain from the sort of bluntness that attracts attention.

So yes, my press release said that Cohen stole Sex.Com. And the PLF agreed to cover my defense. They assigned Portland attorney Susan Eggum to be my lawyer. I had learned about her recently after she had resolved a scandalous case involving unconscionable tactics used by attorneys hired by the PLF. She was receiving kudos in the media for her ethics and savvy. In Portland law, she was hot.

I met her in April, 2000. Susan was crisp, trim, with short black hair and a manner both attentive and extremely efficient. An air of sharpness and clarity surrounded her, but maybe it was just the Portland sunlight coming through the window of her office. We discussed the case, and I knew I was in good hands. She accepted my statements at face value, expressed sympathy for my situation, discussed strategy, and had me out of her office in less than an hour.

This type of crisp efficiency makes some women good lawyers. A man would have interviewed me for two hours, and then taken me out to a long working lunch where we could swap war stories. Women seem more interested in cutting to the chase. They don't vibe to the drama and the hype, and tend to look at all legal tasks as chores. Maybe it's this matter-of-fact attitude that makes women better at multi-tasking. Have you ever seen a woman simultaneously juggling a baby on her hip while sorting laundry, heating a baby bottle, telling the kids not to track mud into the kitchen, and all the while keeping an ear on the Oprah show? The art of doing all of these things is not doing them at once, but rather doing them in sequence really close together. When you put that kind of attention to lawyering, you get a final product like a meal that comes to the table with all of the ingredients prepared properly and presented at the right time. It is logical that nature would select for women with nervous systems well adapted to multi-tasking, since nature hamstrings them with the care of infants while making no countervailing provision for extra time to accomplish all the household tasks that also fall to her lot.

Men, on the other hand, enjoy cooperating with a group of other men to accomplish a single goal, such as chasing down a giraffe on foot for five days and stabbing it to death with sharpened poles. Or getting together a pack of dogs and chasing bears up trees, where you can shoot them with arrows. Given half a chance, men will paint their faces with blood and howl at the moon to announce their conquest over the foe. When this type of mentality is applied without additional refinement to the practice of law, you get a lot of guys trying to hammer every peg, whatever the shape, into the same damn hole. You get narrow issues pursued with monomaniacal zeal and a lack of comprehensive strategy. You get people who are sure of their case, and lose because they never bothered to think that the jury just might agree with the other guy's view. You get a lack of empathy and a lack of insight.

This difference in temperaments has traditionally been resolved in the law by means of the lawyer/legal-secretary relationship. These relationships can be quite lovely and charming, sometimes to the chagrin of the lawyer's spouse, who sees less of him than the secretary, and instead of presenting him with the rewards of work well done, gives him bills, kids to put through college, and a mortgage. Fortunately, lawyers are masters of concealment, so spouses are spared the pain of knowing how deeply these relationships go and how much of a bond develops. When

I worked in L.A., I often referred to my secretary Victoria inadvertently as my wife, and referred to my wife Tara as my secretary. Indeed, it is not uncommon to meet a retired lawyer and his second wife, and discover that she was once his secretary, and that the young woman who put him through law school is no longer on the scene.

A good legal secretary has several of the qualities of the ideal girl-friend. She always listens to everything her boss says. She thinks he is charming, witty, urbane, and whatever nebbishy characteristics he has, are agreeable and endearing. She corrects his spelling, straightens his tie, and reminds him not to be late for court and appointments. She makes excuses for him and can provide convenient alibis on occasion, although only a rogue or a coward shifts his mistakes to his secretary. If, in addition, your secretary is also attractive, such that you have a living adorn-ment sitting in your office to inspire the envious whispered admiration of other lawyers, it can be kind of like having a facsimile of a happy rela-tionship. And it can be tremendously productive.

My wife is my legal secretary, and she has many of the characteristics of the perfect girlfriend. What I particularly like is the way she listens to me eagerly when I'm yelling about how we'll get those blankety-blanks, watches approvingly as I smash my fist into my palm to demonstrate how severe justice will be visited upon the wrongdoers, and then hands me my dictaphone with a tape already in it and says, "Do you want to do it now?" This kind of relationship is stimulating on many levels, and when you've married your secretary, a strange thing happens. She begins to thrive on sexual harassment.

CHAPTER TWENTY-SEVEN

THE HAIL OF LEAD

As I MENTIONED EARLIER, GARY LIKED THE FACT THAT I CARRIED AROUND THE "ART OF WAR." This book confronts the most difficult problem for a military strategist—how to make people fight. Sun Tzu was well aware that soldiers are mostly just peasants in uniform, who don't really want to get up one morning, march off to distant lands, leaving their wives, children and crops behind unattended, so that they can risk life and limb while trying to kill other peasants and burn down their villages, all for the apparent benefit of a lord who lives in a castle. Thus, Sun Tzu's book is full of strategies about how to get people to fight, how to move them into a position where they have no choice, and how to give them the courage that is necessary to win. Soldiers lose courage when there are no victories, and lose resolve when the war drags on too long. As Sun Tzu says in one chapter, "I have heard of some campaigns that were clumsy and swift, but I have not heard of any campaigns that were lengthy and skillful."

One evening in Gary's apartment I was reading to him aloud from another strategy classic, Clausewitz's "On War." I came to a section where Clausewitz explained that, in order to induce surrender, it is necessary that every day bring the opponent news of a new defeat, and that there be no end in sight to the daily drumbeat of failure. Gary quickly seized this idea, and translated it into "Every day has got to be a bad day for Cohen."

I coined the term "hail of lead" to describe a process of sustained attrition dedicated to two purposes. First, to build a favorable record of legal victories with the discovery judge. Second, to keep Bob Dorband so busy he couldn't do discovery against us. To accomplish these goals, I deployed every weapon available in the discovery vault—document demands, depositions, interrogatories and requests for admissions. Still, I needed Cohen's help to make the strategy effective because when a party *complies* with discovery, it's not as good a weapon, since there's nothing to see the judge about. But if a party is non-compliant, like Cohen, and you can keep hauling his lawyer in front of the judge repeatedly, you can build a record of noncompliance, and even get the case dismissed. But the process is labor-intensive.

Victory in discovery is a multi-step process: first you send out the demand for discovery, second you follow-up with a series of letters and phone calls to show that the other guy isn't responding, and third, you file a motion with the judge to compel them to comply with your demand. That's like breaching the walls of the castle. Then there are three more steps, analogous to storming the breach, overwhelming the defenders, and securing control. The opposing party tries to plug the breach by filing an opposition, where he explains that his client is acting totally reasonable in refusing to respond to this ridiculous discovery demand. You go mano-a-mano now, writing and filing a reply brief to rebut these opposing contentions. Finally, you get to the hearing and ask the judge to declare you the victor. Since the rules of discovery are pretty liberal, you should almost always win. If you can't get good at this game, give up civil law, because the good documents don't come easy. In fact, give up trial law altogether, because unless the other guy is a total bumbler, you're going to discover nothing that he doesn't want you to. But if you get good at it, you will have the power to make every day a bad day for the other guy.

Now for the other purpose of the hail of lead: to keep Cohen out of our business. There were witnesses we didn't want Cohen to contact, documents we didn't want him to see. Most of these witnesses and documents pertained to the time period after Gary registered the name in May 1994, and before he filed suit in 1998.

When Gary registered Sex.Com, it was almost a lark. The sort of thing one nerd would say to another: "Guess what I did today? I registered Sex. Com with the Internic." Standard response: "Good move, dude." Net dollars earned: zero. It was that sort of thing. Gary didn't see Sex.Com as a moneymaker in 1994, or he would have put it to work. How did Gary plan to make money in those days? He was one of many Stanford MBAs angling for venture capital in the boardrooms and computer labs of the Bay Area, where a saleable idea could garner millions in investment dollars. Using Online Classifieds, Inc. as his business moniker, Gary registered domain names for things other than sex, like Autos.com, Classifiedads. com, Jobs.com, and that sort of thing. Gary paid $2,000 to buy Match. com to create a dating site. An article in Forbes, the so-called "capitalist tool," gave Gary a full write-up, showcasing him as a wunderkind whose bright idea could turn the profitless Internet into a cash proposition: present the classified ads section of your daily newspaper as an online product, and take bread right out of the mouths of Hearst Corporation and Rupert Murdoch. In 1994, this kind of bold idea launched careers.

Gary's career had been launched. Online Classifieds, Inc. morphed into Electric Classifieds, Inc. With his Stanford degree and high-tech friends like Kevin Kunzelman and Peng Ong, Gary was able to garner venture capital financing from big names like Ron Posner, even roping in Aaron Alter of the famous Wilson, Sonsini law firm to do the corporate paperwork.

Electric Classifieds, Inc., the new corporation, took all of the assets of the old Online Classifieds, Inc. Kremen was for a time CEO of Electric Classifieds, Inc., and he directed the registration of new domain names, sometimes using fanciful corporate identities of non-existent companies as the name of the registrant. Dorband extracted this little nugget from Kevin Kunzelman at a deposition. Kevin, a former Electric Classifieds executive, didn't intend to give Cohen any ammunition by saying this, but it definitely didn't help our case. You see, Cohen argued, the business of registering speculative domain names was what Electric Classifieds was all about—if it acquired all of Online Classifieds' property, then it must have acquired Sex.Com. If Electric Classifieds had acquired Sex.Com, then Kremen could not sue for the loss of something he didn't own. Certainly Electric Classifieds had shown no interest in filing suit, and was, effectively, defunct. It had changed its name to "Instant Objects," and remained a California corporation with former CEO Mark Elchinoff as its Director. And the statute of limitations as to Electric Classifieds, Inc. had long since run. By this analysis, Cohen should get off scot-free.

There was only one way to avoid the problem, and that would be to contact all the upper-ups who had been involved with Electric Classifieds, Inc., and get them to swear that Gary had not given the company Sex.Com, but rather that it had remained his personal property. Of course, you can imagine this was a very delicate process. While Gary was absolutely certain he had not given Sex.Com to Electric Classifieds, we had only one declaration under oath to that effect, signed by his old friend Peng Ong. Peng, as Gary never tired of mentioning, was a billionaire, and had signed the declaration even before I got involved in the case. But the rest were wildcards. I mean, how do you go up to someone and say, "Hey could you swear under oath that I didn't give you something worth millions of dollars?" The finest and most moral of persons might wonder at your motivation in asking such a question, and if even one demurred and said, "I better talk to my lawyer about that," you might find your whole proposition going to hell in a handbasket.

We needed to nail down the ECI insiders, but not rile them up. And we sure didn't want Cohen taking their depositions. He noticed the depositions of a Wilson, Sonsini attorney, and Peng Ong. Cohen teased that he knew Mark Elchinoff did not like Kremen. Indeed, Elchinoff and Kremen were not on good terms, and Gary didn't want to ask him for a declaration. I had to give Gary the opportunity to contact the ECI insiders in the meantime, and keep Dorband from taking their depositions.

We made the field of battle so hostile for Cohen that he could only respond to our attacks. With the hail of lead we kept Dorband running for cover all the time. Gary took up the concept with a vengeance. It could be utilized at every turn. We sent out pointed discovery demands, followed up on them tenaciously, and always filed motions to compel. We sent out press releases, talked to reporters, dug up court records to expose more of Cohen's criminal past, and contacted anyone who might hate Cohen to obtain their assistance. "I want more lead!" became Gary's unvarying demand for action, not theory, for execution, not plans. In his mind, he was astride a fierce war-horse, spurring it from one gun-emplacement to the next, saber held high, urging each crew to fire a full load straight at the enemy ranks. Wreathed in the smoke of battle, rocked by each thunderous cannonade, Gary smiled with glee. He knew he had them on the run. That was a good time to fire more lead! And whenever the silence of the guns reminded Gary that Cohen might be enjoying a moment of peace, he'd rouse us to fire another volley with his one-word imperative—"Lead!"

CHAPTER TWENTY-EIGHT

VICTORY IN THE NORTHWEST

IN SPRING, 2000, I HAD FOUGHT DEFENSIVE DISCOVERY BATTLES with Dorband, opposed NSI's summary judgment motion, defended Gary's deposition, served offensive discovery on Cohen, and was trying to get Rich Diestel up to speed on the case. But I had been unable to conduct discovery, because Dorband had run out the discovery clock with his decoy depositions. I had filed a motion to reopen discovery, but until it was granted, which didn't happen until May 5th, I had to find new ways to hurl lead at Cohen. On March 7, 2000, I filed three complaints in Portland District Court naming Gary as an "intervenor" in cases Cohen had filed against Voice Media, Ron Levi's company, and two other porn operators, Myriad Corporation and National A-1 Enterprises. The Portland Federal courthouse is an amazing new monolith notable for polished granite, stainless steel and water sculptures adorning the pillars with continuous rivulets flowing behind panes of glass. It is beautiful but austere, and although adorned with inspiring maxims of justice, is resolutely devoid of warmth. There is no law library for the use of attorneys, which strikes me as an oversight, as if the judges had forgotten that lawyers traditionally use books to prepare their cases. The law library in the Multnomah County Circuit Court, just up the street, is always jammed.

I'd only handled one case in the Portland Federal Courthouse—a heroin case in front of Judge Redden. The detective who directed the search of my client's house was a big dark-skinned Latino who wore a suit, cowboy boots, and a ponytail about as long as mine. He had a powerful manner, and had talked my client into allowing a search of his house; however, the heroin had been seized from a detached shed in the back yard. I moved to suppress the heroin on the grounds that my client had given consent to search the house, but not the shed. At the suppression hearing I needed to establish that any search outside of the house was beyond the scope of my client's consent, so I asked each of the detectives whether they had the right to dig in the backyard. Each one responded they didn't think so. Finally, the third time I asked the question, Judge Redden squinted and looked over at me asking, "What was dug up

127

in the backyard?" I chimed back, "Oh, nothing, Your Honor. I was just asking it as a sort of 'Supreme Court Question' in order to illustrate the rule of law."

Judge Redden's wizened features transformed themselves into a mask of sudden distaste, as if he had bitten down on a worm and wasn't pleased about it. "Just stick to the facts," he said, "and don't get into anything"—here he paused as if he didn't often speak the word—"metaphysical." Nevertheless, he understood the legal problem, and amazingly, so did the prosecutor, who cut us a deal for 27 months. Hell of a lot better than the seven years my client was looking at.

Gary often described me as a guerrilla fighter. When we went to Portland, we each met with our insurance defense lawyers about the *Cohen v. Carreon and Kremen* lawsuit. I went and saw Susan Eggum, and Gary met with his lawyer, Steve Kraemer. Later Gary told me what he told Kraemer. "I told him that he and his firm were like the American army. The American army is good for a lot of things. They can win a lot of battles. But a guerilla is the best fighter for other types of battles. Mao was a guerrilla fighter, and Charles is like Mao. And I think he's perfect for the job." Gary had a way of saying things that made me feel all mushy inside.

Early on when I began work on the case, I had suggested to Gary that we could do something clever with all of those other lawsuits that Cohen was filing against people, claiming that their adult websites infringed on his "trademark" in Sex.Com. With discovery shut down in the main action, it was time to open up another front in the war. Cohen had filed nine of these lawsuits in Portland Federal Court, and three of them were still pending. Cohen was deliberately racking up these litigation victories in order to announce to the world that, since he was winning trademark lawsuits in federal court, he must have a trademark in Sex.Com. An excellent strategy, because Cohen often sued the weak and defenseless, far from their homes in a venue convenient to his own lawyers—Portland, home of the Duboff firm.

Lawsuits generally must be filed in one of two places: where the defendant lives, or where the wrongful act occurred. Because the Internet is everywhere, it has made it a lot easier to file lawsuits a long ways from where defendants live. Since a trademark infringement on the Internet is visible around the world and in all fifty states, plaintiffs have concluded that lawsuits for Internet trademark infringement can be filed anywhere.

For years collection lawyers in California would sue on debts outside of the county where the defendant lived, making it likely that defendants would simply default. The practice was outlawed by the California legislature in the Unruh Act. Similarly, Cohen won most of his Portland lawsuits by default, and even those who contested these cases rarely did so vigorously, so he was continuing to rack up victories.

It was not helpful to our case that Cohen was collecting these trademark judgments with such ease. I told Gary he had a right to intervene in those lawsuits, because under Rule 23 of the Federal Rules of Civil Procedure, a plaintiff may intervene in a lawsuit if they are so situated that, as a practical matter, their rights will be affected by any judgment entered in the case. It seemed obvious to me that every time Cohen got a court judgment saying he had a trademark in Sex.Com, it weakened Gary's claim. Still, I had never filed a suit in intervention, and didn't know anyone who had. In California, intervention is mainly used to attack voter initiatives, like that crazy anti-Mexican law that required nurses and teachers to rat out their patients and students to the Immigration and Naturalization Service if they discovered that they were "illegal aliens." In a case like that, "illegal aliens" are unlikely to file suit, so the nurses association might start the lawsuit. The teachers would then be allowed to intervene, because as a practical matter, their rights would be affected if the law is put into effect. Finally, the right-wing cranks want to get in on the act, so the Citizens for Safe Borders may be allowed to intervene in support of the constitutionality of the law. As a practical matter, the judge faced with a proposed intervention must ask, "Does the proposed intervenor have an interest in the outcome of this case?"

Usually, the intervening plaintiff wants to intervene and *do* something. But I wanted to intervene and *halt* Cohen's lawsuits so they would not proceed to judgment until after we won Kremen's lawsuit against Cohen. So I was requesting a "stay," the magic word that describes a case that is neither dismissed nor allowed to proceed, but remains in suspense pending the outcome of another case. The argument for a stay was simple. The only person with a right to sue over rights deriving from Sex.Com was Gary Kremen. It wasn't fair to allow Cohen to sue people over the trademark to Sex.Com if he was not the true owner. Furthermore, there is the important "judicial economy" argument, which is basically, "judge, why spend all this time figuring out whether Cohen has a trademark? All you have to do is wait till we win this case down here in San Jose, and you're not going to have to decide anything, because this case is going to go away." Finally, there is the argument that the courts shouldn't come up with different results about the same topics. The Portland courts shouldn't be issuing judgments in Cohen's favor when a California court might find Cohen had no right to even file such a lawsuit. This is called "avoiding the risk of inconsistent adjudications."

Judge John Jelderks, a magistrate judge in Portland, ended up hearing the matter as to all three cases. He set a hearing for April 5, 2000, in one of those huge Portland federal courtrooms, even more impressive than the lobby, with walls as high and thick as a castle, windows like slits set close to the ceiling, and enough milled, joined, sanded and polished wood to account for vast tracts of missing rain forest. We hooked up with Mike Essler and Jim Buchal, lawyers for Levy and Myriad, respectively, who were defending against two of Cohen's lawsuits. When we went to the hearing, Gary was wearing one of the innumerable dowdy sweatshirts that comprise the entirety of his wardrobe above the waist, and strutting like a Hapsburg grenadier looking for a fight. He amused himself by telling Bob Dorband he was going to sue him.

I had assured Gary that I knew how this would be handled, Oregon-style. All the judges who had these cases on their dockets were going to get together and talk about it over coffee. Then they would send all the cases to one guy, and let him or her decide them. We had a good case for allowing intervention, but I hadn't predicted victory. So in that atmosphere of uncertainty and hope that seems to kick up like a high wind when you get too many lawyers together, we listened closely as Judge Jelderks told us what he had to say. Indeed, he told us, the judges to whom these cases were assigned, (who were all Article III judges) had gotten together, and to their surprise, discovered that virtually every judge had one of these Sex.Com cases, and none of them had known about the other ones. I got the impression that this was like each judge discovering there was a bedbug in his bed. The Article III judges had passed all the cases to Judge Jelderks to resolve.

After hearing arguments from Bob Dorband that required the deft application of fallacious reasoning, and some counter-argument from me, as well as a plea from Mike Essler to just stay the case and not rule on whether we had a right to intervene, Judge Jelderks ruled that Gary had a right to intervene, and stayed the cases pending resolution of *Kremen v. Cohen*. This ruling was the beginning of some real anti-Cohen momentum, emanating from the right place — the bench.

A few weeks later, Judge Janice Stewart, following Judge Jelderks' lead, issued a lengthy opinion staying the *Cohen v. Carreon and Kremen* lawsuit. Judge Stewart's opinion observed that Kremen was an Internet pioneer who registered the Sex.Com domain name and claimed that he would have made a "woman-friendly" website had it not been stolen by plaintiff Cohen. Judge Stewart came down heavily on the issue of judicial efficiency, finding that many of Cohen's allegations would have to be resolved in *Kremen v. Cohen* anyway. Finally, she concluded there was some possibility that the action was filed "merely to annoy and harass Mr. Kremen and his attorney." It was a sweep. Cohen was no longer able to use the Portland Federal courthouse as a staging base. I got out the trumpets and flags, and broadcast the victory in an email to all the lawyers on Gary's team using a bold subject line, all in caps — "VICTORY IN THE NORTHWEST!"

CHAPTER TWENTY-NINE

THE SUBPOENA POWER

SEVERAL TIMES GARY HAD TOLD ME SOMETHING SCARY. "When discovery is reopened, I want to serve a hundred subpoenas." Generally, serving a hundred subpoenas could be seen as abusive, excessive, and just plain crazy. Particularly if you're subpoenaing banks and other financial institutions to obtain financial records. You stir up an entire hornet's nest. Banks have subpoena departments with lawyers and paralegals in them, and outside lawyers too. The records you're going after belong to their customers, who make money for them, unlike lawyers who heckle them with subpoenas for financial records. Banks have no reason to like you, no reason to be nice to you, and no desire to give you anything but what the law absolutely requires. If they don't comply, you have to get the judge to compel them to, and that ordinarily requires filing one motion per subpoena, so if you had a hundred non-complying witnesses, you might have to file a hundred motions. Reverting to our magic-metaphor, in a worst-case scenario, we'd have a hundred minor demons screaming to get out of their cages. Sort of like a prison riot in hell, where all the inmates have lawyers. Ugly.

Additionally, it's very hard to get a court to order a bank to produce financial records except in cases where the lawyer is trying to collect a judgment. Cohen, of course, was different. I could subpoena his financial records and succeed in getting them. And why is that? Well, let's return to that classical tactical blunder, filing the counter-claim against Kremen. In the counter-claim, Cohen alleged he had suffered $9 Million in damage due to Kremen's statement to Wired Magazine that he had stolen Sex.Com. When someone says they have lost profits, and they're going to have to prove it in court, you need to get financial documents to show how and why they lost the money. But Cohen was refusing to produce his tax returns, even though he had offered a couple of Schedule "C's" as proof of his prior use of Sex.Com in his initial discovery disclosures. That was his second mistake. You can't use a part of something as proof and then hide the rest, which is something to remember before you pull out a document. If page one of your document looks good, and page three looks bad, you're probably best off avoiding this whole document, or at least not using it to prove your case. Since Cohen had put his financial income in issue, I doggedly harped on his refusal to produce tax returns, working it like a lever to pry open the door of financial secrecy. And when Judge Ware reopened discovery in May, 2000, I bent to the task of preparing and serving over a hundred subpoenas in less than ninety days, many to Cohen's banks.

Serving subpoenas is an occupation with a dark past. In the old days, getting served with a subpoena was a very bad thing, because you could end up missing more than time off work. Witnesses didn't even get witness fees, much less respect. Subpoena is a Latin word combining the prefix "sub" meaning "under," and "poena," meaning "pain." Under pain of what? You might think it meant "under pain of law," thus giving you the alternative of either showing up or suffering pain. But this is not what it meant.

Pain was not an alternative. Rather, it was part of the methodology of interrogation. Many of the early courts were ecclesiastical courts, run by Jesuit or Dominican or Benedictine priests prosecuting crimes like witchcraft, heresy, blasphemy, and bestiality. In cases like these, with souls at stake, capital punishment after a proper confession was the prosecutor's idea of a good plea bargain. Certainly it was inarguably preferable to being burned alive, dunked to death, or slammed into an iron maiden until your feet turned to jelly. These were big cases. Witnesses were sinful, ever since their parents did it in the Garden of Eden, and Satan was everywhere, conspiring with witches to frustrate God's plan. Accordingly, no one could be trusted who had not been tortured, at least a little.

The levels of torture administered were three. For women and the weak-hearted, it was generally deemed sufficient to take them on a guided tour of the torture chamber, allowing them to walk across the blood-spattered floors, look at the implements that glowed red-hot in the torturer's forge, and hear the cries of foolish souls who refused to admit their wrongs or attempted to hide the misdeeds of others. The second stage of torture was the use of the "strappado," a leather strap that would be tied around the wrists behind the back, and used to raise the witness several feet above the floor. The witness would then be dropped and stopped a few feet short of the floor, dislocating the shoulder. Questioning would then be conducted. When an adequate witness statement was obtained, the physician would put the arms back in the sockets, and the witness would be good as new, unless they had a torn rotator cuff or some trivial injury like that. Finally, the third stage of torture was the real deal, the breaking of bones, the searing of flesh, the rack, the thumbscrew, and all the other instruments of persuasion that the medieval mind could devise. So the subpoena has an unpleasant origin, and the word still reeks of coercion. Which reminds me of a story I once heard about interrogation techniques.

It seems that during the Clinton era, the President, who was fond of contests of skill, decided to determine by means of a contest, which was the greatest police agency in the world: the CIA, the FBI, or the LAPD. Three identical rabbits were released into three identical wooded areas, and each police agency was told to bring the rabbit into custody. The FBI surrounded the wooded area with armoured vehicles, fired automatic weapons and incendiary grenades for several hours, while keeping vigilant watch over the wooded area to make sure that nothing escaped. All small floppy things attempting to escape the conflagration were forced back into the flames. After the wooded area had been reduced to fine ash, they declared the rabbit terminated.

The CIA hired operatives in their wooded area, conducting clandestine interviews of rocks, trees, other vegetation and numerous friendly forms of wildlife. After months of networking, the operatives established contact with the rabbit, who turned out to be a double agent working for the CIA. When Clinton was informed of this fact, the investigation was terminated.

The LAPD, deploying their forces from a nearby doughnut shop, surrounded the wooded area with SWAT vehicles and squad cars. Wearing flak jackets and paramilitary gear, and accompanied by uniformed officers, the LAPD operatives entered into the wooded area with a show of overwhelming force. All animals encountered were called "asshole," and forced to kneel on the grass. The sounds of scuffling, beating, squealing, howling and barking issued from the wooded area for several hours. After some time, a squad of uniformed officers emerged from the wooded area, dragging a handcuffed, hog-tied bear, missing patches of fur and hanging its defeated head, while muttering sullenly, "Okay, I'm a rabbit, I'm a rabbit..." So they might've been wrong, but a bear is a big, dangerous animal, and they got him off the streets.

Well, Gary's one hundred subpoenas might have yielded no more benefit than the efforts of the three elite police agencies. Indeed, fully half of the time our private investigators and process servers discovered nothing more than just how many Internet companies concealed their locations with fake addresses and maildrops. But I was about to unveil a secret weapon. It was a supercomputer that had recently been shipped in from Asia. It stood over five feet tall, had natural language programming, a sweet telephone voice, and long black hair down to her knees. She was my daughter, Ana, the subpoena clerk.

CHAPTER THIRTY

ROMANCING THE WITNESSES

I TOLD YOU ABOUT MY WIFE, THE PERFECT LEGAL SECRETARY. We've been married since August 2, 1974, when we tied the knot in front of a Tempe, Arizona justice of the peace with Tara wearing leather lederhosen, and me in a funky t-shirt. We had three kids, Josh, Maria and Ana. Daddy was already in law school by the time Ana got to talking, so she has grown up in an environment where law students and lawyers come tramping in and out of the house, carrying their bottles of beer and stacks of paper. Our kids remember hilarious family moments in our bright blue Santa Monica kitchen, when hopped-up poet-lawyers brandished knives, te- quila bottles, and hastily-crafted rhymes to the sounds of punk rock. All three kids logged scores of weekend hours in Los Angeles high-rise law offices, pretending to be receptionists, copy assistants, and secre- taries, while consuming the abundance of traditional West-L.A. takeout food—awesome lox, bagel and cream cheese brunches, trays of cold sandwiches, and gourmet pizza loaded with everything but anchovies. So spending weekends with daddy cranking out legal paper wasn't really so bad. It gave them an idea of what work is like in the big wide world.

Of the three, Ana was the only teacher's pet. Only due to her do I know how nice it is to have a really great parent-teacher conference in grade school. I certainly had none in my own childhood, and the first two followed my lead, much to Tara's chagrin. *Her* mom was an elemen- tary school principal. The difference between the two older kids and Ana, at least with respect to school deportment, was so notable that when Ana finally entered Ashland High in Oregon, the teachers asked her, dis- believing, whether she was really related to Maria and Josh. These two young pioneers had cut a swath through the school that has never been forgotten. Josh brought the baggy pants craze to Ashland, resulting in the expenditure of innumerable unnecessary yards of cloth, the sort of waste that drives Oregonians crazy. Maria takes her Mexican heritage so seriously that when one of her schoolmates, a proto-Nazi whose father was the head of the local college's criminology department, started talk- ing trash about Mexicans and "poor people," she felled him with a clean right cross, while, interestingly, her teacher made no move to stop her. She was called to the principal's office and issued a criminal citation by a police officer that was summoned to the scene. The slight flush of pride that filled her face when she told me the story abruptly turned to pallor when I reprimanded her in the sternest tones, telling her I was deeply disappointed. She had acted like a Nazi herself, I told her, attacking a person physically for mere words. She got the point, and ultimately delivered an apology to the young man. Maria performed the terms of her juvenile probation bravely, and the incident became a part of local legend, cementing her position in the community as a notorious bad girl.

So how was Ana different? Oh, how about *saintly*? Until the age of 19, which you'll note is after the matters addressed in this book, her mouth could safely have been used as a butter storage device. She got herself into Stanford as a President's Scholar, the only school she bothered to apply to, by wowing them with her unique resume. What's on that resume? Well, no high school grades, that's for sure, because this kid is a middle school dropout. She went to high school for a couple of months, until she decided her siblings were right, but decided to express it a little differently, leaving under her own power. She had done the same in middle school when she concluded her teachers were trivializing the important business of learning. She was particularly shocked when she was criticized for doing more than a project required.

After we moved up to Oregon in 1993 from L.A., Ana hadn't been in middle school more than three weeks before she came up with a great alternative to public education. She asked if she could go on a six-week meditation retreat at the Tibetan-Buddhist temple just up the road from our house. The retreat started every day at 7:00 a.m. and ended at 9:00 p.m. She would be the only middle schooler on the retreat, since everyone else was an adult and most probably over 30, except for the instructors- some handsome young Tibetan boys who had mastered the art of "psychic heat." I'm really not supposed to tell much more because this is esoteric knowledge that is cloaked behind a veil of secrecy. I never even got to see the little tiny skimpy mini-skirt type uniforms people wear when they train in generating the psychic heat. These skimpy uniforms are intended to make you cold, which isn't difficult when the retreat takes place in an unheated barn-like structure in the dead of winter in the Siskiyou mountains of southern Oregon.

Well, I always thought Ana had been studying too hard, and this seemed like just the sort of break she needed. In all seriousness, I told her that she could go to the retreat, and that I would wake her up every morning in time to get there, but she had to promise that when she got enlightened, she would enlighten me first, before all the other beings whom she would thereafter bless with Buddha wisdom. She took the deal, and I performed my part getting her there on time every day. She turned out to be the star performer at the event, inspiring the rest with feats of flexibility and endurance in performing difficult exercises that left others in tears. When the six weeks had ended, Ana had grown four inches, and was barely beginning to work up a sweat on this meditation stuff. She had a radiant smile, a firm step, and a long black whip-like braid that reached the middle of her thighs. This kid was on.

After the retreat was over, her return to school was brief. Somehow those middle school teachers didn't impress her when they came up with assignments such as writing a paper on five things you hope to do, giving as an example "to grow beautiful nails." So it wasn't long before she was back at home again, keeping an expanded meditation schedule and plenty of hours with the computer studying Princeton Review high school materials on CD Rom. I bought her a 12-hour series of videotapes on how to become a superstar student, and she absorbed their contents avidly. Tara and I could help her with some of the work, but after Algebra, we weren't much help with the computer-generated math problems.

People projected a nun-like character on Ana, and she didn't consider it a compliment years later when everyone thought it so natural that she be working in a library. Still, her bookish ways were notable, and extended to the Tibetan language. She studied with a monk at the temple, and also with Alan Wallace, the well known author and speaker on the subject of Tibetan Buddhism.

From Thanksgiving 1999 until March 2000, Ana studied at the Rang-jung Yeshe Institute in Kathmandu, Nepal. Tara had a good time watching over her and reprising her role of twenty years earlier, as an international hippie with the considerable advantage of a functioning debit card. The girls originally planned to stay around six months, which got shortened to three when they decided they wanted better food, air and healthcare than is available in Kathmandu.

From my end, the hectic work schedule was wearing me out, and working so close to Gary was turning me into a wraith. I needed help with the paperwork. The filing was massive, and I couldn't blame the other side either. I was generating the paper blizzard. Keeping the books for litigation costs was a headache. Hiring temps for a couple of hours at a time wasn't cutting it. I needed my woman back. Tara and Ana didn't need much prompting, and on March 1, 2000, they returned in brightly-colored Mongolian garb, bringing paintings, statues, and best of all, themselves.

Tara soon had the books under control, accounts reconciled, and the bills sent out. She next turned her hand to the filing, and corralled the paper blizzard in colored binders on a shelf with document lists, exhibit tabs, etcetera, exactly like they do in the big L.A. firms, because that's where Tara had worked. She has a rigorous code of professional discipline that sums up like this: "Your work will be done perfectly, whether you like it or not." She regards my methods of organization as the flailings of an amateur. She brought order to the case.

Ana started off as a cabin girl on our little litigation frigate, and was quickly promoted to handle the subpoena gun. The gun analogy is apt because the whole goal of subpoena serving is simply to hand the witness the subpoena. You only have to do it once. It's like chucking a harpoon into a whale. After the hook is set, they gotta come. Witnesses trying to avoid being served have engaged in every conceivable evasive maneuver. If you want to learn the meaning of *avoidance*, be a process server.

Filling out a subpoena is a detail job. In addition to the case name and number, you have to state the name and address of the witness, describe the documents you want them to produce, and state a time and place for production. To find current addresses, Ana used online searches and private investigators. Gary composed a most extensive list of documents, the infamous "Attachment A." For the place of production, usually lawyers designate the office of a court reporter, but that's expensive. I decided Kinko's was a good enough place for the witnesses to produce documents. It was easy, I told Ana, to find a Kinko's within a few miles of virtually any witness, using the Kinko's website store-locator. All of this information was integrated into the subpoena by a mind that had no prior experience with banks, private investigators, paralegals or clerks. The subpoenas appeared in her hands, and I signed them. Then she fired them off.

It was a classic example of the old saw in action: "On the Internet, no one knows you're a dog." In the Sex.Com litigation, no one knew Ana was a newly-minted "subpoena clerk." She soon was expert at generating a subpoena to anyone, for anything, and knew the process servers by first name. Her faxes flew fast and far, and were discussed with all seriousness. Soon she was skilled at getting those witnesses tagged. Then came the job of reeling them in.

Tight follow-up on every subpoena we served was an absolute necessity. A shamefully large number of people will simply blow off a subpoena. Ana would call each witness, and with her delicate voice, follow up earnestly and simply. Her first big success was Washington Mutual in San Diego, where she befriended the document paralegal to such an extent that the young lady started calling her for legal advice.

Washington Mutual was where Cohen got his home loan. When you've got a lot of money, you've got to do something with it, and Stephen Michael Cohen was no exception. With some of his Sex.Com profits, he bought a house in San Diego County, in a development called Rancho Santa Fe. When you apply for a home loan, you put your best foot forward in terms of assets, income, and corporate ownership, etcetera. In Cohen's case, this meant providing a list of bank and securities accounts, and declaring his ownership of "Omnitec, dba SEX.COM," a company whose bank accounts were also revealed in the loan file. The loan file showed Cohen bought the house for $3.1 Million. He paid $500,000 down, and borrowed the rest from WaMu on the strength of his other assets—bank and securities accounts held in his own name, and the names of Omnitec, Sand Man International, Ocean Fund International, and other companies. Cohen had come far since he walked out of prison in 1995.

As soon as Ana got fresh records, she copied them for me and faxed and emailed them to Gary. Usually, they'd come faxed back a few hours later, marked with numerous jabbing arrows pointing to circled account numbers, directing us to "subpoena this!" "Follow the money," Gary would chant, echoing Deep Throat. Armed with Gary's prime directive—if it's relevant, subpoena it, cost be damned—we knocked on door after door, tracking down Cohen's financial trail.

The Washington Mutual loan file was like a map directing us to the important places to subpoena. It told us what doors to knock on, and generally indicated the amount of funds likely to be found in each of the accounts. There were accounts at Citibank, Charles Schwab, and Royal Alliance. The biggest ones at the San Diego Wells Fargo Bank, where Omnitec dba Sex.Com had accounts. Within days of receiving the Washington Mutual records, Ana was faxing new subpoenas to a half dozen private investigators to serve on Cohen's other banks.

Ana could get a lot of records on her own, but there were a lot of hard cases out there in the witness world, and those people got passed on to Sue Whatley, an amply appointed tall, blonde, Oregon lawyer with a husky voice made more so by continued application of Salem menthol tobacco smoke. Sue's demeanor is languid in the extreme. Her eyes often do not open more than half way, preferring to look downward. She has a degree in music, can entertain at the piano all night, and a gentle laugh tinged with amused cynical delight. She was the Mata Hari of the subpoena team.

Sue's gift was inveigling her way into the minds and hearts of the witnesses. Talking with recalcitrants, smoothing the way with personal interchanges, and easy, playful emails. Her communications are peppered with personality. She sought to accomplish by wile and seduction what could not be accomplished straightforwardly, and often succeeded. Watching her working the witnesses was like watching someone reeling in a big deep-sea fish. You couldn't always tell which way it was going to go, watching the correspondence and hearing the updates, but then often enough she'd get the documents. One of her big scores was Steve Ramusevic, the accountant for Sporting Houses who gave us copies of the original stock certificates, board of directors information, tax returns, and correspondence concerning the attempted purchase of a Nevada brothel as phase one of the Camp Wanaleiya project. Sue smoothed communications with banks, who had their own lawyers and wanted to talk to a lawyer. What she couldn't cajole, seduce or wheedle out of the witnesses, it fell to me to obtain.

I was the last link in the chain. By the time a witness was dealing with me, romance had clearly failed, and there was only one way left to go — to Kinko's, where I would be happy to have the documents copied at my expense, or to court, where one would be beaten briskly about the head and shoulders with an expensive club.

And little by little, all through the summer and into the Fall of year 2000, the documents began to pour in from state agencies, banks, accountants, courts, telecommunications providers, securities brokerages and law offices, an insane flow of records that began to fill binders, which began to fill shelves. The meaning-to-volume ratio of these documents was not necessarily very high. There might be only two or three pages of useful information out of several hundred, if you were just looking at what you could prove with them in the case. The people in my office were becoming Cohen connoisseurs, beginning to appreciate the nuances and twists of his various deceptions. Each successful subpoena foray expanded an ever-widening circle of inquiry that was creating a three dimensional view of Steve Cohen's long-time pursuit of deceptive business activity, in various states, under various business names. This was the gift we received from the witnesses for all of our labor in romancing them. We got to see the full picture of Stephen Michael Cohen, a picture more clear and detailed than anyone had ever seen.

The biggest danger from studying Cohen so intensely was that you might lose heart in your ability to defeat him. After all, studying the record, you could see he had come out on top again and again. If you thought too long about it, you might hypnotize yourself into defeat, so I made a rule for everyone in our office, that no one could say anything admiring about Cohen. No one should ever speak of his schemes with wonder or amazement, but we should always remind ourselves that he was a thief, a liar, and a conman, and that we would defeat him. It was a joyless inoculation, but a necessary one. One must not fall prey to the enemy's glamour, although one is free to learn from it.

CHAPTER THIRTY-ONE

"SOME CAT IN THE ISLANDS"

As THE ENTIRE BUSINESS WORLD BRIEFLY KNEW IN JUNE 1999, Sir William Douglas, speaking as Chairman of the Board, announced that Ocean Fund International was offering to buy the entire Caesar's Palace operation of seven hotel-casinos for $3.6 Billion. Craig Bicknell reported this development in the June 15, 1999 edition of Wired News in an article entitled "Sex.Com's Pipe Dream." In his article, Bicknell established that the owners of Caesar's Palace said the offer came out of left field, and weren't taking it seriously. Bicknell traced the origin of the offer to an attorney in Salt Lake City named O. Bob Meredith, who said he worked part-time for Ocean Fund, but "couldn't say who sent the message," because "my Alzheimer's is acting up." Elsewhere in news reports, Meredith denied acquaintance with Sir William, referring to him as "some cat in the Islands."

One year later, I still didn't know if Sir William was Ocean Fund's Chairman. And Gary didn't let me forget it. I needed to work with this crazy aspect of the case. To unravel Cohen's web of fairytales, I had to show each one to be an invention, for which no evidence existed. And how do you expose a lie? My favorite method is to assume the lie is true, and then push for proof of other things that must therefore also be true.

For months, Gary and I only speculated about the identity of Sir William Douglas. Then, in December, 1999, in his relentless drift net searches of the Internet, Kremen pulled up an odd fish. An article in a London newspaper indicating that Sir William Douglas did exist, and in fact was the retired Chief Justice of the Island of Barbados. Further, that a London tabloid had published a retraction of a prior article reporting that Sir William was associated with Ocean Fund and Sex.Com. Apparently, Sir William had threatened to sue for libel. Thus, it seemed unlikely he had anything to do with Ocean Fund.

But put that aside. To expose the lie, let's assume Sir William really was the Chairman of the Board of Ocean Fund. He would be a "party witness," and Ocean Fund, as his employer, would be required to produce him for deposition. So I served Bob Dorband with a notice of deposition in December, 1999, which he studiously ignored, choosing instead to dispatch his flotilla of decoys. Discovery closed in the beginning of 2000, and when it was reopened in May of 2000, I filed a motion to compel Sir William's deposition.

The motion was extremely simple. I told Judge Trumbull that Douglas appeared to be an officer of one of the defendant corporations, had made statements concerning the profitability of Sex.Com and Cohen's role in managing the website, and thus Ocean Fund should be required to produce him. In response, Bob Dorband filed a similarly brief opposition supported by a one-line sworn statement by Stephen Michael Cohen that Douglas was not an officer of the corporation.

In my reply brief, I focused my fire exclusively on Cohen's veracity. Drawing richly from files which I had recently obtained from the Bankruptcy Courts in Los Angeles and Denver, I made the most of the surprising whoppers that Cohen had told the Court in those proceedings. The core argument in my reply brief read like this:

> "Cohen's declaration simply cannot be believed. His record as a liar stretches back too far and he will say *anything* that he believes will buy him time to carry on his criminal shenanigans. Mr. Cohen once submitted a declaration in United States Bankruptcy Court in Colorado stating that he had suffered a major heart attack, in an unsuccessful effort to get his personal bankruptcy reinstated . . . . On a second occasion, in August, 1988, Cohen impersonated a lawyer named 'Frank Butler,' and... filed a declaration [stating] that 'Frank Butler' had suffered a major heart attack on September 4, 1988, and had thus missed a filing deadline."

My reply brief contrasted Cohen's deposition testimony with statements made in his declaration and the further statements attributed to him by Sir William in the Ocean Fund press releases. At deposition, Cohen said he hardly knew Sir William at all. This conflicted with Douglas' statement in the Ocean Fund press release: "Stephen and I have an excellent and longstanding working relationship." I was wearing a grin as I finished up the brief:

> "Cohen... has failed to carry his burden of showing that Douglas is anything other than what the press releases say he is: President and Chairman of the Board."

When Judge Trumbull held her hearing on the motion, Bob Dorband played it cool, as if I should admit I was chasing a phantom. Shrugging and frowning in my direction, he argued I was just trying to send Ocean Fund on a wild goose chase, and knew full well that Sir William Douglas had nothing to do with the company. At times like this, the law seems not only to generate irony, but actually to be fueled by it. There was Bob, arguing I knew Douglas had nothing to do with the company, without saying his own client had generated a phony press release. And there was I, who in truth believed that Douglas had nothing to do with Ocean Fund, earnestly contending that he was its CEO.

Judges sometimes appreciate, and comment upon, the ironic postures the advocates strike when vying for strategic advantage, but Judge Trumbull didn't. She just looked at the evidence before her, which showed Douglas to be the CEO of Ocean Fund. The only person contradicting it was someone the evidence showed to be a bald-faced liar who filed false declarations with nary a second thought. She ordered Ocean Fund to either produce Douglas or to provide me with official corporate documents, sufficient to establish that Douglas had nothing to do with Ocean Fund.

Well, by this point, I was confident that Cohen would provide us with a document that would obviate the necessity of producing Sir William for deposition. It was just too easy. And on June 28, 2000, in came the fax. There were three pages, purporting to be the official corporate minutes of YNATA, Ltd., successor corporation to Ocean Fund, stating that on June 21, 2000, the company resolved "that Sir William Douglas is not an Officer or Director or in any way involved with YNATA Ltd. . . . that the Director and Officers of the Corporation hereby represent that they have no contact whatsoever with Sir William Douglas...." The document was entitled "Joint Action of the Directors and Officers" of YNATA, and had four signatures: "Derek Taylor, President; Fernando Rodriguez, Director and Senior Vice-President; Roman Caso, Secretary and Vice-President; and Stephen M. Cohen, Vice-President." The fax also included another document, called "Action of the Sole Shareholder Without a Meeting," bearing the signature of "Rodolfo Gomez-Aguila," appointing Fernando Rodriguez as the Sole Director of the corporation. Rodriguez, in turn, had appointed all of the officers who made the resolution that the company had nothing to do with Sir William Douglas. It was a document set up like a shell game, a sort of automatic-buck-passing device with lots of moving parts. "Ah," I thought, "more nonexistent people to depose!"

Gary was not particularly pleased when I announced that my solution to the shell game was to notice the depositions of all these imaginary Latinos plus the token Anglo, Derek Taylor, to prove that they did not exist either. Gary disagreed. He wanted to attack the corporate documents by presenting them to Judge Trumbull with the argument that they were "obvious forgeries." Problem was, they weren't. The corporate setup seemed convoluted, and the resolution of the Douglas deposition crisis a little too convenient, but I saw nothing in it that would cause Judge Trumbull to immediately conclude that the documents were forgeries. Although it frustrated Gary immensely, the only solution I saw was to call Cohen's bluff again. That didn't happen for another couple of weeks, when Cohen showed up to give another three days of deposition, after having been legally dragged, hog-tied and complaining, back to Beth Ballerini's office on Kettner Boulevard.

And what of the real Sir William? I located his phone number in France through a British private investigator with Caribbean experience. I called Sir William twice, but he never picked up the phone. Further research showed that Sir William was the kind of judge Cohen would have to respect—as Chief Judge of Barbados, Sir William had refused Britain's request to extradite Ronnie Biggs, the perpetrator of The Great Train Robbery of 1963, in which Biggs and his accomplices made off with $7.2 million pounds. A big lie leaves lots of room for nuance.

CHAPTER THIRTY-TWO

IN THE BELLY OF THE BEAST

UNTIL JUDGE TRUMBULL ORDERED HIM TO ATTEND ANOTHER DAY OF DEPOSITION, Cohen refused. Even then, the number of hours to be expended in deposition was set precisely—three days, six hours per day, starting at 9:00 a.m., July 11, 2000. Dorband even tried to keep me from asking any questions at all, filing a motion for protective order, saying that I had asked all the questions that I should be able to ask on behalf of Gary as a plaintiff, and that only Diestel, who was defending against Cohen's counter-claims, should be able to ask questions. Judge Trumbull turned aside this request, and said that Gary's lawyers could spend the time as they chose. Still, I was complimented by the singular emphasis on my role.

Three days is a lot of time to spend with anyone, but as my first deposition of Cohen had shown, it was very likely to be unproductive from one viewpoint—getting the truth. Going to Cohen to get the truth would be the ultimate fool's errand. Why not go to the Mojave to get water, or the Yukon for coconuts? No, there simply wasn't any truth there to get, and yet the time need not be wasted, for in engineering a tyrant's fall, you find his weak point in his strength. Cohen's rigid refusal to disclose anything meaningful about his business dealings led to his downfall. How symbolic it was when we saw the toppled statues of Stalin and Lenin gazing blankly skyward in former Red Square. Their steel bodies, inflexible and unchanging, unable to right themselves, were the mute prisoners of history. Like those rigid sculptures, Cohen's lies had the look of life, but lacked the vital, breathing substance. Once toppled, they too would lie helpless—defeated once, defeated forever.

Cohen wasn't stupid—his gigantic statues weren't easy to topple, because they weren't solid, they were evanescent. He denied everything, revealed nothing, and continued generating deniable disinformation. A helicopter gunship deposition was about to take place, but with a twist. Rather than trying to blow away the structure of lies, we were going to hose it down with concrete, day after day. That process would generate the stiff, attackable structure that could then be toppled and destroyed.

Cohen wasn't about to tell us the truth, so it almost didn't matter what his answers were, as long as they were somewhat definite. Then there would be contradictions, absurdities, non-sequiturs. Through detailed, extensive questioning, we would generate a database of lies. For every question, we would demonstrate, there was more than one answer. Once Cohen's statue of lies was unveiled, it would be recognized as a monstrosity . . . no one would mistake it for the truth. Made static, its structural incongruities revealed, we would reduce it to shards with a single blow of the mallet.

We had recently picked up a new addition to the legal team, Jim Wagstaffe. He co-authors an influential treatise on federal civil litigation that serves as the encyclopedia for California attorneys on federal law. He also fit the description of appropriate co-counsel that was suggested by another attorney Gary and I had talked to: "The guy who goes golfing with the judge." I don't know if Judge Ware golfs, and Wagstaffe is more of a basketball guy, but when Wagstaffe recounted the tale of how he had sat right next to Judge Ware at dinner after Wagstaffe had spent the day teaching him and other federal judges how to do their job, Gary and I knew we had our man.

Wagstaffe joined the case in June, 2000. Gary and I called him "the Wagger," since it was his job to bear our standard and wave the flag. We agreed that he would be our figurehead, and argue all of the motions before Judge Ware, whom he assured us would immediately take notice of his entry into the case. Wagstaffe can cut a charming figure when you're in step with him. He has a shock of hair tinged somewhere between whey and copper. He has a high forehead, strong nose, and large teeth that looked like they would comfortably snap oak twigs as big around as your thumb. He usually wore a herringbone or other woven sportcoat, from which he could have removed the dandruff a little more often. This minor tonsorial oversight was the one indication that Jim was actually wound a little tight. He gives the impression of being a dynamo of mental activity, citing code sections, procedural rules, and precedent setting cases in a steady stream, punctuating his speech with comforting asides like "As you know," or "With which you are certainly familiar."

Wagstaffe appreciated the degree of strategy required to catch a wily character like Cohen. He approached legal issues with zeal and relish, which would shine through an ear-to-ear grin gleaming with those fabulous choppers. And, as long as Gary didn't get crazy in his face, Wagstaffe could tolerate Gary's antics.

On September 5, 2000, Jim, Gary and I had a victory lunch right after Judge Trumbull handed us five discovery motion wins. I thought I had seen everything, but I had never seen a client take his lawyers out to lunch by scoring some backstreet burritos in a restaurant hidden away inside a drugstore, and then taking the lawyers to enjoy their repast al fresco on the grass in a public park. I was churning inside my skin until I realized that Wagstaffe was totally okay with it. He was munching his burrito gamely, and managing not to waste too much mental energy on one of Gary's silly jokes about how this whole place should be re-zoned for a toxic waste site.

At Cohen's deposition, Wagstaffe did a superb job of asking detailed questions, and insisting on specific answers. At the time, it probably seemed to Cohen that the Wagger was getting nothing, but we were compiling our database of lies and inconsistencies. Later, Sue Whatley became well-versed in the minutiae of Cohen's testimony, making it possible to find an impeaching quote to contradict almost anything Cohen chose to say. Wagstaffe couldn't get a coherent story out of Cohen about how Sex.Com had been handed from one shell corporation to another. Cohen would keep squinting, shaking his head, and explaining one wrinkle after another, nearly always ending with the answer that all documents to record the transactions had been lost, or were confidential.

Cohen also had an exasperating habit of running the clock by lecturing the lawyers on how to do their job, while complaining that they were doing it very badly. Wagstaffe usually just let him run on, as did I, since interrupting would just cause Cohen to go on longer, but Rich Diestel always fell into this trap. Cohen completely flummoxed him, and Diestel resorted to counter-lecturing with the addition of many "sirs," to punctuate his sermons with gravity. At times like this, I would just feel sorry for Beth Ballerini. She betrayed no emotion, as still as porcelain, only her fingers moving.

Toward the end of the second day of Cohen's deposition, it had become apparent that we weren't any closer to proving that the shell companies were Cohen's "corporate alter ego," nor had we shown any direct connection between the companies and the theft of Sex.Com. These companies—Ocean Fund International Ltd., it's successor YNATA, and

Sandman Internacional—could get off scot-free with Sex.Com and all its revenue if we failed to prove that they were Cohen's shells. We didn't know anything about these corporations. We didn't know if YNATA was a holding company dealing in valuable commodities and negotiable instruments, as its Articles of Incorporation stated, or whether Sandman really operated a server farm in Mexico where the Sex.Com website was hosted, as Cohen had testified. Cohen had refused to testify about these companies except to release a few teasers. Nor would he produce any documents about these companies, claiming they were not under his control. Without any documentation to show that they were really Cohen's alter-egos, i.e., companies that were financially identical with his own person, it would be difficult to obtain a judgment against these companies.

So the night after the second day of deposition, I worked on my laptop and created two discovery demands, one for YNATA, and the second for Sandman. The notice of deposition to YNATA required it to designate someone to testify about particular issues, and to produce for deposition the phantom directors, officers and sole shareholder who had officially disclaimed having any relationship with Sir William Douglas. The notice of deposition for Sandman Internacional required the company to present a designated witness to testify as to specified matters. When I finished it, I slept soundly, but not very long.

During the last day of our three-day session, I was going to ask questions for the last three hours. It went pretty well until the last few minutes. Gary had been sitting there silently for three days, and it was killing him. Dorband objected to a question I asked Cohen about whether he was using Sex.Com in "interstate commerce." Questioning started bogging down, and then Gary decided to help, telling me, "Yeah, we don't need to go into that." Dorband took the opportunity to interject, "Your client just indicated he doesn't want to spend time on this issue." I looked at Dorband intensely and asked, "You know what?" Then I turned to Gary and pointed my finger at him and said, "He should be quiet." Gary looked like I had slipped a hand grenade between his lips. He swallowed. He said, "Okay." He looked like the grenade was going off, deep inside a secret bunker. You could see him containing the explosion. Dorband got in his dig, "Is there some dissension in the ranks?" I concluded my questioning, and then passed the witness to Diestel.

I'll say this for Gary, I had hurt his feelings with that remark, and badly. But I apologized as soon as the deposition was over, and we never discussed it again. We still had lots of work to do.

CHAPTER THIRTY-THREE

PARLEY

WHEN DO PEOPLE PARLEY? On the eve of destruction, when there's one general dressed in a blue uniform, and another dressed in a red uniform, and they each have 100,000 soldiers massed at their backs, ready to go at each other with muskets, bayonets, cannon, and cavalry. So, just before the sword comes down and the cannons roar, and the horses rage forward, everything stops on a dime, and the two parties get together in a tent on a hill to sit down and have tea. Lives can be saved, fortunes rescued, death avoided and honor protected from discredit. Settlement hides a hundred errors of strategic judgment.

For many lawyers, not to fight the battle is their entire goal. So parley has a long and honorable tradition. I come from the tradition that says you should always settle if you're going to lose, but if you're going to win, settlement should come very dearly for the other side. After having boxed Cohen's ears for three days with three lawyers, and having served him deposition notices that showed we were going after his corporate alter-egos, Cohen should be thinking, "Is it time to settle?"

I wanted to sit down and take the man's temperature. To find out how he felt, and whether, in some safe, secure war-room, far back from the front lines, General Cohen had decided he was ready to throw in the towel.

Cohen had the same idea. I was out in the hallway, and he was loitering in the doorway, sending me these shruggy sort of looks, lightly smiling, the looks that a couple of months later he supplemented with the statement, "You could have been my lawyer," and "it's too bad we didn't meet before all this."

So I said, "Where you going for dinner?"

He responded, "I don't know, where are you going?"

Pretty soon, I'm proposing the idea of having dinner with Cohen to Gary, and he's like, "Why would we want to do that?"

I explained to Gary that it wasn't necessary that we say anything at all, if we were afraid of giving up some advantage. We could just listen. If we kept our ears open, we would probably learn some things. He quickly agreed. So, an hour or so later, I was drinking wine and ordering dinner with Gary to my right, Dorband across from me, and Cohen to my left. The restaurant is called Rainwaters, downstairs from Beth's office on Kettner. Very good food, and very good drinks. We had a couple of bottles of red wine, and everyone seemed to be eating with a hearty appetite.

Cohen's pitch was simple. He had thought that Gary was bullshit, but after talking to Gary for a little while and seeing how we'd been conducting the litigation, he realized that Gary was an old-timer, going back to the beginnings of the Internet, having the hard-wired knowledge that makes the difference between the pioneers and the come-latelys. Sex.Com, he explained, was on the decline. Revenues were down. It was playing itself out. The future was telcom in Mexico, and that's where Sandman was firmly positioned. He'd cut Gary a check for $500,000, and give him an interest in Omnitec, which controlled Sandman. I'd be in on it too. We'd all make bank together.

Dorband is going along with anything. He's just glad the bullets have stopped flying, and he can eat his steak. I would swear his forebears are Austrian, the kind of guys who could combine tea and trench warfare, stab you with a bayonet or ask "one lump or two?"

Then the strange chemistry started to line up. Cohen was talking almost exclusively to me. Gary was talking almost exclusively to Dorband. Pretty soon, Gary pulls out the statements from his securities account and is showing Dorband the current value of his stock portfolio. He wouldn't even show it to me, but he showed it to Dorband, to show him how much money was available to fight this war.

Meanwhile, Steve and I decide to take a walk outside below the antique street lights. While we're out there, he raises his offer to $700,000. I don't have to play it cool. The number's too low. Fifteen percent of $700K I can do in my head. A mere $90 grand. Well it was better, as we say in Oregon, than a poke in the eye with a sharp stick.

CHAPTER THIRTY-FOUR

ON THE TRAIL OF THE SANDMAN

ON THE LAST DAY OF COHEN'S DEPOSITION IN SAN DIEGO, I handed him the deposition notices, one for YNATA and one for Sandman. Those deposition notices commanded the defendant corporations to identify and produce witnesses to testify as to "specified matters." This is the most important kind of discovery that you can use to get to the bottom of things when you're dealing with a corporate defendant. They are called "30(b)(6) notices," because they are authorized by Federal Rule of Civil Procedure 30(b)(6), which was enacted to prevent squirrelly corporate defendants from engaging in games of Tweedledydum and Tweedledydee with plaintiffs who were saddled with the responsibility of establishing that a corporation "knew" or "did" something. Because, as we know or should know, corporations have no real existence, and are what we call "creatures of statute." Corporations do not exist, except to the extent that the law gives them life. The courts long ago ruled that a corporation is a "person" within the meaning of the United States Constitution. But finding a person who is "authorized" to speak for the corporation can be a long and difficult process in litigation. Buck-passing is a way of life in corporate organizations, and it gets worse when the company gets sued. Nobody wants to be the corporate fall-guy.

The theory behind Rule 30(b)(6), is that a corporation *must* have an ascertainable position in the litigation. It *must* know what it has done. It must know what it believes. Where it used to be necessary to take the deposition of high-level "control persons" within a corporation in order to establish what the corporation "knew" or "did," it is now only necessary to propound a 30(b)(6) notice, and the corporation is saddled with the obligation of designating a person to speak for the corporation, to tell what the corporation "knew" or "did." And their word shall be the word of the corporation.

By propounding 30(b)(6) notices to YNATA and Sandman, I had tapped a large stake into the heart of each of these Cohen alter-egos. It was going to take a lot of vampire-hunter type pounding to actually nail the stakes into their chests, but I was going to do it, no matter how crazy it got. Sandman was the first vampire in the crypt, and Dorband agreed to allow the deposition of this Mexican company, assuming we were willing to go to Mexico. Cohen had proposed Tijuana for the venue, but after the well-remembered assassination of a Mexican presidential candidate there, I insisted on Ensenada, about 60 miles south.

Cementing my reputation as a guy who would drive incredible distances to do crazy things, I decided to drive to the Ensenada deposition from my home in Oregon, picking up Gary along the way, since he wanted to be at the deposition. There was method to my madness, since I intended to drop off my royal blue Grand Cherokee Jeep in L.A., where a charity would pick it up and give me a tax write-off. Gas prices had gone sky-high, and I figured the Ventura County Rescue Mission could afford fillups better than I. I'd drop it off on the way back from Ensenada, and Gary and I would fly back to our respective destinations, departing from Burbank International for San Francisco and Oregon.

So I fired up the old rig early one morning a couple of days before the day of the deposition and drove to San Francisco. I arrived at Gary's office around noon, but it was hell getting him out of there, and we found ourselves stuck in Silicon Valley rush hour. We kept driving all night until we reached National City, south of San Diego. On the way, Gary exhibited his latest weird trip . . . talking with Cohen on his cell phone. Cohen was teasing Gary, driving him crazy, feeding him ideas, playing with his mind. In the dark, south on I-5, I kept hearing Gary's cell phone ring. It's Cohen again. And again. In National City, we stayed in a fleabag hotel, and prepared for the trip to Ensenada the next morning. Gary was interested in impressing everybody but me. From his point of view, I was his partner, who slept on the couch.

Next morning we had to cross the U.S. border, buy Mexican insurance, and drive about sixty kilometers of toll road to Ensenada. Although we were running a little bit behind, Gary wanted to eat breakfast, so we had to do that. When we got to the hotel in Ensenada, the deposition had been underway for an hour. Being late is never really a good idea. In addition to the Sandman designee deposition, we'd also agreed to take the deposition of Roman Caso, Vice-President of YNATA Corporation and one of the people who had signed the resolution denying any relationship between YNATA and Sir William Douglas. Diestel had decided that it was more important that I be present for the deposition of Roman Caso than for that of the Sandman designee, who had turned out to be Stephen Michael Cohen. Sandman turned out to be a corporation owned wholly by himself and his wife, based on Mexican incorporation documents that Cohen produced and I was able to decipher. Cohen's testimony consisted of a smug lecture about the true meaning of Federal Rule 30(b)(6). He and I fenced extensively about the difference between "personal" and "corporate" knowledge. It was mildly amusing.

The real surprise came when Roman Caso sat for deposition. As soon as he realized he was being videotaped, he expressed his complete consternation, and protested that he had business to do, had been waiting all day, and could not be expected to do this sort of thing. Speaking in Spanish, he said Cohen had lured him there by saying it was for some sort of negotiation. He claimed to have no knowledge that a deposition had been scheduled. Admittedly, in Mexico they rarely are. Speaking Spanish, I attempted to explain the situation, while Cohen tried to placate him, also in Spanish, by calling me a "pinche pendejo," which is essentially "fucking asshole." Caso was having none of it. He looked at Cohen with suspicion and anger, stating "I'm not sure who's the asshole here." Then, he stormed out. Shortest deposition I've ever attended.

Like Ronald Reagan, one of Gary's heroes, Gary had slept through the action. After getting his breakfast, the whole business of taking depositions was too much for him. When I returned to the parking lot, Gary had one leg poking out the passenger window of the Cherokee while the warm Baja sun baked his bones. We could smell the sea and hear the rattling of the dry beach grass. The trail of the Sandman lead nowhere.

CHAPTER THIRTY-FIVE

THE HILLS OF RANCHO SANTA FE

ON OUR WAY BACK FROM ENSENADA TO L.A., where we were to catch our return flights to San Francisco and Oregon, Gary decided we should stop and see Cohen's mansion in the hills of Rancho Santa Fe, south of San Diego. I didn't feel any need to do this, especially given the fact that we were driving north on the 405 freeway with planes to catch at the end of our trip. But Gary overcame my resistance, of course, and we took the Rancho Santa Fe exit. Since we were going to be doing what I call a site inspection, I stopped and bought a disposable camera that took panoramic pictures. If Cohen's house had cost $3 Million, I figured it must be quite a spread, and I wanted a record.

The next thing was finding the house. We had the address—17427 Los Morros Road, but needed better directions. Gary had the answer. He would call his pal Bob, who was holding the fort back at Gary's house on Third Street in San Francisco, and have him look at the address on Maps.com. The only problem with this plan was bad cellular phone reception. My phone wasn't doing anything, and Gary's phone was barely working. So there we were, on Gary's cell phone to Bob, driving around in the hills trying to follow Bob's directions as he read them off a computer screen, all the while losing signal while we looped and dipped through the coastal terrain. The neighborhood was impressive. All of the names were in Spanish, like Flores Drive, or Santa Maria Way. Finally, after about six calls to Bob and the same number from him calling back, we managed to find the place. It was tucked away in a large orange grove, and there was a big SUV parked in a horseshoe driveway. An agricultural road went up the east side of the property, so Gary and I hiked in that direction. From there we could see the tennis court, the large swimming pool, super-deluxe playhouse, and the enormous central residence. I couldn't get good photographs from the road, so I climbed up into a eucalyptus tree to get a better shot. Gary was scared we would get busted. We waited with bated breath as a farm laborer drove by in a truck. We got our pictures, headed back to the road and found our way back to the freeway without further help from Bob.

Gary had been right about going to see it. The concrete experience of seeing Cohen's wealth was provoking and inciting. You could see all he had that we didn't have, because we hadn't won the case yet. Everything became concretized. It took shape in physical reality. We knew we could get there with the right moves.

If you look at the distance on the map from Rancho Santa Fe to Burbank, California, where we were catching our planes, it really doesn't look that far. That's because they don't show you all the cars stopped on the freeway. The 405 freeway is the subject of at least one punk rock homage that I have listened through, and painfully. This strip of freeway, particularly the part that runs between San Diego and Los Angeles, is brutal. The smog is thick and unrelenting. At the wrong time of day, between 2:00 and 7:00 p.m., your average speed can't get much better than 5 mph in the tough spots, 50 mph when it's going great, and 20 mph on average. Everybody's talking on their cell phones in their cars, the heat haze and the smog is rising all around, and you feel less than anonymous. If you died of a heart-attack in your car, people would just drive around you.

Eventually, I spotted the familiar landmarks. TRW. The Herbalife building. The gigantic donut near the airport. Las Tijeras Boulevard, that's "the scissors" for those of you who don't speak the native language.

Around Fox Hills, aka "Black Beverly Hills," it became obvious that it was time to get onto the surface streets. Gary concurred, being an old southlander himself, and we got onto Sepulveda Boulevard. Pushing forward, I gassed up at the Chevron on Olympic and Sepulveda, where I remember a lady once survived a shooting because of a leather jacket and a small caliber bullet. We bought sodas and other liquids and proceeded north through the heat toward Burbank. I got there in time for Gary's plane, and was making frantic phone calls to the Rescue Mission I would give my Cherokee to, hoping they could pick it up before my plane arrived. Gary seemed to be experiencing some remorse at leaving me there with this situation, but his plane had to go, and we had what passed for a personal moment.

The young lady from the Mission that I talked to on the telephone understood me perfectly. I do redneck real good. When the tow truck driver arrived, it was almost as if he had come from Oregon. Poor people helping poor people. I gave him the car, took the receipt, signed over the title, and said sayonara to the big beast that had tailed the Sandman all the way to the edge of the sea.

I had no time for sentimental goodbyes. Inside the Burbank airport, everything was okay. My plane was leaving on time, and I was leaving with it. I bought a couple of magazines, stood in line and caught the big bird back to Oregon.

CHAPTER THIRTY-SIX

ON DYING GROUND

Sᴜɴ ᴛᴢᴜ ꜱᴀʏꜱ ᴛʜᴇʀᴇ ᴀʀᴇ ɴɪɴᴇ ᴋɪɴᴅꜱ ᴏꜰ ɢʀᴏᴜɴᴅꜱ on which battles may be fought. For example, there is ground of contention, which would be beneficial to either side able to seize it. There is light ground, which is when you enter shallowly into enemy territory, intersecting ground, which gives access to a well-trafficked location, and heavy ground, which is deep inside enemy territory. There is also bad ground, like mountain forests, steep defiles and marshes, and dying ground, where Sun Tzu says, "you will survive if you fight quickly and perish if you do not." Sun Tzu gives particular advice for the conduct of military activities on the various grounds. On light grounds, do not linger; on bad ground, keep going; on heavy ground, plunder. On dying ground, there is just one thing to do — fight.

As frightening as it sounds to be on dying ground, the old adage is, "put them on dying ground, and they will live." Sun Tzu explained:

> "If they fall into dying ground, then everyone in the army will spontaneously fight. This is why it is said, 'Put them on dying ground, and then they will live.'"

From May 18 until August 21, 2000, we were on dying ground.

I'd always told Gary, from the very beginning, that it was risky to fight with NSI over the property issue, because if we lost it, Cohen would say that what's good for the goose is good for the gander, and since it wasn't property, he couldn't steal it. And on May 18, 2000, directly on the heels of the court's order granting summary judgment for NSI, Dorband filed a motion for judgment on the pleadings ("MJOP") arguing precisely that. The third amended complaint started out with ten claims for relief. We were down to three claims — conversion, unfair business practices, and declaratory relief. The new tort of domain name theft was proving maddeningly difficult to define in established legal terms. Dorband had moved the judge to dismiss conversion and declaratory relief, attacking conversion first, and using the force of its collapse to take down the declaratory relief claim. Then he would direct a motion at the last remaining claim, for unfair business practices, and the game would be over. There were excellent reasons for this two-step strategy.

The Federal Declaratory Relief Act allows the federal courts to sort out disputes between people and companies even before grounds for a damage lawsuit arises. For example, you can sue an insurance company for declaratory relief if they threaten to refuse to defend you in a law-suit, even though arguably, you haven't suffered any damage yet from their refusal to defend. Pleading a claim for declaratory relief is about as simple as saying, "I am the plaintiff, this is the defendant, and we have a dispute I want the court to resolve with a legal judgment." The only hitch is, declaratory relief cannot operate in a vacuum. The court can only ad-judicate your rights if you have some rights to maintain; otherwise, the court will dismiss the case for lack of a "case or controversy."

If declaratory relief provides no independent source of legal rights, why bother putting it in your complaint? Because it allows the judge great flexibility in fashioning a remedy, allowing him or her to make any order that "justice requires." Now that's nifty—justice with a scalpel. In our case, we needed an order declaring Gary to be the owner of Sex.Com, and directing NSI to transfer the registration into his name. The source of Gary's rights was his ownership of personal property that had been stolen. The injury to his property rights could best be remedied by a dec-laration establishing Gary's ownership and directing NSI to deliver pos-session of Sex.Com to its rightful owner.

Dorband didn't quarrel with the basic proposition: "The declaratory claim, by its own terms, arises from plaintiff's alleged 'ownership and possession' of the Sex.Com domain name." Based on the ruling for NSI, Dorband argued, it was clear that the law of conversion didn't provide a remedy for Gary's loss, and since declaratory relief gave him no ad-ditional rights, Gary's declaratory relief claim was meaningless. As Dor-band put it: "If a domain name cannot be converted under California law, it stands to reason that whatever the defendants did... it does not amount to an invasion of a legally protected interest under California law...." Dorband also had an excellent fall-back argument. Under the de-claratory relief act, the court can exercise discretion not to decide a legal issue, especially a novel issue under state law. So if his argument was not sufficiently convincing to clinch an affirmative win for Cohen, Dorband invited the judge to avoid the issue: "Based on the Court's recognition that the issue of applying an ancient legal remedy (conversion) to a modern intellectual property concept (domain names) is essentially a determination better left to the State of California, the Court should decline to exercise its discretion."

Judge Ware had observed in his order granting NSI summary judgment that unfair business practices laws provided a remedy for the theft of intangible property interests, such as business goodwill. But that wouldn't help much, because if Gary's claim was for loss of business goodwill, it had no value. Gary had never built a website and had no customers, so he had no good will and lost nothing when Cohen took the registration for Sex.Com. The judge might call Gary's interest in Sex.Com a "mere expectancy" of future earnings, "too remote" to give rise for a claim of damages. He might end up with an acknowledged, but worthless piece of theoretical property.

So we were entering a narrow pass. At times like this, the mind concentrates, and the past dissolves. If you think about all the time you've sunk into the case, and how it's maybe just a hair's breadth away from being lost, you can't think. But if you let yourself go, the fear of imminent destruction will bear you along on a wave of energy. Like shooting the rapids in a rubber raft, moves come to you instinctively, you process the information and steer the right course. Pushed relentlessly forward, the moments bore me along on a swift current. I needed to put the information together, and use Wagstaffe's people to assemble our most impressive product yet. Since they had only recently joined the case, they knew nothing about the facts, and were still getting up on the law. The opposition to this motion was our first project together, and we worked smoothly to integrate our thoughts and writing. It was exhilarating to have them share the intellectual adventure of the case, and the additional firepower was more than welcome.

Argued as a matter of pure legal theory, the motion was surgically clean. There was no evidence to consider, there were no facts to weigh. There were just abstract issues to decide, let the chips fall where they may. If the law decrees that a thief must go free, then free he must go, and it is the judge's duty to dismiss him. Plaintiffs go home disappointed every day from the courthouse. It's no great heartbreak for the average judge, and no surprise that the wealthy often emerge victorious.

Most lawyers, looking at the motion, would not even try to think of a way to bring Cohen's character into issue, but we had to do it. We had to get some moral suasion going. We had to argue that courts do not sanction thievery, and that where necessary, the law must be stretched and fashioned to respond to new threats to ancient rights.

But in response to a motion for judgment on the pleadings, you're not supposed to submit any evidence. How could I bring in evidence about Cohen's past, so the judge could understand that Cohen was a thief, and he should not get the assistance of the court to pull off the theft? Judge Ware had to understand that Cohen was a bad man with a clever lawyer! How could I do it? I decided to submit only a narrow category of documents which are "judicially noticeable." Court records are always judicially noticeable. Convictions, divorce decrees, bankruptcy filings, declarations filed in litigation, and statements made on the record by judges, are all judicially noticeable, because their accuracy is inherently reliable. As it happened, within the narrow category of judicially noticeable documents, Cohen had generated a plethora of damning records.

In January 2000, I compiled a stack of documents about Cohen I called "The Big Book of Evil Deeds." It was about two inches thick. I created it for a special occasion that I haven't discussed yet, that is, when Cohen filed an ethics complaint against me with the Oregon State Bar. Everyone has heard that lawyers are supposed to obey certain ethical rules. Nobody has any idea, of course, what these rules might be, since as the old lawyer joke says, lawyers are replacing rats in lab experiments these days, in part because there are some things even rats won't do. Lawyers seem to be willing to do any damned thing, from saying toxic waste dumping is ecologically beneficial to making a stolen election a fait accompli. What is it that lawyers can't do? Well, according to Cohen, I couldn't do press releases that call him a thief.

When someone makes an ethics complaint to the Oregon State Bar, an ethics investigator immediately sends you a letter with a copy of the complaint, and you get two weeks to respond.

My response to the Bar was essentially this: "I did nothing wrong, and before you get all involved with this, consider the source." With my letter, I enclosed the Big Book of Evil Deeds, which included copies of Cohen's conviction for bankruptcy fraud, phony declarations he signed under the name of Frank Butler, the RICO complaint Cohen filed against his wife and her lawyers, and copies of the Oregon RICO lawsuit he had recently filed in Portland against Gary and myself. The Big Book, more than a ream of spiral-bound paper, weighed in at nine pounds, and was certain to receive an honored spot on the ethics investigator's credenza. Cohen responded to the Big Book in a letter saying it just showed how unethical I was, that when confronted with serious allegations, I would just throw more mud. The ethics complaint died a natural death a few months later.

The Big Book of Evil Deeds, however, became a hot item. Gary loved it, and I had Kinko's cranking out dozens of copies. I sent them to journalists who appreciated solid documentation to back up their stories on this amazing con man, Steve Cohen.

When the time came to file opposition to the MJOP, I pulled out the Big Book and began work on the second edition. Since January, we had obtained the files of two bankruptcies Cohen had filed in Denver and L.A. We had also obtained records showing that Cohen had incorporated a slew of California and Nevada companies. And I had plucked a beauty of a quote from Judge Judith Keep, denying his request for bail pending sentencing after the jury had convicted him of bankruptcy fraud: "You have lied to the Courts." The Big Book became a slimmed-down and more substantive packet for Judge Ware entitled Plaintiff's Request for Judicial Notice (the "RJN"). The RJN provided evidence of four relevant facts:

(1) Cohen had established a pattern of theft by deception and forgery,

(2) Cohen had repeatedly lied to the courts,

(3) Cohen had never claimed prior to 1993, that he had used Sex.Com as a service of the French Connection; and,

(4) Cohen had admitted that Sex.Com was personal property, and thus was barred from disputing that claim.

Although past crimes and conduct are generally not relevant to a court proceeding, the intelligent advocate will try to find ways to fit into the exceptions. Three exceptions applied here. First, past convictions for crimes involving deception are always relevant to a party's credibility, so the bankruptcy conviction was relevant to Cohen's entire denial of liability. Second, when past actions add up to a pattern of deceptive conduct, they are admissible to show the deception was part of a conscious plan, not mere happenstance. Third, under the doctrine of "judicial estoppel," a party cannot "play fast and loose" with the courts by taking inconsistent positions in different cases. For example, in the Portland trademark infringement cases Cohen filed sworn affidavits saying Sex.Com was his personal property; accordingly, he should be "estopped," i.e., prevented, from disputing that the name was property. And when he stated in his 1986 Denver bankruptcy that he owned *no trademarks, copyrights or other intellectual* property, that should bar him from now claiming that he used Sex.Com as a trademark since 1979.

The RJN framed the issues as a dispute between a convicted con man who used the law to make his thefts more secure, and a brilliant dot-commer who was playing it straight. Should Cohen get the benefit of his cynical manipulation of the legal system, which had continued nearly unchecked for decades? The answer seems obvious. With that moral argument in place, we just needed to give the judge some case precedent finding it unlawful to appropriate intangible property without the owner's permission. And that intangible property had to be unprotected by trademark, copyright, or other legal basis. If we could do that, we would be in a good position, because Judge Ware had specifically said, at the status conference in early May 2000, that he would allow Gary to have his "day in court" against Cohen, even though he was granting summary judgment for NSI. Judge Ware wanted to do the right thing, but beyond the moral argument, we needed some support in case law.

Because Dorband was attacking the declaratory relief claim by way of the conversion claim, we wanted to support it by showing we had a valid unfair business practices claim. A California appellate case from 1951 called *McCord v. Plotnick*, supported this position solidly. The court decided *McCord* on the basis of a U.S. Supreme Court case called *International News Service v. Associated Press*. This must have been considered a "high tech" case in its own day. Plaintiff alleged that every day, the Associated Press would buy the plaintiff's newspaper, and using a new-fangled device called a telegraph, would transmit the contents of plaintiff's newspaper to defendant, who would use it to publish defendant's paper. When plaintiff sued for unfair competition, the Associated Press objected that the news articles were not copyrighted, that they were publicly distributed, so they were not confidential, and thus plaintiff had no claim. The argument was rejected by the Court:

> "If that which complainant has acquired fairly may be sold fairly
> at a substantial profit, a competitor who is misappropriating it
> for the purpose of disposing of it to his own profit and to the
> disadvantage of complainant cannot be heard to say that it is too
> fugitive or evanescent to be regarded as property. It has all the
> attributes of property necessary for determining that a misap-
> propriation of it by a competitor is unfair competition because it
> is contrary to good conscience."

This language from *International News*, quoted by *McCord*, was vi-
talizing to our case. It provided a good model for the judge to chart his
own course in the wilderness of new technology and clever schemes.
The Supreme Court's analysis that theft of evanescent assets is an unfair
business practice, seconded by the state courts in *McCord*, gave us the
substance we needed to hang on to the declaratory relief claim. *McCord*
also struck a positive moral tone, supporting the argument that Cohen's
exploitation of the legal system should not be tolerated any longer. While
some might have doubted whether Gary's registration of Sex.Com was
something he had acquired "at substantial cost," few could doubt that
it could be "sold fairly at a substantial profit." And unless we wanted to
encourage thievery, that profit should not go to a thief.

We cited another case that had a technological twist, and lightened
the brief with a touch of humor. In *Downing v. Municipal Court*, a fellow
who had been selling slugs to cheat the San Francisco parking meters filed
suit to prevent the prosecutor from charging him with vending machine
theft. The slugs didn't cheat vending machines, the swindler argued, because the parking meter wasn't a vending machine, since it dispensed no
product, and the privilege of parking a car for a few hours wasn't "property." The judicial response to this argument was dismissive:

> "The fact that a new machine has been invented, and a new
> means, method or scheme devised to evade a lawful condition
> for its use does not destroy the effect of the law."

Since the theft of Sex.Com was an unfair business practice under
the dual authority of *International News* and *McCord*, rather than falling with the conversion claim, the declaratory relief claim should remain
standing, because it was separately supported by the unfair business

practices claim.

On August 21, 2000, Judge Ware's opinion was filed. The conversion claim was out, but declaratory relief stayed in, because said the judge, it was "at least" supported by the unfair business practices claim. On dying ground, we lived.

CHAPTER THIRTY-SEVEN

BECOMING THE ENEMY

IN HIS DISCUSSION ON "BECOMING THE ENEMY," Minamoto Musashi advised warriors to consider the enemy's perspective. My copy of Musashi's strategy, "The Book of Five Rings," was a classic of tasteless publishing. Someone with a twisted sense of humor had defaced the venerable work with a cover photograph of a paranoid-looking businessman in a Burberry coat, wielding a copy of the Wall Street Journal as his weapon, sizing up a hulking samurai in lacquered armor, wearing a helmet adorned with flapping banners. It must have been printed during the Reagan era, when the yen was way up, our national self-image was in the toilet, and all things Japanese were enviable. Man, that was an ugly cover! One day, in a last ditch-attempt to procrastinate work a little longer, I pulled out my knife and excised the goofy picture from the cover in a frenzy of distaste. On the procrastination front, the gambit was highly successful. The project must have consumed at least five minutes and a foot of packing tape. The crude facelift also improved the book's utility, since I now wasn't afraid to be seen reading it in public. One day, sitting in an airport bar while working on Gary's case, I read this section:

> "Even a burglar caught in the act is thought to be formidable when he blockades himself in the house. But if you put yourself in his position, you will see that he feels helpless, that everyone in the world is against him. He who is blockaded himself is like a pheasant, while he who is waiting outside is like a hawk."

Reflecting on Cohen's situation, I realized that he had locked himself into a fortress. Although he looked and acted secure, one thing was sure—he was in there, and he wasn't leaving. A siege would seem to be the obvious solution, but Sun Tzu advised against costly, time-consuming sieges only as a last resort. The prize tends to be destroyed in the course of a siege. Many castle walls, once breached, give access only to a ruin full of suicides. To abort this process, a siege must somehow be reasonably swift. Caesar Borgia developed a swift method of concluding a siege using focused firepower. He set up a cannon, and fired one cannonball after another at the castle walls, always at the exact same spot. The wall caved in within a day, Borgia's troops stormed through the breech, and the cruel and innovative Italian added another jewel to his crown of conquests.

I figured it could be so with Cohen. Since we had State Farm on our side, providing additional firepower, we could afford a Borgia-style siege. We just had to keep blasting away at the same spot, until it caved in. The weak point in Cohen's fortress was his refusal to disclose his financial records. Confident in his strategies, unaware that stone walls can be breeched, Cohen was satisfied to ignore our continuing assault. Cohen didn't worry that it might provoke suspicion to hide behind a cloak of confidentiality and forgetfulness at depositions, to refuse to produce documents in response to our demands, and to rely almost entirely on witnesses who were either dead or living abroad. He apparently didn't realize that it was suspicious to live in a crime capital like Tijuana and do business exclusively through international corporations with straw-man directors and confidentiality agreements guarding their financial records. He must have figured that if big, mainstream companies could set up foreign subsidiaries, invoke confidentiality and the Fifth Amendment to avoid producing damaging information, and use bogus shelters to avoid taxes, why couldn't he? This argument, however, would merely put Cohen on the same level as Enron with a smaller capital base, and would not make his conduct lawful.

Like the Republicans say, it's all about defining your adversary. Perhaps without realizing it, Cohen allowed us to define him as the kind of person who receives an abbreviated version of civil justice. By resisting our discovery so resolutely, he demonstrated that his claims were unworthy of thorough consideration. They deserved to be terminated with a sharp blow of judicial impatience. Though he denied it to himself and the court, Cohen was identifiably cast from a mold that has turned out large numbers of offshore-based intellectual-property thieves who play corporate shell games, disobey court orders, conceal assets, and use scorched-earth litigation tactics to exhaust their foes. Trial judges have developed a special body of law for disposing of these atavistic characters. When presented with enough evidence to prove that a party is a bad-faith litigant, exploiting the system, a judge can simply ignore their arguments and enter judgment against them. Where the basis for dismissal is a history of egregious discovery abuse, the appellate courts won't second-guess the trial judge's decision. This doctrine is a blunt instrument for dispatching litigants who hire criminally stupid lawyers willing to clog the courthouse with faux lawsuits in exchange for an hourly fee. With his history of "lying to the courts," and his current position as a rogue pornographer exploiting a stolen domain name to reap undeserved profits, Cohen was easy to define as a classic intellectual property thief who should go directly to jail, without passing "Go."

Being averse to sieges, Sun Tzu advised luring enemies out of their fortified castles by attacking something or someone precious to them. Thus, proper samurai houses—basically a shed with a good conference room—were often burned by their owners, and were designed to evoke no attachment. But it's one thing to be detached about losing your house, and quite another to remain calm as the enemy attacks friends and relations.

In May 2000, Diestel served subpoenas on Cohen's ex-wives Karon and Susan, and Susan's daughter Chandra. Gary and I had served a subpoena on Midcom, where Cohen worked in a cubicle next to Lee Fuller during the exact time period when Cohen stole Sex.Com. We also subpoenaed Fuller and Midcom's owner, Barbara Cepinko. We subpoenaed some of Cohen's other confidantes dating back to the Tustin sex club, the French Connection, and the prison years. Each of these people knew about Cohen's dealings with Zolp, Sporting Houses, Ghiglieri Fine Arts, and one would assume, Cohen's acquisition of Sex.Com. As soon as he found out we'd served these people, Cohen would try to contact them. It probably wouldn't be a lot of fun to get one of those phone calls from Cohen. Just imagine if one of your friends buried stolen loot in your back yard and swore you to secrecy. Then one day, the sheriff called and asked to take a look around your property. That wouldn't be fun.

By mid-May, Cohen had identified Diestel's additional firepower as the source of the subpoenas that his friends and relations were receiving, and was busy plugging leaks. Toward the end of May, we were closing on the date for Karon Cohen's deposition in early June, when Cohen unveiled a new strategy—a peace initiative. Just as we were getting ready to sink in our knives, Cohen offered Diestel a dismissal of all Cohen's counterclaims against Gary. If we allowed Cohen to dismiss his claims against Gary, Diestel would be off the case, thus nullifying all the effort we'd spent getting State Farm onboard and bringing Diestel up to speed. Cohen's entire counterclaim would have caused us only to chase our tail instead of spending time building our case. It would be far more satisfying, and productive of good results in court, to kill Cohen's counterclaims on the merits, rather than allow him to withdraw them. If he'd thought farther ahead, Cohen would have dismissed his counterclaims before Diestel filed Gary's answer, because now that Diestel had filed an answer, Dorband needed Diestel's agreement or court approval to file a dismissal.

Peace sounded great to Diestel, of course, so I had to ask him. Was Cohen intending to dismiss the counterclaims permanently, with prejudice? Since Dorband hadn't specified, I assumed he was offering to dismiss the claims *without* prejudice, which would allow Cohen to refile the case at any time. I was right—that was all that Cohen was offering, and I wasn't buying. Cohen's tactics reminded me of Slobodan Milosevic's peace proposals, which he used to rest his soldiers and build up supplies before launching another offensive. We could not afford a Bosnian peace accord, I told Gary, who agreed that any truce offered by Cohen would be a trick. I called Diestel immediately, and wasn't surprised by his response. As a California state court litigator, where a dismissal never requires "leave of court," and anything that clears the calendar is a good thing, my idea to oppose dismissal seemed topsy-turvy. Proving that he wasn't in it just for the money, Diestel didn't understand why I wanted to abort the peace process. He asked quizzically, "What can I do if he wants to dismiss his counterclaim?"

In an excited tone of voice, I said, "You can object! You can demand a dismissal with prejudice or no dismissal at all! You can demand that he pay your attorney's fees as a condition of dismissal!" Those things are all available under Federal Rule of Civil Procedure 41, and Diestel wasn't surprised to hear that we could block Cohen's exit. It was just counter to his experience to frustrate an adversary's attempt to surrender. He could have cited Sun Tzu's exhortation: "Never fight an enemy who is going home." I would have responded, however, that Sun Tzu did not advise against fighting enemies who are *pretending* to go home. Still, Diestel wasn't ready to assume that Cohen was planning to blithely dismiss his counterclaims one day and re-file them at leisure. So I argued another point—what difference did it make if Cohen dismissed the counterclaims at this point, when he still had the Portland federal lawsuit pending against both myself and Gary? We had to oppose this here, now.

On the Friday before the week when Karon Cohen's deposition was to take place in Florida, since Diestel remained uncertain about how to respond to the peace proposal, I sent him a letter demanding a strategy meeting with Jose Guillermo of State Farm. Meanwhile Dorband, who undoubtedly realized that Diestel's delay meant he wasn't going to dismiss, filed an *ex parte* motion to dismiss the counterclaims, and a follow-on motion to quash all of the subpoenas Diestel had served on Cohen's friends and relatives. Of course, Dorband filed his papers at 2:45 on Friday, June 2nd. This was a bit of a shock, because a Rule 41 motion to dismiss claims or counterclaims should not be filed *ex parte*, and must be filed as a "noticed motion," giving the opposing party two weeks to file a response. An emergency motion provides a very short, uncertain window for response, and allows the judge to essentially grant the "ex-parte" request instantly.

I wanted Diestel to at least use that short, uncertain window for response that had opened on the evening before the weekend. On Monday, June 5th, Diestel could have filed an opposition, but he hadn't. I couldn't wait any longer, so at 6:30 a.m. on Tuesday, June 6th, I flew into San Francisco, arriving in Diestel's office at 10:00 a.m. There's nothing like stating your requests in person. I wanted an opposition filed, in writing, to prevent this *ex-parte* motion to dismiss from being granted. We haggled amiably as he agreed to call Judge Ware's clerk and tell her that he would be opposing Cohen's ex parte motion to dismiss and quash subpoenas. Diestel called the clerk on his speaker phone, and she told us something that saved my weekend. The judge had already denied Cohen's *ex-parte* motions, ordering Cohen to refile the motion to dismiss as a regular noticed motion, and referring his motion to quash subpoenas to Judge Trumbull for decision. How surprising – all the obstacles to taking Karon's deposition had dissolved. Judge Trumbull's calendar was so backed up there was no danger of her deciding a motion before Karon's June 9th deposition.

The threat of peace had been scuttled, at least for the moment. While it is not always true that everything your opponent wants will injure your case, when you are dealing with a wily and dedicated foe like Cohen, represented by a skilled and able mercenary like Dorband, you can be virtually certain that anything they want to do has been efficiently designed to injure your case, and you should frustrate all of his efforts.

The way this story turns out demonstrates the correctness of this assumption. Dorband re-filed the motion to dismiss the counterclaims, putting it on the regular motion calendar. Diestel opposed the motion, arguing that the case should be dismissed with prejudice, or only after Cohen paid all Gary's defense costs. At the hearing, Judge Ware was ready to give everyone what they wanted. He would grant Cohen's request for dismissal, and grant Gary's request to make it *with prejudice*. Diestel was surprised, and I was not, when Dorband reversed course and withdrew his motion to dismiss during oral argument, over a month after he had started the entire drama. This maneuver didn't please Judge Ware, but Dorband cited precedents that allowed him to change position at the eleventh hour, and Judge Ware stayed his hand. Cohen's counterclaims against Gary were allowed to stand.

This was of course what Gary and I had earnestly desired. Not that Gary enjoyed being the target of Cohen's frivolous counterclaims, but they *were* the key to keeping State Farm in the case, and we couldn't do without State Farm. Gary wanted State Farm to destroy Cohen's counterclaims completely, not have them dismissed by stipulation so Cohen could hide them in the closet and then pull them out again whenever he found it convenient. Wagstaffe suggested that Diestel attack the counterclaims using California's new "anti-SLAPP" law. "SLAPP" is short for a "Strategic Lawsuit Against Public Participation," the type of lawsuit developers might file to punish a group of homeowners with legal fees and threats of humongous liability for opposing a local land-grab. To halt the filing of these anti-free-speech lawsuits, the California legislature enacted an anti-SLAPP law that allows judges to quickly dismiss meritless lawsuits filed to interfere with Constitutionally-protected free speech. Cohen's bloated claim for nine-million dollars in damages resulting from Gary's statement to Wired magazine was clearly a SLAPP suit. Indeed, the very idea that Cohen, an ex-con running a porn site from a Mexican safe-house, could even *be* defamed was kind of a hoot.

At that time, though, the anti-SLAPP law was a bit newfangled for Diestel, and since it would be costly to file, State Farm wasn't moving in that direction. Tactically, however, it was an excellent time to attack Cohen's counterclaims, because Cohen's eagerness to dismiss, alternating with his refusal to accept a dismissal with prejudice, had raised questions in Judge Ware's mind about his motive for filing the counterclaims in the first place. The innumerable shades of grey that had enshrouded the case for years were beginning to sort themselves into clear areas of black and white.

CHAPTER THIRTY-EIGHT

WHERE THE BODIES ARE BURIED

I HAD PLANNED TO TAKE KARON COHEN'S DEPOSITION ever since I called her on my cellphone just before sunrise one morning in mid-summer 1999. I'd risen early after a few hours sleep on the couch in Gary's living room. I went to the unused back bedroom, and dialed the Florida phone number I'd gotten from my private investigator Paul Nyland. As I gazed down into the overgrown garden behind Gary's apartment, a suspicious Karon answered the phone. She asked how I had gotten her unlisted phone number. I was chatty and friendly, but she was dead serious, and asked quite a few other questions before she decided I really didn't work for Cohen. Once she decided I was the lawyer for one of Steve's enemies, she turned talkative, and entertained me for nearly an hour with Cohen stories.

She told me how Cohen had stolen her life savings from a brokerage account while he was in prison, forcing her to hire a lawyer to get it back. Cohen hadn't forgiven her for daring to keep her own money, either. After he got out of prison, he stalked her for years. One time she discovered him sitting right next to her on a barstool in Florida. She didn't recognize him at first, though, because he had grown long hair and a beard, and was wearing sunglasses. When she realized who he was, she left the bar and went back to her car. When she reached it, she discovered all four tires had been slashed. Cohen, she said, had kept turning up in unexpected places, causing her problems in myriads of ways, until she made a committed effort to disappear and cover her traces. She hadn't heard from him in years.

Karon spoke with the honest accent of a lower-middle class southerner, sounding like someone who had never thought she was smart enough to outsmart Steve Cohen, and had just hoped she could outrun him. My phone call was an awkward reminder of a painful past, an opportunity to vent, and a reminder that Steve was still casting a shadow over her life. She was willing to give testimony, if the case required it, so long as her current whereabouts could be kept a secret from Cohen. She knew all about The French Connection, and the lawsuit by the software-makers. She had been there when Cohen was arrested for bankruptcy fraud. As for Sex.Com, she had never heard of it, or heard Steve talk about it. These were just the things I had hoped to hear from Karon, so I added her to the short list of people who had known Cohen back in the day, and weren't either dead, bought off, or unwilling to talk.

I went across the street and bought coffee for both of us, and went back to the apartment to wake Gary with fresh java. Gary had a voracious appetite for positive information, and the news that I'd just chatted with Karon was better than breakfast. On that particular day, however, funds were still in short supply, so actually deposing Karon remained on the list of things we'd do when we got money. Now that Diestel and State Farm were on the case, the time had come. Diestel's private investigator contacted Karon. She had suffered some health setbacks since we had spoken, and was less willing than before to give a deposition, but after some negotiation, she agreed to give a deposition at Volusia Court Reporters, in Daytona Beach, Florida.

I had only been to Florida twice before. During the summer of '74, Tara and I had hitchhiked from Colorado to Florida, up to Michigan and back to Arizona, a rolling courtship we carried on in other people's cars and houses, concluding in marriage back in our hometown of Tempe. During our trip through the south, a top-forty hit by David Bromberg haunted the airwaves, recounting the tale of a "sweaty, stinking trip through southern hell." The song could have been our soundtrack. On our way to Mississippi to see Tara's relatives, a cracker dry-fired a revolver in my face from a passing car, causing me to think I was imminently dead. So we skipped Mississippi and detoured to the beach in Pensacola, Florida. In Pensacola, we cooked fried shrimp and hush puppies, sang songs in the campground with a couple of young dudes, and tried to make love in a sleeping bag in our pup tent. David Bromberg was right–even sex feels like work when you're sweating that much. When we woke up, we turned our thumbs north, only to narrowly escape death in a nightmare ride on the wrong side of Green River in Tennessee with a crazy cracker who fortunately repented of his ways before raping Tara and killing me. We made it to Memphis alive, and after a day of bird watching in Audubon Park, continued hitchhiking north, getting a ride on the single bench seat of a blue 396 Chevy Ranchero next to a fat, slightly depressed, but utterly harmless, white boy. He did ninety all the way to Michigan, and it wasn't too fast for me. I had returned to Florida only once, in the early nineties, to defend the deposition of an elderly plaintiff in an accounting malpractice case. That turned out depressingly enough. My client, a holocaust survivor who lost a bundle in Texas residential real-estate bonds, also lost his malpractice lawsuit, and died when he got my letter telling him he'd lost.

Florida, named "the flowery place" by Spanish explorers, has apparently been entirely taken over by developers who scrape off the vegetation, line the coasts with high-rise hotels, drain swamps, build homes on bogs, and cover the rest with a thick layer of asphalt and concrete. Daytona Beach is a car drive away from Orlando, so I scheduled myself to fly in the day before Karon's deposition, after which I would drive to Miami and meet an investigative reporter specializing in Caribbean money scandals. The next morning I would fly out of Miami. When Ana gave me the tickets, I stuffed them in my briefcase without a second look.

At the Orlando airport, I rode a train from the flight terminal to the main airport. Disembarking from the train after sailing through the gleaming tunnel, I was momentarily surprised to be greeted by the most famed diplomats of the Magic Kingdom—Mickey and Pluto. I suddenly remembered—Disney *owns* Orlando! The airport was essentially an embassy manned by 'toons, where life-size statues of Bugs Bunny, Elmer Fudd, Porky Pig, Daffy Duck, and the Tasmanian Devil remained on guard against an invasion of reality. The airport shops and restaurants were uniformly decorated with movie memorabilia, dulled by a thin layer of condensed cigarette smoke. Walt Disney himself, a stickler for pristine clarity, would have been livid to see the magic dimmed by a lack of white-gloved attention. For at least one jet-lagged lawyer, the unity of civic reality and Hollywood fantasy was existentially nauseating.

After a quick pint of cold beer, I walked to the rental car area. Diestel was standing in the Hertz line, litigation case in one hand, a soft suit-bag slung over his shoulder. He upgraded his rental to a sharp-looking gold Mustang GT without comment. My car was reserved with Avis, and I had no upgrades to apply, but the little blushes of jealously passed as I realized I didn't care what I drove, as long as it had a CD player and was big enough to survive a collision with an SUV. In my plain vanilla four-door, I drove down two-lane blacktops, past white clapboard buildings, east toward the Atlantic coast.

Daytona is a little town with a big racetrack that lives for NASCAR. Walk into a bar during the off-season, and you have the entire floor to yourself, all four thousand square feet of it. As I entered one of these barn-like enclosures, the absence of the race fans was palpable. I missed them myself, and felt I should apologize for not being one. It required no imagination to visualize the place stuffed with hundreds of guys in race caps, jostling each other in a masculine fashion, swilling twenty-ounce cups of Bud Lite, shooting pool, and talking about fuel injection. This place was for *them*, I realized. The pert waitresses and sports bar decor made me thirsty, but I had no cause to linger. I could get swozzled in my hotel room on a six-pack of yuppie beer or some Stoli, for the price of two plastic cups of Lite. And in my motel room, I wouldn't have to sit there like a bar-stool ornament while the bartender flipped from one cable sports channel to another, working his way through his cigarette slowly, one eye squinched against the smoke curling past his slick dark hair, until at last he deigned to ask me what I wanted, and painfully poured me a draft. One beer, extracted from the unwilling, consumed in my role as the unwanted, was all the southern hospitality I could stand.

After leaving the sports bar, I cruised the empty streets of Daytona briefly, looking for some "there" to experience or observe. Since my quest for something, *anything* to hold my attention, was utterly fruitless, I headed out to the motel row down by the beach, separated from the rest of Daytona by a long, watery inlet. I drove across a narrow bridge to the windswept coast, a narrow finger of land pointing south, looking vulnerable lying alongside the enormous Atlantic. Diestel and I had rooms at the same place, a circular concrete and glass high-rise with a big lobby, plush restaurant, and rooms overlooking the sloshing gray-green sea. Diestel and I had dinner together in the restaurant downstairs, mulled the next day's prospect like the grizzled survivors we were, and retired early to our separate lodgings. Upstairs in my room, I got my materials organized for the next morning and went to bed early, teased into sleep by the murmuring ocean, barely audible through the sealed window-glass.

The next morning, Diestel, Dorband, Karon, and I met at Volusia Court Reporters. Karon said she wasn't feeling well and wanted to finish quickly, so we started immediately.

Karon married Cohen in Las Vegas in 1990, moving from West Virginia with her adolescent son into a two story house on Via Pardal in

Trabuco Canyon, where Cohen mysteriously enjoyed free rent. Chandra Boydstun, Cohen's daughter from a previous marriage, joined them, and there on Via Pardal, all three were held prisoner by Cohen's paranoia. They weren't allowed to have visitors, and were forbidden to answer the door, to prevent the Sheriff from serving papers. Cohen used video surveillance to protect himself from unwanted intrusions. As Karon testified, "He had a camera set up in his office in the bedroom and he could see who was at the door. I mean, we could go in and out. But we wasn't to answer the door to anybody. If you saw parcel post, something like that, he had to answer the door, he answered it himself."

Cohen held multiple licenses to perform security and property-recovery business. He was licensed as a locksmith, a repossessor, a private investigator, and a contractor. He got into business repossessing cars through Action Auction, owned by a fellow named Heitz. Using his repossessor's license, Cohen wormed himself into some sort of partnership with Heitz, but ruined Heitz's relationship with the Highway Patrol. I related this with LA bankruptcy court filings that revealed Cohen's use of YANTA (*not a misspelling* of YNATA, but rather *another shell company*) to buy and loot a towing company. Perhaps the YANTA name was a play on the Spanish word for tire, which is "llanta," pronounced "yahnta." The joke would be apt, because tires are made of rubber, so they bounce, and after some use, wear out. Karon had been officially designated in corporate filings as the Director of YANTA, and when I showed her the documents, she was not surprised, although she laughingly declared that she had nothing to do with the company, had never gone to a board meeting, and knew nothing about the company. It was just like Cohen, she explained, to include her in the paperwork without telling her.

Cohen never paid the bills—they went straight to the trashcan. He had five telephone lines, but paid no phone bills, because they were billed to the names of other people. Cohen procured stolen cell phones from thieves and reprogrammed them with telephone numbers he plucked out of the air with a scanner from cars driving by on the freeway. He sold the hacked phones, that worked "free" until the cell phone companies disconnected them. Although this left some of Cohen's buyers irate, he shrugged them off. I suspect many of his customers were happy with their purchases, and knew exactly what they were getting. Stolen cellphones are perfect communication vehicles for criminals, just like stolen cars are always used by experienced holdup men.

Despite knowing he was involved in illegal doings, Karon believed Cohen to be a lawyer. Early on in their relationship, he had shown her his suits, and his name in a book full of attorneys. He sometimes got up in the morning to go to court, to appear in his own cases, and sometimes to make appearances for other lawyers. Sometimes he would have papers laid out in the morning that were signed with Frank Butler's name, but she couldn't remember seeing Cohen actually forge the signature. Since the topic of Frank Butler had come up, I asked her if she had ever heard of Butler having a heart attack, as Butler had apparently sworn in a declaration filed by Cohen.

CARREON: Did you ever hear him say that Frank Butler had had a heart attack?

KARON: I don't recall. Just that he's out of the country one time. I don't recall.

While Karon had no recollection of a heart attack by Frank Butler, she seemed genuinely bemused by my question about whether Steve himself had had a heart attack, as he had sworn in court filings.

CARREON: Did you ever know of Steve having a heart attack?

KARON: Steve Cohen?

CARREON: Yes.

CARREON: My husband? (In a tone of confusion)

CARREON: Yes.

KARON: No. I didn't know he had a heart attack.

CARREON: Had you ever heard that he had a heart attack back in '87, like in maybe April or May of 1987? I know you didn't meet him until a few years later but did he ever tell you 'I had a heart attack back in '87?'

KARON: He didn't tell me about that. I never heard anything about that.

CARREON: Did he ever go to a cardiologist or heart doctor?

KARON: Steve never went to the doctor. He'd go just because he could get prescriptions pills one time free. He had Kaiser insurance and he got the pills, brought them home and didn't take them.

Life with Cohen was not very exciting: "He was always at home all day long. Every evening we went out to get the mail, out to eat. That was pretty much the regular routine all the time." Another part of the routine was cleaning up after the sex parties Steve hosted at "The Club," a suburban playhouse for swingers in the City of Tustin that Cohen once described to me as a business where he "got paid by rich guys to fuck their wives." Well, in LA, that's probably a job that needs doing.

The Club boasted a mailing list, newsletter, and all-night parties replete with finger food, drinks, lubes, and acres of rumpled sheets. Members of the club got free memberships to the French Connection BBS. Karon cleaned up with help from young Latinas, many of whom were shocked, and sometimes unwilling to clean up the wreckage of a gringo orgy. Disgusting! Somehow I doubt that Cohen provided rubber gloves. Eventually, neighbors complained, and the DA charged Cohen with running a house of prostitution. Apparently, Cohen didn't tell the jury, as he told me, that he *was in fact* screwing women for cash, which would be prostitution, albeit it of the pleasant sort, and walked out of the courthouse a legally not-guilty man. The story had gone out on TV, though, and while Steve was proud of his visibility as a free love entrepreneur, Karon was humiliated, and lost the companionship of her son into the bargain. The young man returned to West Virginia rather than share a roof with a man who had been charged with running a whorehouse.

Eventually, the free ride came to an end. The cops came to the Trabuco Canyon house, looking to arrest Cohen.

KARON: He told me not to be scared. Because the police had come and surrounded the house and someone was ringing the doorbell. Which we couldn't answer. He wouldn't allow us. Then I guess they left. He tried to get in his car and leave. The way he was doing it was very suspicious, trying to sneak out. They surrounded the house and I saw him get arrested.

CARREON: They surrounded the house and then demanded he come out and he went?

KARON: He wouldn't come out. They left and went down the road a little bit. He got in his car to take off and they got him.

CARREON: Oh. So he actually attempted to escape?

KARON: Yes.

After the arrest, the unhappy family moved out of Via Pardal, and Cohen hired Mike Mayock to fight the charges. At trial, Cohen was convicted of bankruptcy fraud and related crimes, and remanded to the custody of the Bureau of Prisons. Judge Keep denied Cohen's request for bail pending appeal, prompting Cohen to call her a "cunt" on his way out of the courtroom. He immediately received a set of handcuffs and a yellow jumpsuit as a reward for his eloquence, and began serving his sentence at low-security Lompoc Federal Penitentiary, where according to Karon, Cohen pretty much had the run of the place.

CARREON: Did you have strange experiences regarding Mr. Cohen and his use of the telephones at Lompoc?

KARON: I called that Lompoc prison one night . . . and I told them my husband just got through calling me on the phone.

CARREON: About what time of night or day was this?

KARON: I don't know. It was dark. I'm really not sure what time. Nine. Ten. I'm not sure. Eleven. It was dark. And they say there is no possible way. They are only allowed like five minutes a day on the phone and there is no way he could be on the phone and I said I know his voice, it was his voice and he was on the phone. So I guess eventually they went and checked and said he was in bed. Later he told me - when I went in to the last visit in Lompoc and told him it was over. I said "You're not getting any better at this situation." He laughed and said that they came to his room and he acted like he was sleeping when they come to check on him.

Inmate status posed no serious obstacle to Cohen's larcenous schemes. When Karon married Cohen, she deposited the $75,000 death benefit from her first husband's life insurance into an account in the name of Repossessor's Inc. Without explaining how *his* creditors would attempt to seize Karon's money, Cohen moved the account to a Shearson securities brokerage in North Carolina "to avoid creditors." But when Cohen went to prison, Karon learned she had no signature authority on what she thought was her own account. When she called Shearson, they told her Cohen had removed her name from the account using a fax authorization. When she questioned him about it during a prison visit, he told her she didn't know what she was talking about.

KARON: And I called the company myself. And they said, 'I think it was faxed over, as far as I can remember' and I go, like, he's in prison! How can he be faxing you over information? So I told them, I threatened them with my attorney, that I wanted my money, and I wanted it back in my account. That's how I had to pay my bills. He was in prison. If they didn't—he didn't tell them about being in prison. I said if you don't believe me you call Lompoc. I give the number and everything. He's in prison, doing this from prison. Because I did not give him authority to do it.

CARREON: Did you get your money back?

KARON: After about two, three weeks, yes, threatening them.

CARREON: Who paid you? Shearson Lehman?

KARON: Uh huh. He later went on to tell me that well, when I come out of prison I won't have any money. I told him that didn't give you no right to take my money!

The Shearson caper was the last straw for Karon. She filed for divorce. I knew both Karon and her divorce lawyer had been sued in the RICO lawsuit that Cohen filed from prison. I thought Karon would recognize the RICO complaint, but she had never seen it before. She had never been served and knew nothing about the lawsuit that alleged she and various others conspired to "purloin" the French Connection.

Karon didn't have to hear more than a few lines of the complaint before she declared confidently: "Basically what I think is happening here is he's too embarrassed about what had happened and he's trying to throw the blame on me..."

Even though Karon hadn't seen this particular frivolous lawsuit, she was painfully familiar with Cohen's tactics for hijacking the judicial process: "You have to miss work. You have to go to an attorney. Then he pulls up all kinds of stupid stuff in here you didn't do, didn't say, it didn't happen, but he's representing himself so it doesn't cost him any fee. But a person like me, you've got to keep taking off work. You've got to pay your money. And it's no fun. And the judge told me at one point. 'He has the right as a citizen to sue whoever he wants,' but he can keep throwing it out if it's not true. So basically he can sue me all he wants or anybody else."

Karon was very familiar with The French Connection, on which Cohen, under the screen name "Tammy," played Systems Operator, "sysop" in bulletin board parlance. Karon had been a French Connection member, and regularly chatted with people online, but had never heard of Sex.Com. Her testimony confirmed my belief that Cohen had forged the French Connection screen printouts attached to the Sex.Com trademark application. Karon recognized Richard Klaus's video of the interface, but had never seen the screen captures Cohen filed in support of the Sex.Com trademark application.

Karon recalled that Cohen did not easily surrender his hold on her, often calling from prison to urge her to keep The French Connection running. It was hers now, he told her, for everything she had done for him, and she should keep it going for the profit potential. Cohen was a true pioneer in the era of prison labor out-sourcing, but typically turned the concept on its head, getting a free person to work for a convict. Karon remembered: "he would call me from prison and have me on the line the whole time until it was finished." But Karon couldn't deal with the complexity of it all—phone bills in the names of people she didn't know, technical issues, and the whole mess. One day users started calling to say the system was down. Karon looked in the room where the computers had been stored, and the whole system was gone—computers, modems, and all. I asked her if that made her feel better, but she had her own response to the disappearance:

CARREON: You probably breathed a sigh of relief?

KARON: I could care less.

CARREON: And after that you never logged on to The French Connection again in your life?

KARON: I didn't want to log on to Steve, The French Connection, or anything that had to do with him.

As the deposition wound to a close, Diestel, Dorband, and I were all of the same mind. We had invaded Karon's privacy long enough, and she had given us all she could. Dorband quickly abandoned his cross-examination when it became apparent that Karon was incapable of saying anything helpful to Cohen. In response to one of Dorband's last questions, Karon explained how she came to give up on Cohen: "I gave him a chance, if he would go straight, and stop doing things like that. I could forgive for the past. But he just continued to do things illegal."

CHAPTER THIRTY-NINE

MY MIAMI

DIESTEL AND I ATE LUNCH TOGETHER after Karon's deposition. He was starting to trust me. It couldn't hurt that Karon had proven several of my theories right. The encounter with one of Cohen's most vulnerable victims tapped a vein of outrage. Diestel had far more sympathy for Karon than he had ever shown for Gary. He was angry. It showed in the way he ate his lunch, chomping with tenacious resentment. After lunch, Rich took off for the airport in his gold Mustang, and I hit the road in my four-door refrigerator.

I got onto I-95, the big traffic artery that drains straight down the leg of the state into Miami, siphoning traffic onto the counterclockwise arc of Biscayne Boulevard, a broad beachside motorway that tracks the curve of the shoreline. I rolled into town with the setting sun shining through the back window as my car hurtled east along the sweeping concrete curve. With light shining all around me, I smiled and took the exit ramp into Little Cuba. Because the weather is similar, I couldn't help comparing Miami with LA, where I lived for ten years. LA never ends, it just sweeps around and loops back on itself like a never-ending snake of red and white lights, coming and going. People sleep and salve addictions in LA neighborhoods, but they don't seem to live there. In LA, everyone is going somewhere, and nobody stays anywhere.

In Miami people are living, hanging out, walking down the streets. Young Cuban women wear tight dresses and high heels, walking like prizefighters, extending a challenge to which many a man feels compelled to rise. Sometimes the traffic moves so slowly, it feels like drivers are just taking a good look at the women, and no one seems to mind. Intrigued, I resolve on seeing the town later, and start looking for the office of the investigative reporter I'm there to meet. This guy has blown the lid off a couple of Caribbean money-laundering scandals. He's not clear how he can help us, and I try to sound like I know what I'm talking about, but the idea of chasing Cohen's offshore millions doesn't appeal to me. In all my years of lawyering, I had only recovered large amounts of money from banks, insurance companies, and large corporations. I agreed with

Willie Sutton — one must go where the money is.

Gary thought he could seize Cohen's offshore accounts, though, and he wanted me to talk to this guy to see what I could learn. The reporter confirmed what my online research had taught me — the Caribbean has more swindlers than the beaches have crabs; the islands provide employment for a small army of English-style solicitors; and, the army of solicitors services the needs of thousands of corporations, each comprised of little more than a stack of papers, a mailbox, and a bank account. Not surprisingly, the solicitors have no interest in perforating the secrecy of their clients' dealings. But there was a ray of hope, said the investigator. After the BCCI scandal, the British imposed the Proceeds of Crime Act on its protectorate nations in the Caribbean and, if you could find a lawyer to handle your concerns, the laws were on the books to help you track down and recover stolen millions. But that was a huge "if," because most island solicitors refuse work that might make them unpopular in the few really good clubs and restaurants. On most islands, which are small by definition, being unpopular can be very uncomfortable. And should you suffer an accident, there are so few police to conduct an investigation.

The investigator had a date in a short while with his Colombian girl-friend, who didn't speak English. When I asked if he spoke Spanish, he said no, that they actually had a language problem but in some ways, it was better that way. I understood. In Miami, it's more about what you *do* than what you say. With the investigator gone to make sign language with his Colombian girlfriend, I went back to my room, spread the entertainment weekly out on the apricot-colored bedspread and studied the ads. Looking for a nice, pleasant dive, I settled on "Churchill's, A Sort of English Pub," which seemed to host rowdy rock acts on Northeast Second Avenue. Big-city addresses on streets with small numbers are always interesting to investigate. I drove into the deserted downtown, leaving the cool air of the shore behind, directing the prow of my generic rental into a dark slice of unfamiliar city.

Approaching Second Avenue, the neighborhoods began to look run-down. Then there were young black guys standing in the bus lanes, offering a chance to score. This was the perfect place and the perfect vehicle in which to get my brains aired out, but I hoped my ponytail would mark me as a defense lawyer. Something worked, because even stopped at the lights, I wasn't approached with baggies extended. The pervasive presence of the edgy entrepreneurs suggested to me that Churchill's might be the real deal. Then I saw it up on the right–a one-star dive in a cratered neighborhood, butt up against a row of crack houses.

Walking through the dimly lit doorway, I discovered the place was somewhere between beautiful and falling apart. Behind the big, oval bar, stood a tall gal with a wide mouth, red hair, a slightly insolent tilt to her head, and some flamboyant neck-gear. A big pile of refrigeration equipment hulked near the back wall. Two people sat on the far end of the bar. I sat down at the empty side, and ordered a Bass ale that the redhead quickly delivered in an icy glass. Swampy air flooded the place with a sticky scent that slowly made me feel slick with sweat. I slumped down in the chair and drew the night air and solitude around me. The spooky guys dealing drugs weren't allowed to enter, but their eyes kept lancing through the doorway as they walked past.

Eventually, Plutonium Pie, a power trio, started up their equipment and blasted a few big chords from their five-foot Marshall stacks, followed by some guitar riffs that settled into my brain like acid splattered randomly across a steel plate. I ordered another Bass ale and settled back. As the band got going, I noticed the musicians shared similar features. All three had long wavy hair, black as coal. If I had to guess, I'd say they were descendants of the Dravidian people who inhabited the Indian subcontinent before the Aryans invaded.

Only five people including the barmaid and myself were watching this gig, but the Plutonium Pie people didn't seem to notice as they blasted through a bunch of great-sounding original stuff. The drummer flailed the skins confidently, her hair a dark, penumbral halo around her young face. The bass player was always right where he's supposed to be, and the guitarist stood like a calm, dark god, working the neck of his instrument, commanding platoons of power chords to destroy each other. Pretty soon I was dancing around like a fool next to the sprawling metal coils of disemboweled refrigeration equipment.

It continued that way for about an hour. Then the band took a break to go out on the back porch for some beer and conversation. I bought a round for all the band members. They started rolling joints with that self-assured manner musicians have, like smoking pot was their right in exchange for making music. The swampy night air out on the back porch was thick enough to eat. The porch ran the length of the back of the house, with makeshift shade-creating structures, all destroyed by the sun. Even in the dark, with the pot smoke drifting on the tepid breeze, everything felt sun-beaten. The wood was rough and splintery, the plastic frizzy, the cotton awnings frayed. There was even sunburned refrigeration equipment out there. I wondered idly if Churchill's doubled as storage space for some air-conditioning repairmen, or if they never bothered to haul away the guts of their beer coolers after tearing them out. After the tea party, the Pie played another couple of tunes. Then it was 2 a.m. and time to close. By the time I left, I was tight with everybody, and made a mental note that Miami could be a nice place to self-destruct, if I ever had the inclination.

Back at the hotel, it was time to get myself organized, packed to go, and horizontal on the bed to catch downtime. I settled down, pulled out my plane ticket to see what time I had to be at the airport, and discovered that my plane was leaving in six hours from Orlando, the same place I flew into. Not Miami, where I was. Ana did not get this right. There was not even any point being very mad about it, because I had to save all my energy for a long night's drive. I packed and checked out of the hotel the same night I checked into it.

My efforts to get back to Orlando turned out to be for naught. A few hours into the insane project, my eyes kept closing as I tried to keep my car between the fuzzy white lines. I pulled over in a restaurant parking lot and reclined the driver's seat to get some rest. As warm daylight and morning traffic noises filled the car, my resolve to reach Orlando at any particular time dissolved like honey melting in the sun. Curled up behind the steering wheel, I abandoned myself to several more hours of luxurious, who gives-a-fuck oblivion. I had missed a plane, for the first time in my legal career. No worries. I was only going home.

CHAPTER FORTY

QUEEN OF LIES

THE SHOWDOWN WITH BARBARA CEPINKO HAD BEEN A LONG TIME COMING. Barbara owned Midcom, an Orange County personnel place-ment company for government contractors, from whose offices Cohen had faxed the forged letter to NSI. Gary had longed to sue Barbara and Midcom back when he hired me, but I had steadfastly refused to do it, seeing no sense in multiplying the number of our foes, or filing claims based on thin evidence. Searching for dirt in courthouse databases, Gary had discovered that Midcom, Barbara and Cohen were all being sued for sexual harassment in Santa Clara County by Tammy Robinson, a former Midcom employee. Robinson's complaint was stuffed with juicy tidbits that rang true, like Cohen talking up Camp Wanaleia and making salacious remarks.

Hoping to find a lawyer who would do what I wouldn't, Gary had me call Robinson's lawyer to try and interest him in filing another suit against Barbara and Midcom, for conspiracy to aid in the theft of Sex. Com. He wasn't interested. Midcom's lawyer, Robin Offner of San Diego, had turned the Robinson case into a sinkhole of attorney-time, filing over a dozen discovery motions. Robinson's lawyer wanted out of the case, and no more of Midcom.

Deposing Barbara had always seemed likely to generate conflict, so it was comforting to coast in behind the deposition subpoena Diestel had served on Cepinko in his capacity as Gary's defense lawyer. I could have served my own subpoena, but didn't want to invite flak. On the appoint-ed day, Gary and I walked into the dusty brick Midcom office building on Tustin Boulevard in Anaheim, California. Midcom's double doors were secured with keypad locks that Gary said were required by government regulations. We met Barbara in the white-walled Midcom conference room, windowless and devoid of decoration. The room was so sterile it seemed as if they'd stripped it just for us.

Barbara sat at the end of the conference table, lounging at her ease, looking a little frowsy, and altogether too comfortable. Diestel was set-ting up quietly. Dorband was absent, and in his stead appeared Robin

Offner, an urbane young lawyer who rose to shake my hand. I sized him up — medium height, wrapped in a dark sportcoat comfortably buttoned round a waist filled out by the good life. He had thick dark hair, a tanned face, dark eyes and brows, and soft lips that seemed pleased with themselves. Gary returned Offner's offer of a handshake by sticking his arm out stiffly at shoulder level, leaning away from Offner, and sighting down the length of his arm with one eye. Sometimes Gary liked to play gangsta. Offner accepted the weird handshake without change of expression.

Barbara neither extended her hand nor rose from her chair, instead casting me a mischievous grin accented by a single bucked tooth. She and Cohen went back all the way to the days of The Club. In her late forties, with a figure that had certainly seen good days, Barbara seemed like a woman used to getting her way without excessive effort. Her blowsy demeanor suggested she'd look good with a martini in her hand.

We were ready to start when Robin told us that only *one* of Kremen's lawyers could question his client. Robin's position was ridiculous, but nothing in his appearance betrayed it. Barbara assumed the role of a captive damsel who would be happy to testify, once her dragon gave his permission. Diestel puffed annoyance at encountering bullshit so early in the day. Cohen was pulling the strings through Offner, and Gary's anger was swelling on our side of the table.

We had to punch through. I pulled out my Rules of Civil Procedure, reviewed Rule 26, passed Robin the book, and told him it said nothing about how many attorneys could depose a witness. I then began intoning Judge Trumbull's name ominously, as if her magical edicts were mine to dispense, telling Robin that the Judge clearly ruled in prior motions that *all* of Mr. Kremen's attorneys were entitled to ask questions of witnesses. I explained that Mr. Diestel and I had completely different jobs requiring separate lines of questioning, and had to conduct separate examinations of Ms. Cepinko.

Clutching his pen in a hooked right hand, Gary wrote on a page of blank paper that he'd turned parallel to the edge of the table, like a lefty. He didn't look up, but his torso swelled with waves of angry breathing, his features knotted up, and his eyes darted angrily. He was ratcheting himself into a rage. His body language said he would fire everyone if he did not get his way. I called for a break.

Diestel, Gary, and I headed out the push-button doors in a knot of turmoil. Standing in the powdery light pouring through the windows that lined the hallway, Gary was snorting, about to go postal with his bare hands and teeth. Diestel and I assuaged his concerns. Not to worry! We would both throw ourselves against the foe and get what we'd come there for. We would both question Cepinko–no retreat! Diestel and I were in complete agreement–we had to prevail. Making Robin Offner unhappy was no problem, especially when we considered the alternative.

When we got back in the room, Robin was more accommodating, and we quickly worked out a deal that allowed both Diestel and I to question his client. Diestel started questioning Barbara, and for a short time, Gary's rage subsided to occasional emissions of steam, like a volcano itching to wipe out a small town. But brimstone was soon raining again as Diestel, unfamiliar with the Midcom facts, got bogged down in bookkeeping. During Diestel's first break, Gary told me to take over. Tell Diestel to move aside. When I told Diestel what Gary had said, he shook his head with a bemused smile, and in a tone of mild disbelief, said, "You guys are really something."

Getting a kick out of the obvious conflict on our side of the table, Barbara exuded amused skepticism as I faced her. I started with the paper record—Cohen's Midcom paychecks. Barbara gave Cohen some kind of job after he got out of Lompoc, but she couldn't remember why she paid him $600 a week, plus a house and car allowance of $900 a month. Barbara said she'd hired Steve to answer phones, but also said he usually worked in the wee hours of the morning. When I questioned how often the phones rang at Midcom during those hours, she just laughed as if it were so funny that I would try and trip her up with those cute little lawyer tricks.

Barbara had seen the Sporting Houses stock certificates I showed her, bearing her name, but insisted they meant nothing, because they were worthless. Steve had made all Sporting Houses decisions, and spent all of the money. She had hosted Sporting Houses meetings in that very same room where we were sitting, but she had simply made the space available as a courtesy to Cohen. Barbara remembered Sex.Com vaguely as a subject only Steve understood or cared about. Yes, yes, Steve had told the Sporting Houses directors that Sex.Com was worth millions, and he wanted to buy it, but there was no money, and it was all so long ago. So very long ago. As she drifted ever farther from the probing point of my questions, she became as languid as Cleopatra gliding on the flooded expanse of the Nile, sliding effortlessly out of my reach.

Barbara had actually given me a lot of good ammunition on the corporate alter ego front—it was obvious that from her viewpoint, Sporting Houses was a sham corporation that Cohen used for his exclusive benefit. But with her languid demurrals and coy deflections, Barbara had deprived me of the satisfaction of a good adverse interrogation. Like Cohen, she deceived with practiced ease, leaving the impression that the entire exercise has been a waste of time.

Trying to close with a good show, I made one last stab at disturbing her composure. In the Ashton-Tate case, Richard Klaus swore in his declaration that Cohen had taken him to the Midcom building, through the keypad-locked doors, showed him the Midcom computers, and told him they operated The French Connection. As a result, a judge had ordered Federal Marshals to seize Midcom's hardware. Squinting slightly at Barbara, I asked if she knew Cohen had lied about her and violated her company's security just to embellish a confidence spiel. Did she realize her old friend had invited disaster to her door? Barbara didn't dispute Cohen's responsibility for the raid. Back when it happened, she'd asked Steve if he'd brought the law down on her, and he denied it. When the Marshals came to seize the machines, she had to spend all day on the phone, until at last the Marshals left without the computers. Yes, she admitted, back then it was a big problem, but in retrospect, it was just more silly Steve stuff. She smiled.

CHAPTER FORTY-ONE

THE RUNAWAY STAGECOACH

BACK IN OREGON, Ana was learning the traditional lore of the subpoena clerk. Taking her work to heart, she served one witness after another, harvesting praise and ten dollars an hour—better than the Santa Barbara library and not as dusty. The office was humming. Tara, resplendent in Nepalese silk clothing, long blonde hair shining, had settled into the new office I opened on East Jackson in Medford with Peter Carini. The move increased my floor-space by a factor of three, making it easy to work with my new staff.

Tara decorated the place in a Roman theme, and in the lobby we hung a large painting of a classical visage and an abstract banner. For a touch of pistolero-chic, we put out the big brown pigskin couch Tara shipped back from Guadalajara in the mid-nineties. We laid Tibetan rugs on the floor, and brought in our high-backed leather chairs, in Early Spanish Inquisitor style. We were getting respectable. Tara settled into her own office, where she tracked the gobs of cash we spent on investigation, service of process, deposition transcripts, copying, after-hours pizza, and sandwich runs.

Susanne and Ana shared an office with the filing cases and document binders. Susanne checked in to work regularly at one o'clock in the afternoon. She would show up, settle down at her desk and spend a little time pawing through her purse looking for a mirror or a Paxil, whatever. She was a great blonde creature with sleepy eyes, smiling, sad cheeks and gentle, pouting lips. Taking her station, talking into the telephone soft and low and deep, laughing that "huh, huh, huh" of hers that is knowing and wanton, conspiratorial. Sue enjoyed writing memos adorned with humorous asides, blending character sketches of the big players in the online skin trade with off-the-cuff comments about the personalities she was encountering in the subpoena enforcement project. She sometimes struck up email relationships with lawyers for witnesses or their attorneys, which often helped us to get the documents we wanted.

After Judge Ware reopened discovery in June 2000, we went after Cohen's financial records with subpoenas propounded to his bankers,

193

something you ordinarily wouldn't do. But with Cohen begging for it by refusing to produce his own financial records, he left the door open for us to go directly to the source – the moneychangers themselves. We were particularly interested in Sporting Houses records from the Las Vegas Wells Fargo, and those of Omnitec, from the Anaheim Hills branch, near San Diego. By August, we were receiving a steady stream of bank records that Ana scanned into PDF files and Tara filed in three-hole binders. We bought new shelves to hold the dozens of binders.

To be sure we got compliance from all of our subpoena-recipients, we kicked off "Operation Pushbroom." Operation Pushbroom was named after the job of sweeping up after the horses in a rodeo parade. I saw a lot of rodeo parades as a child, since my nanny, Trini Noli, was part Apache, and her children loved horses. The parades would happen right downtown on First Street in Phoenix, a couple of blocks from my house, the cowboys wearing satin outfits with silver spangles, the child majorettes twirling their batons and tossing them high in the sky. Amid all this splendor, I noticed that the beautiful horses were crapping all over the street. Then I saw how the pushbroom people cleaned it up. They never walked past it – they swept it all up in metal dustpans, dumped it into their rolling trashcans, then moved ahead to the next pile of crap.

Operation Pushbroom was based on the same principle – give all the crap the same treatment, and don't let any of it get past you. Ana listed all the witnesses on a big chart, marked them off the list when we received their documents, and narrowed the field to those few non-compliant witnesses who had to be compelled by court order. Nobody was permitted to fall through the cracks. Wells Fargo was looking for a crack to fall through. From the time we served them, Wells Fargo did nothing but delay. Ana and Sue spoke repeatedly with the Wells Fargo people, who would pull tricks like calling Ana with four or five people on the line at once, to interrogate her aggressively for the sake of intimidation. Everything Wells Fargo did was tentative. They always hedged their response, and were shameless about requesting one extension after another. I mean, it's one thing to ask for extensions of time to produce voluminous archived documents, and quite another to simply dilate the time for response indefinitely, which was Wells Fargo's established M.O.

In an effort to shut us down altogether, Cohen had Dorband file a motion to quash all of our subpoenas. He argued that our subpoenas were burdensome, because they directed the recipient to produce every document that in any way related to any person or business listed on a three-page list called Attachment "A." Judge Trumbull denied Cohen's motion to quash the subpoenas because none of the *witnesses* had objected to the burden of responding, and Cohen had no standing to seek relief from burdens that might be suffered by third parties.

Attachment "A" was a comprehensive document, as was the manner of its creation. Gary produced the list based on computer research, primarily using Google to drill down into records that frankly, I'm not sure were meant to be public knowledge. In those days Internet security was a topic of little attention, and people built websites with wide-open backends, as if they were parking their data on the dark side of an asteroid, where no one would ever run across it. Welcome to the world of the search engine! Gary searched for, discovered, and interpreted online documents that revealed the relationships that formed the infrastructure of Cohen's online empire. By subpoenaing all documents discussing the people and businesses we knew were involved with Cohen, we forced Cohen's secret associates to call their lawyers. It was probably because Attachment "A" was so thorough in tracking the net of Cohen-controlled money that Wells Fargo was at great pains to avoid releasing the documents in its possession.

Wells Fargo had been hiding behind Cohen's motion to quash, so as soon as it was denied, I faxed Judge Trumbull's order to Wells Fargo. Cohen then threw another hurdle in our path by sending out personal letters on his own stationery, threatening any bank that violated his privacy with civil liability. The letters infuriated Gary, who asked if he could send some personal missives of his own, but Wagstaffe and I wouldn't let him.

Emboldened by Cohen's letter, Wells Fargo continued stonewalling unto the eleventh hour. All Wells Fargo documents are electronically archived in Phoenix, Arizona, and were available for immediate production, but Ana and Sue were at their wits' end. They had spent weeks talking with a lady in Phoenix named Barb Bakutis, a Wells Fargo document custodian. Her accomplice in The Big Stall was Felix Fierro, also officed in Phoenix. Sticking with my pushbroom, I sent the right letters to Barb and Felix, inviting them to schedule a conference call with Judge Trumbull's calendar clerk. Pushing forward doggedly with mundane scheduling tasks makes a threat credible, and only credible threats induce adversaries to accede to your demands. As we talked about scheduling the hearing on a motion to compel production, I heard a sound in Barb's voice that suggested she was eager to produce the documents, and was seeking clearance from some unnamed superior.

Just as Barb was about to crumble, our subpoena gun grievously misfired. I had filed a motion to compel compliance with a subpoena I'd served on Salt Lake attorney O. Bob Meredith, the fellow who took the credit for faxing out the press release announcing YNATA's phony take-over bid for Starwood, the owner of Caesar's Palace. I figured he would have some documents, and for about a month after I contacted him by phone, he repeatedly promised to produce everything he had, some-times even saying he was "on his way to Kinko's" right then. But he never sent anything. When he got my motion, O. Bob called Judge Trumbull's clerk to object that the subpoena we had served was not enforceable, be-cause he was in Utah, and the subpoena was "issued" from the Northern District of California. In a short ruling, Judge Trumbull refused to enforce a subpoena that hadn't been "issued" by the district where the witness had been served. The terse ruling left me feeling sheepish, because she cited only one authority for her decision—Wagstaffe's book on Federal Civil Procedure. This ruling was a clear case of form triumphing over substance, because the courts don't "issue" subpoenas at all–lawyers do–and correcting the error simply meant typing "Utah" on the subpoe-na instead of "Northern District of California." But the Judge had ruled, so it was time to cope with the fallout.

O. Bob had revealed my error at a bad time, because the discovery completion deadline was looming uncomfortably near. If I had to deliver new subpoenas to all of the witnesses residing beyond the jurisdiction of the Northern District of California, it would be a costly fix for a technical oversight. The entire subpoena project was in danger of foundering. If O. Bob didn't have to produce in response to a badly-worded subpoena, then all of the witnesses in the Eastern, Southern, and Central Districts of California, and those in all of the other forty-nine states, could also refuse production. With a single phone call, O. Bob had tied my tail in a knot.

Wells Fargo was going to take full advantage of the snafu if I didn't fix it quickly. So, having indulged my sorrows for about fifteen stunned minutes after reading Judge Trumbull's order, I called Ana to attention and we cranked out corrected subpoenas before we left the office. Fortunately, the dear child didn't claim to have anything else to do that evening, and by the next morning, we had served corrected subpoenas on Wells Fargo. I called Barb Bakutis immediately to keep things moving.

As she had no doubt been coached by Cohen or Dorband, Barb raised the issue of the O. Bob ruling, but I was desperate, and mowed down her objections, reminding her that Wells Fargo had the prior subpoena over two months, that she had already located the documents, and that the new subpoenas I had just served accorded with the requirements of law in every respect. Admittedly, there was very little time left for Wells Fargo to produce documents, because they had delayed so long that the discovery cutoff was fast approaching. But that was *their* fault, I reminded her.

The Wells Fargo subpoena people are trained differently from bank tellers, who are supposed to give up the government-insured cash without a fuss. Maybe we should insure their records too, because as it is, they hold out as long as possible, hoping the party seeking records will go away, and providing documents only when actual court action appears imminent. The incentives are all on the side of non-production, and banks rarely get in trouble for not producing documents. To secure Wells Fargo's compliance, I had to restart the mechanism of compulsion repeatedly.

Finally Barb called and told me she was ready to send the documents. I hardly dared believe it. I wanted to stop breathing, to make sure I didn't screw something up. Before she ran the copies, she wanted a check for $700, for costs of copying the Anaheim Hills and Las Vegas bank records. I said I would fax her a copy of the check if she would please start copying the records immediately. She agreed, so I sent a letter confirming our agreement, and faxed a copy of the check.

She called back after she got the fax to ask how to deliver the documents. I suggested she ship them COD, so I wouldn't have to send her a check. She thought a moment, and said that sounded fine. Ten minutes later, she called back to start the insanity all over again. She couldn't send the documents to my office. She had to deliver them to the exact Kinko's locations prescribed in my subpoenas—Las Vegas records to the Kinko's in Vegas, and Anaheim Hills records to a Kinko's someplace in San Diego County.

Astonished, I asked her the obvious question. Weren't all of the documents right there in Phoenix? Why then would she split them into two boxes, and ship one to a Kinko's in Vegas and the other to a Kinko's in San Diego, when she could send them all to my office? She just had to do it that way, she said. I sent her the seven-hundred dollar check via Fedex, crossed my fingers, and held my breath.

CHAPTER FORTY-TWO

INCIDENT AT CHULA VISTA

CHULA VISTA IS SOUTH OF SAN DIEGO, north of the Tijuana border. Gary and I had spent a night at a Budget Motel there on the way back from Ensenada, after the absurd circus of the Roman Caso / Sandman deposition. Chula Vista cops probably look at everyone like a suspect, and they took pointed note of my big, blue Cherokee as Gary and I rolled into the motel parking lot. The town looked boring as hell, we were tired, and we had beer for dinner. There was nothing to stay awake for, so we turned out the lights. As we lay in our separate beds, I fell asleep with Gary quipping occasionally about random issues.

Next morning, we breakfasted at a restaurant serving nothing but white flour pancakes anointed with colorful syrup, gleaming eggs, and bacon flattened under steel weights. This was no doubt the perfect welcome for persons fleeing poverty and low caloric intake in lands to the south. Stressed-out waitresses chucked plates on the sticky tables, and a snarly cashier gave me free steely silence with my change. When we left Chula Vista, I didn't expect it would require any further attention from me, as it seemed to be falling in on itself quite nicely. I was wrong, though. Thanks to Steve Cohen, the name of Chula Vista is forever burned on my mind.

One day in September, returning to my office after spending the morning representing shackled men in green pajamas and plastic flip-flops, as I walked through the front door, Ana and Sue were excitedly shouting in unison, "Cohen stole the documents!" Turning to Tara, who seemed fairly calm, I saw her nodding with lifted eyebrows that told me that, yes, it was true, Cohen had stolen the documents. After a few moments, all three communicated the gist of the problem — someone had gone to the Chula Vista Kinko's, used Diestel's credit card number to pay for all the copying of the Wells Fargo Bank documents, and walked off with both the copies and the originals! We had no Wells Fargo documents!

Standing in the hallway of my office, I screamed a couple of obscenities and Cohen's name, and then suddenly, in the midst of shouting, felt myself overtaken by clear, calm thinking. I realized a great blessing had befallen us. It was just a question of whether we could properly take advantage of it. I cross-examined Sue quickly to confirm the key facts. She had talked to Diestel and the Kinko's manager, and confirmed that Diestel had been in San Francisco when the documents were picked up at the Chula Vista Kinko's by a man who looked a lot like Cohen, and told the copy clerk to charge the copies to the credit card number Diestel had previously provided by phone. It was a very smooth Cohen maneuver. Knowing all of the details of the copying arrangement, he used his knowledge to execute a last-minute gambit to upset a game I'd spent months putting together–but I knew I could turn this to our advantage.

Most lawyers wouldn't have agreed with my optimistic assessment of the likely outcome of Cohen's theft. Viewed legalistically, Cohen had barely committed a misdemeanor, a theft of a copy job worth less than fifty bucks. Not exactly Court TV material. But any proper legal sorcerer would know that Cohen had committed an unforgivable sin against the very source of magic itself. Those documents had become the *property* of the court. They were *evidence*, the sacred ore from which legal alchemists extract the gold of truth. Not being a true initiate, Cohen did not sense the magnitude of his error. We could also easily infer that the documents contained damaging information, because he certainly didn't need to steal his own bank records—he was presumably free to look at them at any time. Thus, he must have been stealing them in order to prevent me from examining them, and there could be only one reason for that.

I went to work quickly, falling into prosecutor-mode. I needed a police report with witness statements, a description of the subject, a description of the stolen item, and an identification of me as the victim. Victims, as you no doubt have heard, have *rights*. Susanne got the Kinko's manager on the phone. Our conversation went like this:

"Hi, this is Charles Carreon. I understand there is some problem with my copying job."

"Well, yes sir, this guy came in and said he was one of the lawyers on the case and claimed the documents."

"Did you see him yourself?"

"Yes."

"You gave him the documents?"

"Yes."

Pausing a moment to get the pitch of my voice just right, I launched the emotional javelin: "Well, my God, that's a theft! Call the police!"

I literally held the receiver two inches from my mouth and screamed this into the phone, because I knew I needed to motivate the manager to make a police report, because without a police report, there is no crime. A police report is prepared by a cop, who is really a junior magistrate, a street judge. The courthouse judge never sees crimes that haven't been worked up initially by a cop. In the mind of a judge, a crime that hasn't been investigated by a cop essentially hasn't happened. If you can't get a cop interested, you're definitely going nowhere with the courthouse judge. On the other hand, if there was a police report, it would provide *prima facie* confirmation that Cohen had committed another crime. I knew the Chula Vista police wouldn't go to Kinko's at the request of an Oregon lawyer, unless perhaps, I could also offer them free Winchell's donuts, which seemed too complicated. It would be simpler to get the manager of Kinko's to report a theft, which would definitely prompt a police investigation.

There was of course a hitch I could foresee, and I bet Cohen had, too. Nothing had been stolen from Kinko's. They got paid for their copies, albeit with Rich Diestel's credit card. Thus, Kinko's couldn't be the victim of the theft, in much the same way that NSI was not the victim of the theft of Sex.Com. While Cohen had certainly gotten copies at Deistel's expense by impersonating him and using his credit card, that might be a little abstruse for the Chula Vista cops. Besides, Deistel wouldn't want to appear as a "victim" on the police report. No victim, no crime. But since I had paid Wells Fargo $700 for the originals that Cohen also stole, I was the biggest loser here, and those documents were my property. I was a victim.

It is the victim's prerogative to demand that the person who has committed a crime against them be prosecuted. While I did not expect that misdemeanor charges would ever be filed against Cohen, I intended to proceed along that road. One thing you'll quickly learn in the criminal law business is that positive identification of the subject is key. It's usually a climactic moment, when a victim or eye witness identifies the defendant from the witness stand, usually in terms of "that man sitting there next to the defense lawyer." In almost every case where it happens, it is the most compelling, direct evidence. If a woman points to the defendant and says "He stole my purse," conviction is certain unless the defense attorney can somehow dislodge the solidity of this identification from the jury's mind. Of course, a surveillance video recording the defendant committing the crime is even more convincing.

Kinko's, of course, had a security video, and thus we had undeniable evidence out there, and all we had to do was get our hands on it. Suddenly everything was falling into place. It was as if gold had fallen into a sack, and all I had to do was tighten it up. I had only one big worry, and one big question. I was worried that something might happen to that videotape before we got it. And I couldn't help wondering how Cohen, who installed video surveillance at his Trabuco Canyon squat to monitor visitors, could have overlooked this hole in his plan? I wouldn't be comfortable until I had my hands on the videotape.

Surveillance videos recording crimes in commercial locations often disappear, probably because business owners often think of crime on the premises as an embarrassment and potential source of liability. I learned this fact at some cost in a case where my client had been shot and her boss murdered in an attempted carjacking at a downtown LA gas station. We'd sued the gas station because there had been two prior murders on the premises, and they had no security guard. The surveillance video should have depicted my client, screaming for help, covered with the blood and brains of her dead boss, staggering into the gas station, her face ripped into hamburger by the blast of a twelve-gauge, sawed-off shotgun. But by the time I got on the case, three years after the shooting, there was no such videotape, nor were there any videos of the numerous shootings, assaults, robberies, and other crimes recorded among the forty or fifty police reports that recorded the sorry history of a hellish location in simple cop-speak. I lost the trial, and forty-seven thousand dollars in costs expended by my firm, after the jury concluded that while the gas station had certainly been negligent with regard to security, the attacker was such a bad man, that even an armed guard wouldn't have deterred him. I would have won if I'd had that video.

So this time, securing the video was my first priority. During my first conversation with the manager, I had emphasized that he must pull the video from the machine immediately, copy protect it, and give it to the police as evidence when they interviewed him about the theft. He understood, and agreed to do everything I asked. With those wheels in motion,

I made another call to Beth Ballerini, and she gave me the phone number for Jerry the videographer down in San Diego, who had recorded all of Cohen's deposition testimony. I called Jerry and told him the problem. He was delighted to assist me, and said he would immediately make a copy of a video deposition of Cohen and deliver it to the Chula Vista police so that they could make a comparison between Cohen and the thief in the Kinko's security video.

A day later, Sue told me that Detective King of the Chula Vista Police Department had called to say that, based on his comparison of the man in the Kinko's security video with the video of Cohen at his deposition, he was "90% sure" they were both the same man. He had prepared a police report, recording this conclusion, and was making a copy of the security video for our own use. When it arrived though, the video was difficult to watch, because the Kinko's security system actually had seventeen cameras recording a series of one-second images sequentially from each of the seventeen cameras. So images of Cohen were dispersed all over the tape, mingled with irrelevant shots of random people and copy machines. It took a video editor a few days to prepare the edited video, showing only images of Cohen in temporal sequence.

While we were waiting to receive the edited video, Diestel called to say he had received a large packet of Wells Fargo bank documents in a FedEx envelope without a sender's address. The records appeared to be for Omnitec and other Cohen accounts. The sudden appearance of at least some of the Wells Fargo bank records was almost as disturbing as Cohen's theft of them. I immediately concluded that Cohen, sniffing the criminal theft charge in the wind, had decided to undo the crime. If Diestel and I got our documents, after only a brief delay, then legally there was no theft, just a deviation from the delivery schedule. Cohen was attempting a pretty clever save, I thought. It hadn't occurred to me that he might have planned to return the documents even before he stole them.

At last the edited videotape arrived. Sue and Ana were burning with excitement as they led me into their office, and turned on the old Mitsubishi TV. Their faces were filled with joy as Ana pressed play on the remote.

In a series of grainy black and white still pictures, Cohen appeared on the screen looking bored, wearing a sweatshirt and leaning against the cash register. We watched in silence as he claimed a bulky stack of documents, about a foot thick, and tucked it under one arm. We continued watching as he turned away from the counter and walked toward the exit. He pushed his way through the double doors, and they closed behind him. Good stuff, I thought to myself, and leaned forward to hit rewind so I could watch it again, but Sue held me back and said "Wait, watch this!" The doors then opened, and Cohen came back through them. He reached into the FedEx supply rack next to the door, pulled out one large, floppy FedEx envelope, tucked it under his arm with the stolen documents, and walked back out the door. That was obviously the FedEx envelope Cohen planned to use to send the documents on to Deistel. Laughter and high fives were spontaneously shared all around. Peter Carini checked in to see what all the ruckus was about, so we showed him the video and uncorked some red wine. It was absolutely the best short movie I had ever seen, although it helped to know the plot.

CHAPTER FORTY-THREE

THE PIPELINE

GARY AND I WERE ATTEMPTING WHAT MACHIAVELLI CALLED THE MOST DIFFICULT OF ALL ENDEAVORS—"to change the established order of things." Changing the established order is almost impossible, because those most able to change it are comfortable with the existing system and have no incentive to seek change. This is why Gary's efforts to enlist pornographers to overthrow Cohen always came to naught. They were used to living with Cohen as the god of Sex.Com, and had no desire to destabilize an arrangement that worked for them.

Wagstaffe and I filed Gary's motions for summary judgment and preliminary injunction in August 2000, hoping for a swift adjudication, but Judge Ware didn't cooperate. As the days of autumn blew by, Judge Ware delayed the hearing several times, and Gary, his funds dwindling rapidly, suffered like one sentenced to hang at dawn. The same messenger–time itself–could bring good or bad news. It was only a question of which came first. The cock's crow would sound when his money ran out. The reprieve would come when Judge Ware said, "the domain is yours."

Only Gary knew when he would run out of money, but for me the date had effectively arrived in August 2000, when Gary refused to pay any more fees, and fell behind on reimbursing me for litigation costs. Seeking to assure my future security apart from Sex.Com, I took on a drug case for the Federal Public Defender, and did a one-week trial in Eugene with Peter Carini as co-counsel. It was a big case, involving twenty pounds of meth, three delivery charges and two conspiracy counts, and it sucked up a lot of my time. Gary was furious, but contained his anger, since he knew that Wagstaffe's loyalty would not survive any suspension of fee-payments, and therefore even my divided loyalty was valuable. Fortunately, the outcome of the Wells Fargo document subpoena brought good news that watered all of our hopes.

One day in late September, I was down in the Bay Area with Gary when Tara called me on my cell phone. She sounded happy, which always makes me happy, but it was more than mere domestic pleasantry. She was calling with really good news. She and Ana had deciphered the money flow from Sex.Com, and there was a lot, *like really a lot*. I asked her if she meant a *whole lot*, and she said yes, a *whole lot*. She was proud and happy that for once I was right about a case being worth something. Tara said that she had emailed me the flowchart she and Ana created, showing multiple money streams flowing into Cohen's bank accounts. Every month, one Jordan Levinson would transfer at least $400,000 from his account at Union Bank in Fort Lauderdale to Omnitec's Anaheim Hills Wells Fargo account. Gary and I read the memo and perused the charts later at his Montgomery Street office. We were very impressed with the clarity of the eleven-page memo, but the raw numbers commanded our special attention. Some months, Levinson wired as much as a million dollars to Cohen's Omnitec account.

When I realized Sex.Com produced $400,000 per month, my mind flared into white heat, like a mound of coals injected by a bellows with a flood of fresh oxygen. I was exultant–I would get paid! Memo to all legal staff: *We have to win.* The discovery of the huge cash flow, while nothing like the astronomical numbers totted off in Sex.Com's press releases, was still big money for lawyers. It was a tremendous relief to know that there was a large flow of cash coming from Sex.Com, because my bet was on the continuing value of the name as a source of endless profits. This was the fall of 2000, and bad news about the deflating "New Economy" was beginning to roll in, so I was glad that the optimism of my early days on the case had been justified.

The good news from the Wells Fargo documents came just in time to replenish our motivation to write persuasive reply briefs that would compel Judge Ware to grant our motions for summary judgment and preliminary injunction. Judge Ware had given us more time than we had wanted, but the Wells Fargo documents made us grateful for the delay. When you added in the Kinko's document theft, which highlighted the importance of the Wells Fargo records, we had a lot of new ammunition. By forcing us to store up energy to attack with accumulated momentum, Judge Ware had given us an opportunity.

Sun Tzu compares a force attacking with momentum to a raging flood tossing boulders like pebbles. A good way to generate a raging flood is to build a dam, then break it. Judge Ware's slow docket dammed up our forces. The Wells Fargo documents were the waters rising behind the dam. The videotape of Cohen stealing the Wells Fargo documents would serve as our dynamite, to break the dam most dramatically. When momentum is with them, says Sun Tzu, even cowards fight bravely, and when it is against them, even brave men run.

The Wells Fargo documents recharged my personal momentum and drew it into a single focus. Before seeing the money memo, my obsession had been naïve, based on conjecture and faith, like Moses before he reached the river Jordan. But when I glimpsed the vast river of cash actually flowing from Sex.Com, I turned from a mere believer in vague future riches to the possessor of actual, objective knowledge of just how rich I might become.

Thus, toward the end of October, in a mood of resolve and quiet optimism, Tara, Ana, Sue and I packed boxes filled with three-ring binders of documents into the Camry, and headed south on I-5 to the Bay Area. Fiercer than we looked, our little foursome comprised the core contingent of Gary's troops. Sue knew Cohen's lies virtually by heart. Her copies of his depositions were feathered with yellow stickies, cross-referencing lies that often lay three and four levels deep. Tara had devised a total document management system that contained every piece of relevant paper in a growing library of three-ring binders. Ana could put a hand to any banking document or other business record that she had subpoenaed from anyplace in the world. I was a functional madman, as obsessed as any paranoiac with unraveling a complex plot that was *actually* a fantastic reality. I could use my encyclopedic knowledge of Cohen's lifetime of crime to prove that virtually every transaction in which he had ever engaged was a fraud.

We were scheduled to spend three days, from Saturday morning until Monday evening, in Wagstaffe's office overlooking the San Francisco Bay Bridge. Modern lawyers get a lot of work done by locking themselves away in a silent skyscraper with a crew of colleagues. On the weekends, elevated offices lack food, co-workers, and excuses for distraction. Instead of halls filled with lawyers and staff, you have silent carpeting, empty doorways, ubiquitous office machinery, and the galley slave of the modern legal attack-ship—an overtime secretary chained to her computer. The bright expanse of the world is sealed outside floor-to-ceiling windows that don't admit a breath of air. The outside world is for ordinary people, and as we look down from our glass cellblocks, the child heart within us palpitates silently, held hostage by an omnipotent taskmaster. Entombed in such vast, silent warrens, the spirits of many lawyers drudge, wraith-like, attending to tasks that one law professor called alternately evil and inconsequential. When the game is afoot, however, the endless carpeted hallways, ringed with glass cages, become the staging bases for profes-sional warriors who delight in conquest. Peering into each paper-clut-tered office, amid the spill of open law books and the drafts of briefs in process, a warrior sees a forge, glowing with heat, gritty with dust ground from the sharpened blades of deadly intellectual weapons.

Jim Wagstaffe's young associates, Pam Urueta and Michael Von Lowenstein, were two fine young liberal lawyers who liked to go home at reasonable hours. Fortunate in their careers, perhaps innately gifted, wise in their choice of schools and bosses, I liked them, but unencum-bered by the burdens of hoarding cash to raise children, they had de-veloped a different orientation on the law. Huddling in Michael's office, assuring us that their legal work was nearly complete, it was evident that Pam and Michael were only there because Gary was Wagstaffe's client, Wagstaffe was their boss, and Wagstaffe was joining us in the skyscraper over the weekend.

So it was with pleasure that the Oregon crew welcomed the arrival of Gary Kremen, the pivot of our personal history. He took one look at what Pam and Michael had thus far produced, and was immediately, silent-ly seething. This is the danger of showing a demanding client an early draft–they may tend to think that the work is inadequate, their case is foundering, and victory is in doubt. Much worse is the effect when one has been claiming that the work is nearly complete, as Pam and Michael had been. But Gary reacted efficiently. After blasting off a few rumbling voice mails to Wagstaffe, warning that things were looking a little sketchy on the Pam and Michael front, Gary crashed out on the conference room floor for a solid nap.

Soon Gary's snores were resounding ominously down the hall. In the dim light of a San Francisco morning filtering through the floor-to-ceil-ing windows, the rise and fall of his capacious abdomen gave him the appearance of an unconscious leviathan beached on a foreign shore. Mi-chael and Pam obsessed over this problem. Proclaiming earnestly that he needed to go home and sleep in his own bed, they tried to leverage Gary's strange behavior into an excuse to escape the office, or at least to get rid of Gary, who had disturbed their procrastinations. Sue, Ana and

I, however, might have been keeping guard over the tomb of King Tut-
ankhamen, the way we protected Gary's prostrate form. He would not
be wakened or moved. Eventually, he would rise from oblivion and command us. That was the order of things.

The young associates upped the ante, calling their boss. When Wagstaffe called me to ask about the situation, I assured him there was nothing unusual going on with Gary. He needed his sleep. He was bothering
no one. So with Wagstaffe's blessing, Gary slept on. Michael fumed. I suggested to Michael and Pam that they dedicate themselves to producing a
better brief before Gary woke up. I could feel the love.

Shortly thereafter, Gary woke up and started cracking his whip.
When Wagstaffe arrived, Pam and Michael realized that their fate was
sealed. Only an excellent brief would secure their exit from our intellectual prison. Gradually, they assumed an outwardly docile manner, fun-
neling their aggression into their writing, as is appropriate, and the work
product continued improving. With Gary demanding that Pam and Michael add more facts to their arguments, Sue was able to feed them relevant quotes, demonstrating her total mastery of Cohen's testimony as
she consulted her well-thumbed, cross-indexed transcripts of Cohen's
numerous depositions. Eventually, Michael even woke up to the need
to cite the *McCord* case, where the California Supreme Court authorized
judges to enjoin the theft of intellectual property. I was comforted to
know that this controlling precedent, later cited by Judge Ware in his own
opinion, would be included in our briefs.

While Pam and Michael nailed down the legal issues presented
by forged titles and invalid trademarks, I dug into the financial documents. In their money memo, Tara and Ana had neatly summarized the
recurring monthly transfers of hundreds of thousands of dollars from
Levinson in Florida to Omnitec in Anaheim Hills. When I studied the
memo closely for the first time, however, I suddenly realized something
that was obvious, but had escaped my attention as a crucial fact. *Cohen
drained the Omnitec account every month.* All the money flowed out via
wire transfer to numbered accounts in Luxembourg and other offshore
money havens.

The legal implications of this fact had escaped me until that very
moment. Gary wanted to recover more than just Sex.Com; he wanted to
freeze Cohen's bank accounts, seize the Rancho Santa Fe mansion, and

also grab a little house on the Mexican border that Cohen had stolen from an unfortunate man named Godinez. That was a tall order, and seemed unachievable until I realized that Cohen drained the Omnitec account every month. Until then, I hadn't seen the single fact that would convince the judge to grant such a variety of unusual requests.

I grabbed the binder of bank documents and walked down the hall to talk to Wagstaffe. As I walked through his office door, he looked up from his computer and smiled with strong teeth, and his silvery-red beard bristled with energy. I sat down, showed Wagstaffe my summary of the Omnitec bank records, and asked him if he thought it would strengthen the argument for an asset freeze. He understood exactly what I was saying. The Omnitec account was simply an offshore pipeline. We could focus on the pipeline to provide the one thing that had been missing from our factual record—convincing proof that Cohen was putting the stolen Sex.Com money offshore, out of reach of the U.S. courts. The bank records showed that Cohen had been putting his ill-gotten gains beyond the reach of U.S. law for years. At least thirteen million dollars, I calculated, had already disappeared from the country through the Omnitec Wells Fargo Account.

From the birth of a legal inspiration to the drafting of an admissible declaration can be a bit of a distance. As the hours of the last day of our three-day weekend ticked by, my declaration became compendious. I wanted to give Judge Ware and his clerks one place to find all of our financial evidence. I wanted to dramatically emphasize how Cohen had risen from rags to riches with only two tools—Sex.Com and his criminal imagination. Because a judge can only order restitution of funds that can be traced to an unlawful source, I needed to establish that all of Cohen's post-prison wealth was traceable to his theft of Sex.Com.

Most of the documents I planned to attach to the declaration were as familiar as old friends, and I was excited to introduce each one in the proper dramatic order. The divorce papers Cohen filed from prison "in forma pauperis" proved that he was broke in prison, and presumably was still broke when he left in 1995. Photographs of the Rancho Santa Fe property depicting Cohen's mansion, pool, tennis court, and playhouse—showed how rich he'd become in the last four years. The bank record of Omnitec's $500,000 down payment on Cohen's Rancho Santa Fe house showed Cohen using Sex.Com money for his personal benefit.

An unsigned tax return subpoenaed from Cohen's accountants showing less than $40,000 income for 1998–showed that Cohen lied to both the courts and the IRS about his wealth. Omnitec bank records referring to "Sex.Com DBA Omnitec," and a bank officer's handwritten notation that "Steve Cohen is Omnitec," proved that Cohen, Omnitec and Sex.Com were an indivisible trinity. Statements from Cohen's securities accounts and bank accounts subpoenaed from around the nation showed that, aside from a few hundred-thousand dollars, almost all of the Sex.Com money was offshore, having been funneled through Omnitec to foreign banks. To the pipeline argument, my last exhibit was Cohen's check on the Omnitec account for seminar fees at "The Offshore Institute."

During several hours of our third day of all-out effort, Wagstaffe and Gary sat shoulder-to-shoulder, huddled over the form of the proposed order we would submit to Judge Ware for signature. I didn't need to be involved, because Gary had taken my advice to make the order his "wish list," and had written up one that would have made Santa Claus sweat. The way it turned out, if Judge Ware signed it, Gary would immediately assume total control over Sex.Com and virtually all of Cohen's property subject to U.S. legal control. Cohen could fight all he wanted, but if that order got signed, it was equivalent to assassinating his entire case in a single blow. Based on Cohen's own confessions about the Dimmick letter, and the damning evidence I was putting in my declaration, both Wagstaffe and I believed we had the evidence to justify such an order, but lawyers still like to proceed incrementally, and don't like to look greedy in front of the judge, so we would both have asked the judge for less relief. Gary wouldn't let us do it. The wish-list idea had stuck, and we were stuck with it.

So we had to convince Judge Ware to give us the asset freeze. From the legal doctrine viewpoint, the hard pull was that Gary was a private individual, and the main case on freezing bank accounts to prevent "a dissipation of assets" before judgment was a federal case that allowed the Republic of the Philippines to freeze deposed dictator Ferdinand Marcos's bank accounts to recover millions he and Imelda stole from the government during his years as a U.S. puppet dictator. Getting Judge Ware to apply this precedent had initially struck me as a long shot, because in the Marcos case, the plaintiff was a nation impoverished by a fallen tyrant, seeking restitution of hundreds of millions in stolen tax dollars. Gary, on the other hand, had filed a registration form to establish his rights to six letters and a dot, waited three years to sue, allowing Cohen to build up a hoard of Sex.Com cash, and could be characterized as an opportunist seeking a windfall. Worst of all, since Sex.Com had been under Cohen's control for five years at this point, without proof that he was doing something to hide his money from seizure after judgment, there was no reason to seize his assets. For example, no judge would freeze Ford's assets on behalf of a plaintiff who sued them for incinerating his family in a defective vehicle, because all judges believe Ford will be around to pay the judgment, even if only from a bankrupt estate. Putting seizure of assets ahead of a finding of liability is, after all, a bit draconian – a lot like making an accused wait in jail until their case comes up for trial – and as you know, the rich rarely have to do that. Cohen, of course, would insist that he should enjoy the same legal presumption of reliability and honesty as Ford Motor Company. I could hear Dorband saying it now – "Of course Mr. Cohen will pay any judgment rendered against him! He has millions!"

That argument wouldn't hold much water in the face of evidence that Cohen was spiriting money offshore at the rate of $400,000 a month. We could get that asset freeze order, because the Omnitec account was nothing but a pipeline for pumping cash offshore, and in fact, the vast majority of the Sex.Com money was already gone, and would never be recovered. By tracing Cohen's rise from a broke ex-convict to a supernova in the pornography firmament, we made a common-sense argument that effectively traced all the funds to Sex.Com, and placed the injunctive relief lever firmly in Judge Ware's hand.

On Monday afternoon, we had to call the courthouse to ask for permission to submit the Kinko's security video as evidence. When Sue called and asked the clerk, she was asked to wait, then the clerk returned to ask what type of video it was. Sue explained that it was a security video of Mr. Cohen stealing subpoenaed bank records from Kinko's. The clerk seemed surprised, and after a further delay, presumably to talk with the judge, returned to the phone call with considerably more animation to say that, yes, we could definitely file that video. Sue's declaration attached the video, which included a clip of Cohen's deposition for the sake of comparison, along with the police report recording Det. King's "90%" estimate of the thief's identity.

The vibes were getting positive around Wagstaffe's office. Pam and Michael were allowed to depart with the sun still in the sky, leaving Wagstaffe to polish their draft. The Bay Bridge was cloaked in the encroaching dusk as we pushed up against the seven o'clock Fedex deadline. We were making seven copies of every document, and Wagstaffe's copy machine was in constant operation as each written work reached final, was proofed, signed, and copied. One by one they stacked up in the back hallway of Wagstaffe's office, waiting for the Fedex guy to arrive. The copy machine racketed on, producing seven reply briefs, seven proposed orders, seven copies of Sue's declaration, and at last, seven copies of my declaration, revealing the marvelous, amazing, $400,000-per-month pipeline. The explosive videotape was taped into a manila envelope that we stapled to the last page of Sue's declaration, and placed on top of the whole stack. If it had been a shooting war, we would've sealed it with a kiss and a short inscription, scrawled in lipstick, "To Cohen, with Love."

CHAPTER FORTY-FOUR

THE MAGICIAN AND HIS PHANTOMS

THE DAY AFTER WE FILED OUR MASSIVE REPLY BRIEFS and declarations, Wagstaffe told me that he'd finally read through my declaration and voluminous exhibits with full attention, and was pleasantly surprised to see that we had convincingly proved all of Cohen's sham companies were nothing other than Cohen's corporate alter-egos. Wagstaffe thought I'd given Judge Ware good reason to "pierce the corporate veil," under the alter-ego doctrine. He said he figured I was gathering up useful information with all of the discovery I was doing, but hadn't realized it would end up being so comprehensive and convincing.

The alter-ego theory had assumed even greater importance for us when we realized that we had never sued Omnitec, because Cohen had obscured its significance quite effectively. The long-desired Wells Fargo bank records alone revealed the central role of Omnitec. No wonder Cohen stole them from Kinko's. He had laundered the Sex.Com profits through five companies. Most of them were decoys, like Sporting Houses Management, Ocean Fund International and YNATA, that nominally "owned" Sex.Com. Others, like Omnitec and perhaps Sandman, were primarily bags of money that inflated as the money came in, then deflated to be sure that, as the YNATA name promised, they would "never amount to anything."

The alter-ego doctrine is based on the reasonable proposition that a company has to operate on the same set of laws as a person, because at most, incorporation turns an inanimate stack of papers into a pseudo-human. A person can't be allowed to immunize themselves from the consequences of their conduct simply by using a corporation to perform unlawful acts, so the doctrine holds that if a corporation is merely the alter ego of an individual, and has no true separate character, the acts of the corporation, and its legal liabilities, are binding upon that individual. Like many other legal doctrines, it rarely works as intended. For example, no court would pierce the corporate veil of the corporations that hooked children on cigarettes, or killed workers with asbestos, or despoiled countless acres of public lands with toxic waste. Such a result would be antithetical to the true purposes of our corporate system, which protects the individuals who drive our economic juggernauts from being judged too harshly when they occasionally steer us onto the reefs of mass misfortune. Someone has to run the world of industry, after all, and who but the rich would know how? While you may reject such a doctrine, the courts pretty much abide by it. On the other hand, amateur frauds like Omnitec that produce no apparent benefit for society are a fit subject for corporate piercing. This may seem ironic, because compared with Enron, that created money that never existed, Cohen's business model was actually more legitimate – at least the money he stole was real!

That real money, however, coursed its way through numerous illusory companies. We got the last piece to Cohen's puzzle when we traced the flow of Sex.Com money to Omnitec's Wells Fargo accounts, and thence to offshore banks. Omnitec's role in the business was so central that Cohen probably created Ocean Fund, YNATA and other companies primarily to conceal its existence. By leading us down the Sandman's trail, and in search of Vito Franko and Sir William Douglas, Cohen kept us barking up trees that held no treasures. Small wonder Cohen seemed amused by our efforts to unwind his twisted tales. Nevertheless, piercing Cohen's serial deceptions was necessary to engineer his final defeat, because Gary had to defeat YNATA's claim that it was a "bona fide purchaser for value." To conceal the fact that YNATA's acquisition of the domain was merely Cohen passing the domain from his right hand to his left, all Cohen had to do was contend that YNATA was actually owned by someone besides himself, to forge their signatures, and to procure their non-attendance at depositions. Since one who seeks to "pierce the corporate veil" in Federal court must prove by "clear and convincing evidence" that the doctrine applies, Cohen was hoping he could defeat our efforts to unmask his corporate alter-egos by propping up phantoms and charging Gary the expense of proving they were nonexistent. The burden was on us to prove that he was YNATA, and if we couldn't produce such evidence, YNATA might prevail. It took a long time to dissolve all the phantoms. We just needed to keep Cohen talking. When someone is lying, there is no such thing as asking him too many questions.

The opportunity to get Cohen under oath one last time arose fortuitously. You may recall that Judge Trumbull ordered YNATA to either produce Sir William Douglas for deposition, or produce some corporate document to show that he was not in fact a YNATA corporate officer. This ruling must have delighted Cohen, who, seeing one more opportunity to forge his way out of trouble, had provided Dorband with the corporate resolution signed by several "officers" and YNATA's "sole shareholder." The resolution pointedly stated that Sir William Douglas had stopped working for YNATA *the day before* I served the notice to take his deposition. Besides Cohen himself, four imaginary persons had signed the resolution, which was just a few pages, and looked like a basic forgery project that had presented no challenge for Cohen. All this forgery was very good for us, I reminded myself, because winning in court is often based more on proving that your adversary is lying than proving that you are telling the truth. Thus the William Douglas story, tired as it was, continued to serve as a handy battering ram, cut from Cohen's own corrupt timber.

When we insisted on deposing each of the signers of the resolution, Cohen played his position like a poker hand. He raised the bet. We wanted to poke holes in the YNATA corporate veil? We could pay for the right. During Christmas 1999, he'd tried to send me to Russia, Israel, Greece, and other distant lands with poor security. Now he found another use for hazardous venues. The corporate officers of YNATA were all in Caracas, Venezuela. Why could they not leave Caracas? Dorband explained that they could not obtain US entry visas. Why? Because they had all sold arms to Iran and Iraq in violation of the UN arms embargo. They were, in other words, gun runners, whom we would have to visit on their home turf in what was then the murder capital of the free world, a place where you could check into your hotel one night, and get hosed off the pavement before coffee the next morning.

Cohen's Caracas gambit stimulated a round of soul-searching on the Kremen team. Gary was furious, and didn't have the money to send me to Caracas, but he didn't want Diestel to go alone. Diestel had his bags packed, and Wagstaffe thought he should go. If he didn't, then Dorband could hold the depos, claim we'd had our shot at cross-examining the witnesses who would be unavailable for trial, and move to admit that un-cross-examined testimony at trial. That was a nasty prospect, but I argued that it was totally unreasonable to expect me to go to South America, and Gary to pay for it, after we had all three wasted our time and money traveling to Mexico for the sham "deposition" of

Roman Caso, who discovered after his arrival that he was urgently required elsewhere. Gary backed my position, and we planted our heels. I wasn't going to Caracas.

State Farm probably preferred having Diestel file a motion to compel YNATA to produce its officers for deposition in California over sending him to Caracas. It was certainly cheaper, and worth a try, so Diestel drafted and filed a declaration that recited the Roman Caso story to explain why we didn't want to embark on another hegira through Latin America. We showed Judge Trumbull the resolution signed by the YNATA corporate insiders and asked, essentially, "What's up with that?" YNATA can file declarations here, but its officers can't abide the heat of our laws? YNATA submitted no supporting evidence for its inability to produce its officers for deposition in the U.S., aside from a note in Spanish from a purported Mexican lawyer.

Faced with yet another goofy international discovery scenario, Judge Trumbull considered the lessons of recent history, and concluded there was no need for Kremen's lawyers to travel to Caracas and repeat a farcical experience. Ruling from the bench, she ordered YNATA to produce its officers in California, and to present a designated witness in San Diego to testify as to specified topics within YNATA's corporate knowledge. Judge Trumbull was tired of Cohen's game, and never ruled in his favor again. From what I could conclude, virtually all of the territory in her mind had been liberated by Kremen's forces. Although it was not her job to determine the merits of Gary's position, I suspect that, if Judge Ware had asked her for a thumbnail summary of Cohen's case, she would have said, "Hang him."

The depositions of imaginary people never happen. Although Judge Trumbull ordered the YNATA directors and officers to testify in the United States, they never came. Dorband's bland letters responded to my demand that YNATA produce its officers as ordered by simply stating that Cohen could do nothing to procure their presence, nor could the corporate officers themselves travel here in violation of visa restrictions. It was all too convenient, and devilishly frustrating for Gary. Cohen appeared to be using the signatures of people allegedly in foreign countries to add an international glow to his forgeries, while shielding their origins from inquiry. Still, Dorband's mask stayed in place, and the existence of YNATA's officers was untested. To all appearance, Cohen was getting away with forgery again.

It was thus especially important that Judge Trumbull had also ordered YNATA to designate a witness to testify in California. The corporation didn't need an entry visa to get in the country – it was already present before the court. We could anticipate that, even if he were subpoenaed to testify at trial, Cohen would deny knowledge of YNATA's activities, and characterize even his signature on the forged corporate resolution as the artifact of some clerical task to which he had accorded little attention. So it was essential to get some human being on the record who was authorized to testify for YNATA. Judge Trumbull had ordered the deposition to take place in San Diego, and the only question was who Cohen would find to occupy the witness seat in Beth Ballerini's conference room. As the day for the deposition approached, Dorband wasn't forthcoming about who that would be.

As November 4th, the date set for the deposition approached, Dorband temporized, avoiding phone calls, buying time. We had reached, and he knew it, that point in the hunt when the predators are closing in on the quarry, having kept it on the run for long enough to induce exhaustion. In the hunt, pursuers take turns keeping pressure on their prey, to deprive it of rest and drive it to collapse. Bob Dorband was tired. You could see it in his face, hear it in his voice. We, on the other hand, had sighted the pulsing jugular of cash, like a vein beating hard on the neck of our prey, Omnitec, a lumbering beast full of tasty blood and fat to appease our hunger. Cohen was too arrogant to pay attention to Dorband's lagging stride. Playing the role of a mad genius who had planned for every contingency, he was not expecting any reversals. He didn't realize that Bob Dorband had tired of fronting for a humongous liar, had stopped caring about the outcome, and was beginning to let the chips land where they might.

As the hail of lead that was daily trained in his direction took its toll, Bob's writing lost its zip. Instead of sounding pithy and biting, his arguments seemed short and inadequate. He had bandied words well at the pleading stage, where only theoretical principles were at stake, but once we started to trade heavily in facts, he found that he could rarely cook up a convincing story from Cohen's stock of lies. Cohen's record of weird conduct had been thoroughly documented in the court's records, so there was an inexhaustible source of evidence to support our claim that he was a lying crook who breathed deception. Dorband's job had thus been reduced to that of the loyal courtier, insisting that the King certainly did have clothes, and of the finest.

Still, Bob fulfilled his role with dastardly aplomb to the bitter end. He never dropped his sword for an instant, never pled for quarter, and never betrayed a hint of despair, regardless of the odds against him. Dorband earned my resentful admiration as he slogged on through the fall of 2000. As the weeks stretched out and the frequency and intensity of our attacks steadily mounted, Bob kept up a stream of correspondence or avoided communications, as circumstances required, conceding nothing, disputing whatever was disputable, and scoffing at the purported significance of whatever he could not deny. His loyalty was manifest by the rigor of his efforts.

Clever advocates always keep silent about bad facts as long as possible, because the earlier you reveal them, the more likely it is that your adversary will use them against you. Following that rule, Dorband kept us in suspense about who YNATA would present as its witness on the fourth of November until a few days before the deposition. I shouldn't have been surprised by Dorband's disclosure that Cohen would appear as YNATA's witness, but it seemed like such a bad move on Cohen's part that I actually was. Then again, remembering how badly Roman Caso had performed as the Sandman designee, I figured Cohen probably knew better than to try using a puppet a second time. When Ana heard that Cohen would testify for YNATA at the deposition, she talked Gary into letting her accompany me as an assistant. I loved the idea, since Ana's ability to keep paperwork organized had grown to the point where she did it better than anyone but her mom. Gary surprised me by deciding to skip the trip, and got a kick out of authorizing Ana to go in his place.

Ana's presence at the deposition completely changed Cohen's demeanor. Gone were the lewd comments, the sneers and jeers. I had less need of attitude as well, having finally gotten fully prepared to question him about the issues that would come up at trial. With my documents in chronological order, premarked with exhibit numbers in one big binder, I was ready to begin my march on the capital of Cohen's deceptions—YNATA. Although Cohen's shell game had lost much of its mystery, the best time to ask questions is when you know the answers. Over a year after my first, vertiginous meeting with the master-deceiver, I had learned a great deal about Cohen's affairs. Directed by Gary's indefatigable research, our barrage of subpoenas had produced hard data that revealed the extent of the wealth Cohen controlled. I assumed that Cohen was fully aware of how much we knew, since we'd put it all into the documents we had already filed with Judge Ware. It was a far different situation than the one I'd faced the first time we met.

Cohen knew we had Levinson's Union Bank records showing monthly deposits to Omnitec's Wells Fargo account. He knew we had brokerage statements referring to "Omnitec, DBA Sex.Com," and other financial documents that proved he owned Omnitec. He knew we had the loan file for his place in Rancho Santa Fe that proved he bought the house with Omnitec funds. He knew he had signed all those Omnitec checks and wire transfers. But when I showed Cohen these records, he seemed unaffected, and peeled off new lies like a series of hundred-dollar bills fresh from the mint. Cohen's latest lies were intended to rebut the claims we'd made in our latest filing, by denying that all Cohen's money came from Sex.Com.

Omnitec, Cohen explained, was "a bill-pay company," and very little of the money in its accounts came from Sex.Com. The Wells Fargo Anaheim Hills records showed different, of course – all the money came from Levinson, the Sex.Com bagman. Like most corporate criminals, Cohen would calmly trot out the latest lie, then fade into vagueness when asked to provide corroboration for his assertions. He couldn't give details about Omnitec because he wasn't there to testify on behalf of Omnitec. When I asked him to explain what YNATA knew about the financial affairs of Omnitec, its wholly-owned subsidiary, he refused on the grounds that he was bound by a confidentiality agreement that was conveniently located in Venezuela. Further, it would be a violation of Venezuelan criminal law to breach the confidentiality agreement. His memory was conveniently vague on all details. Diestel, sitting quietly to my right, shook his head in gentle disgust as the new lies befouled the room.

One question, and only one, provoked Cohen to depart from his script of wholesale denial and out-of-the-loop executive ignorance. After he agreed with me that YNATA derived its claim to ownership of Sex.Com from the rights of Steven Michael Cohen, I asked whether YNATA had any *other* basis for claiming ownership of the domain, if Steven Michael Cohen's rights to Sex.Com were proven to be invalid. After Dorband declined Cohen's request to answer the question for him, Cohen launched into a proclamation of his deep, abiding faith that Kremen had no rights, had no standing, and never would be found to have any rights. Therefore, he concluded, YNATA would never have to deal with the issue, and it was irrelevant.

Most people, not suffering from brain damage, recognize their signature on the documents they signed. It is a hard question to deny when your signature is staring up at you from the page and someone asks: "Did you sign this document?" But when I showed Cohen a dozen or more checks and wire transfers he'd signed on behalf of Omnitec, he refused to identify his own signature even once. He couldn't remember when or why he signed the checks, assuming he'd signed them at all, which he declined to concede.

Cohen adhered to a disciplined act of self-obliteration. Committed to denying his role in any recent transactions involving Sex.Com, he nevertheless was forced to appear as a witness for a corporation whose workings he was at pains to conceal. In defense, he argued that in fulfilling his duties as YNATA's designated witness, his personal knowledge was irrelevant. As YNATA's designated witness, he officially knew nothing, and would gladly testify to it. His phantoms were meant to be the focus of your attention, and to them your attention was duly directed.

CHAPTER FORTY-FIVE

NOTHING LEFT TO TRY

IT WAS LATE NOVEMBER 2000. We were tracking the progress of our weapons arcing toward ground zero. They met a little anti-missile defense in the form of motions to strike the declarations of Carreon and Whatley, with their wild tales of Cohen's evil deeds, but the days of easy deflection were over for Cohen. We vaporized his obstructions, and our weapons continued en route to their targets.

Judge Ware had finally set the hearing for a date we hoped would stick – November 27th – and the entire Oregon team was coming down to see what our efforts would produce. Although Gary invited us all to stay at his new place on Third Street, it was an aesthetic purgatory in a run-down industrial district across from the wharfs. Gary had lost old Bob Deschl as his computer geek and pizza procurer, replacing him with a tweeker named Crab whose sleeping habits were irregular. Crab bragged about his remodeling skills, but gritty brick dust coated everything in the house for months, including the bed sheets, rendering it uninhabitable by members of the fairer sex. Not that Gary seemed to mind. He called his new headquarters Dogpatch, named after the bar down the street, and was building out a dungeon in the basement, forging a new, kinkier image.

With victory approaching, and relief in sight, crappy lodgings were more than I expected my wife, child and fellow-lawyer to endure. So Tara, Ana, Sue and I stayed at the Lighthouse Hotel in Pacifica that has great views of the pounding surf, and is just twenty minutes north of the San Jose federal courthouse.

The morning of the 27th, the weather was sunny as Tara steered the Camry South on the 280 through the rolling green hills that fringe the Pacific coast. We sailed past the exit to Half-Moon Bay, the Stanford campus, and Sandhill Road, and rolled into San Jose, down the broad curving streets, and into the parking lot south of the Federal Courthouse. Inside, we met up with Wagstaffe and Pam, who would be arguing the trademark issue after Jim tackled the main issue of conversion of personal property. The bright, sunlit areas on the second floor of the courthouse were rather solemn, but our mood was bright. Diestel showed up, smiling with friendly anticipation. Ana and Sue talked cheerfully with everyone. Tara and Diestel hit it off. In the last year, Gary's team had swelled to three firms and eight lawyers – two from my office, two from Diestel's, and four from Jim's.

Then Gary showed up with a copy of the San Jose Mercury News. There it was, on the front page, below the fold, with a color picture of Judge Ware – an article about the case. Wagstaffe had finally come through with the publicity he said he could conjure, and it was the first time an article about the case had hit the print media. All prior articles had been digital only. Somehow, the fact that the mainstream news had already picked it up made it seem more likely that we would win. How, after all, could Judge Ware tell the whole world that Cohen, a convicted con-man, should keep what he had stolen? Perhaps Gary had been right all along, and what was simply needed was that everyone should know that "the guy stole it!"

In the courtroom, Jim, Pam, Gary and I sat down at the large conference-sized counsel table next to the jury box, settling into the blue leather swivel rockers edged with faceted brass tacks. Tara, Sue and Ana sat in the gallery on our side of the aisle – the left side, as we sat facing the bench. It was one of those moments that make you proud to be a lawyer, despite what you know about the profession. The surroundings pull it out of you, as you contemplate the majestic symbols on the wall, and enjoy the physical separation between those who sit at counsel table and those who do not. You appreciate the size of the room, the solemnity of the bailiff, the mental isolation of the court reporter, the indulgent power of the clerk who takes business cards and speaks with the advocates. I for one cannot forget, when standing in a federal courtroom, that this is the place, for good or ill, where right and wrong are distinguished from each other in our society, in a free-for-all of debate and argument, a fast-changing flow of facts and rules that only experts can navigate.

When the case was called and we introduced ourselves, Judge Ware seemed his usual self, but his opening words suggested something more. He began:

"Well, although this matter has been before this court in a number of different ways and in a number of different motions, and I'm familiar with the background, I'm presented here with an opportunity to adjudicate the case summarily on an argument that, as a matter of law, there's a basis for declaratory relief being granted in favor of the plaintiff and requesting certain injunctive relief."

Alluding to the large volume of our submissions, Judge Ware continued:

"I doubt if I would have enough time in the day today if you wanted to repeat all the arguments that you've made in your papers, but I wanted to give you a brief opportunity to say by way of oral presentation to the court anything you would wish to add."

Jim began. Directing Judge Ware's attention to the forged letter, he laid out the facts in parallel statements:

"There's no dispute that the signature at the bottom of this page from Ms. Dimmick is forgery. There's no dispute as to that fact. No one is arguing that this document effectuated a transfer of this domain name. There's no dispute that Ms. Dimmick had no involvement or connection with Online Classifieds, none whatsoever. In fact, there is no dispute that Mr. Cohen prepared this letter with his friend Vito Franco. There's no dispute that the first line of this letter saying that Mr. Cohen supposedly had numerous conversations with Ms. Dimmick was a lie. He had no conversations with her."

With a series of gentle nods, Judge Ware confirmed the indisputability of this trio of facts. Jim continued attacking the letter, saying it was "implausible, to say the least, that an Internet company that sells online advertising would not have a connection to the Internet." Judge Ware's face showed that he agreed with this proposition. Judge Ware also appeared willing to infer that Cohen had substituted his own email address for Gary's on the registration form so that, as Jim put it, "if NSI actually checked up on the bizarre letter, they would call up and say 'Did you mean to transfer?' and he would have impersonated Mr. Kremen." Since ordinarily, an error in the contact fields of a computer document wouldn't give rise to an inference of fraudulent intent, Jim deftly sprinkled mud in Cohen's direction, alluding to his theft of the Kinko's documents: "I would ordinarily not make that assumption, if we didn't have a substantial history of this man impersonating people his whole life, and he's done it in this case, impersonating a lawyer to get documents."

Using the knife of undisputed facts to reveal the place where the decision had to be made, Jim cut to the heart of the issue:

"The signature is forged–it's undisputed. It's forged *ab initio*, and all title transfers fail as a matter of law; therefore, the domain name must be returned and NSI has already submitted itself to your Honor's jurisdiction to do that, to return the domain name."

Latin phrases sometimes seem to say more than the English equivalent, or at least lawyers like to think so. Take the term *ab initio*, which means "from the beginning," and provides the root for words like "initiate" and "initially." Beginnings are fundamental to the distinctions the law must draw to establish who owns a piece of property. Ownership rights arise from lawful beginnings. Illicit beginnings generate only illegitimate claims of ownership. Law distinguishes legitimate rights from illegitimate claims. Property law is almost entirely the product of inheritance litigation, and English property law denied bastards the right to inherit a crown, a fortune, or a title. In essence, we were arguing that Cohen had a bastard's claim to Sex.Com, and nothing more. He was a pretender, a usurper, a man without good title, and Gary Kremen was the true heir.

Judge Ware had taken it all in. Cohen's claim was void from the beginning, because as the old rule says so simply, "no lawful title can arise from theft." But the law has another principle of great age, which is that only those with "standing" can bring a civil suit to correct a civil wrong. Only someone who stands to inherit has standing to contest a will. Only the defrauded person can complain of a fraud. And only the person who owned a piece of property *when it was stolen* can file a civil complaint for conversion. Referring to Cohen's standing argument as a "piece of confetti," Jim dismissed "the suggestion that Mr. Cohen somehow can get away from summary judgment because the domain name was not owned by Mr. Kremen." His argument is an excellent example of how to keep the focus on your opponent, even when the attack is on your own client's status:

"It's perhaps glib, but let me say it, your Honor. His argument is that 'I stole from someone, but I don't know from whom. It wasn't Mr. Kremen.' That's not his standing to make that argument. He is not here. If someone else wants to come into this courtroom and say, 'We're the owner,' they have the power to do that, but that's not before your Honor."

So Cohen had no standing to contest Kremen's standing! Wagstaffe had stolen Cohen's weapon and deftly turned it against him. Judge Ware's face showed satisfaction at this artful turn of phrase. Nevertheless, artful phrases are not enough to win summary judgment, where every essential fact must be indisputable. We needed to remove every cloud on Gary's title to Sex.Com, particularly those cast by his own careless statements at deposition. Fortunately, Gary had managed to obtain declarations from five of his former business partners at Electric Classifieds, Inc., whom I will call the "ECI Insiders." As you may recall, ECI purchased Online Classifieds, Inc. (OCI). The ECI Insiders all swore that Sex.Com had always remained Gary's personal property, and had never been assigned to OCI. Wagstaffe now laid the declarations of the ECI Insiders on the table:

"Attached as Exhibit F to my declaration are all of the declarations from people at OCI that say we never acquired Sex.Com. There is no witness in this case who says that OCI acquired Sex.Com and Mr. Kremen's testimony, if it is read with any care whatsoever, does not say that Sex. Com was transferred to OCI."

The team hadn't been all of one mind about including the declarations of the ECI Insiders, because Pam and Michael were inclined to shy away from the issue, and didn't even mention the five declarations in their legal brief in support of summary judgment. But Gary and I knew we needed the declarations, which had cost Gary a lot of time and effort to obtain. I had not addressed the problem at the writing stage, and it's not the best practice to just toss some declarations in to the record for unexplained reasons. Nevertheless, at the last moment during our three-day marathon in Wagstaffe's office, I had pointed out to Gary that his painfully garnered declarations weren't being included in our submissions. After a short discussion with Wagstaffe, who agreed with our thinking, he attached them as Exhibit "F" to his own declaration. Watching Judge Ware's approving look as he took in their importance, I was very glad Gary had been able to obtain them, and that I had made the necessary fuss to get them into the record. The ECI Insider declarations put paid to Cohen's "standing" argument with a five-pointed seal.

Jim wrapped up his argument by passing the torch to Pam, continuing his use of festive metaphor: "So the trademark piece of confetti–Ms. Urueta can address that." Pam had decided to *burn* the confetti by arguing that *no one* could trademark Sex.Com. This is called proving more than you need to, but for Pam it was easier than understanding all the facts. The USPTO had already determined that Sex.Com was a descriptive mark that Cohen *could* trademark by showing that, despite its descriptive character, the mark had acquired "secondary meaning." I had no argument with that conclusion, and simply contended that Cohen had tricked the USPTO into approving the registration with false statements. Cohen's declaration that said he'd used Sex.Com in commerce long before he stole the domain in 1995 was a complete invention, and all the use of Sex.Com he'd gotten since he stole it was illegitimate. We could have gotten Cohen's trademark registration set aside for fraud, while preserving our right to trademark the domain lawfully. However, to make such an argument would have required Pam to have a greater grasp of the facts in the USPTO file, and frankly, at the time, I was not fully up to speed on trademark issues, so Pam's strategy became our strategy.

Pam was operating like many intelligent young lawyers do–entirely on theory, and thus she took a theoretical tack that destroyed the future to secure the present:

"When analyzing whether or not Sex.Com can be marked in the first place, the court needs to look at the word 'sex.' Mr. Cohen makes the argument that Sex.Com is not generic, it is descriptive, but even that argument, your Honor, fails. For a descriptive mark to be trademarked it needs to acquire secondary meaning, and all Mr. Cohen has done is offer thirteen declarations, submitted by friends of Mr. Cohen's, that go to the prior use of Sex.Com."

Just thirteen declarations? On any ordinary day, that sounds like a lot of evidence–thirteen declarations should be enough to bulwark the arguable validity of a trademark that the US Patent & Trademark Office had already concluded was protectable as a descriptive mark possessed of secondary meaning. Thirteen unrebutted declarations, as these all were, would seem likely to raise an issue of fact.

Pam needed to explain why thirteen declarations meant nothing:

"Those thirteen declarations don't establish secondary meaning, and even if they did, those secondary meanings aren't a survey of the relevant market. Mr. Cohen needs to show this court that, worldwide, a consumer would associate Sex.Com with YNATA, and he has failed to do that."

Now this was a good point–Cohen's declarations didn't even attempt to establish secondary meaning. Ironically, it would've been easy to do so, because every day, lots and lots of people type "sex.com" into their browser and hit "return." One might presume they knew what they expected to find there. The statistics necessary to make a good "secondary meaning" argument were all there in Cohen's computer, and he didn't use them.

As her argument went on, Pam meandered deeper into theoretical realms, arguing there was no "likelihood of confusion" between Gary's "use" of the domain and Cohen's operation of the website. That was strange territory because Gary had never used Sex.Com at all, so any claim of confusion was absurd. Gary had no use, so how could it ever have conflicted with Cohen's use? Pam theorized that Gary might some-day market chocolate chip cookies through Sex.Com, and that would not infringe on Cohen's use of it as a sex site. Theoretically, she posited, Co-hen might come back to court with a trademark claim if Gary abandoned the theoretical sale of chocolate chip cookies and reverted to selling por-nography. She had run so far into the woods that she was running out the other side.

At the time, however, I had no criticisms. Pam's words were just a merry tinkle in my ears as I watched Judge Ware's face, the mirror of my fate. Reading the transcript today, Pam sounds like a fruit loop, but Co-hen's case had been marked for death, and Judge Ware was happy to hear a nice young lady prattle on with such confidence. He could adopt her argument. It was probably correct, or not too far wrong. More impor-tantly, Cohen's number was up. Judge Ware was going to pull the trigger.

Dorband stood up, and began by arguing, as he had for years, that Gary lacked standing to sue, because the domain had been registered in the name of Online Classifieds, Inc., a non-existent corporation. Al-though Judge Ware tried to maintain the appearance of judicial neutral-ity, he failed. His face registered disgust as he listened to about a hundred words of Dorband's argument, then began rebutting it vigorously with his own counter-argument. Cohen, said Judge Ware, had used a forged letter to acquire the domain! His claim was based on no valid title! He had no standing to object to Gary's standing! He had stolen documents produced under subpoena!

It warms an advocate's heart to hear the judge reciting his own argu-ments, and I swiveled in my chair at counsel table to pass amazed and delighted looks to Tara, Ana, and Sue, who reciprocated with subtle nods.

When Judge Ware concluded there was nothing new from Cohen's side, he set aside legal issues and just asked Dorband where Cohen was. When Dorband said Cohen wasn't there, and didn't have to be, it was not what the judge wanted to hear. He was sick of phantoms, of conjuration, of endless wordplay. Like a lion tamed by an enchantment, suddenly recovering his ferocity, he turned on the enchanter. His cool exterior dissolved, and sharp angles of displeasure showed in the folds of his robe. It was time to back off, but a weary Dorband dug in his heels, his silver head bobbing somewhat as he deflected one after another of the judge's hostile questions. Judge Ware seemed shocked by the mildness of Dorband's deflections, as if some emotion from him, some acknowledgement that the spell was unwinding, was required.

Judge Ware had wanted to be sure that Dorband had no evidence to rebut the claims of actual fraud and theft. We had exposed the workings of Cohen's larcenous machine in our papers, and Judge Ware had apparently examined them in detail. He had clearly watched the video. Only that could explain his rage, barely restrained by judicial decorum, which revealed itself as a slow detonation proceeding in Judge Ware's consciousness. That suppressed explosion was setting off an even bigger charge of outrage that had slowly accumulated in the judge's mind, fed by all the evidence drawn from our briefs and exhibits — Cohen's lifetime of crime, his liberal use of forgery to take what was not his, the network of phony companies with nonexistent directors, the pipeline of cash, the entire map of Cohen's Big Lie. Though it had all seemed unlikely upon first hearing, we had proven it all, even down to catching Cohen on video stealing bank records.

When Cohen decided to steal the Wells Fargo documents, he blithely staked the last of his personal capital on a wild bet, probably without even thinking about what he was doing. When the camera caught him at his game, he lost everything. After that, Cohen was just a thief, and the judge knew how to deal with thieves.

Judge Ware had been fully primed when he took the bench. He knew all he needed to know about Steven Michael Cohen, and nothing Dorband said had changed his mind. He was now permitting himself to go ballistic. His voice began to rumble like thunder. I turned back toward my crew and gave them the raised-eyebrows look. They returned the same look. It was real. We had arrived on the plain of judgment.

Like the wind that announces the onset of a sudden storm, Judge Ware swept the last of Dorband's arguments aside, and declared that he was ruling in Gary's favor on everything. He was directing NSI to immediately put the registration in Gary's name. He was freezing all Cohen's real estate and monetary assets, and he was going to require Cohen to pay a bond into Court to secure the judgment he intended to levy against him. He would reduce his order to writing during the noon hour, and we could pick it up after lunch. So that Cohen didn't pull any clever tricks before then, he told Dorband to call Cohen immediately and tell him that the freeze order was effective *now*.

The thunder of Judge Ware's voice had barely subsided when Dorband asked whether he was imposing a temporary or a permanent injunction. Judge Ware answered that it was permanent. Dorband then ventured to ask about the trial date. Judge Ware took umbrage at the very notion of a trial, as his response made clear: "Trial? What trial? There is nothing left for a jury to try!"

CHAPTER FORTY-SIX

THE KING IS DEAD, LONG LIVE THE KING

As GARY'S TEAM POURED OUT OF THE COURTHOUSE, victorious and exultant, we tasted the sweetness of complete vindication, and immediate attention from TV news. Gary urged me to step forward to get my share of the acclaim, so he, Wagstaffe and I addressed the cameras in turn. We had lunch at the nearby Spaghetti Company, and frankly, the event felt incongruously ho-hum. Jim, Pam, Gary, Tara, Ana, Sue and I gathered 'round the table and congratulated each on the work, but the true festive feeling that characterizes most courtroom victories was lacking. For one thing, the work was anything but done. After lunch, Wagstaffe and Pam headed back to their office, and I returned to the courthouse.

Although Judge Ware had spoken his order from the bench, warning Dorband to phone Cohen immediately and tell him not to move a dime from his left pocket to his right, this was only a stopgap through the lunch hour. We could pick up the written order at one o'clock. At one o'clock I was at the door of the judge's chambers. I waited a short while until Judge Ware's large, impassive bailiff opened the door and handed me the order.

I read each page eagerly and with amazement. Judge Ware had given us everything. His Order was virtually unchanged from Gary's original wish list, in fact he'd just signed what we gave him, with minor alterations. He had filled in a number where Wagstaffe and Gary left a blank for how much Cohen should pay as a bond to secure his right to proceed to trial. It was $25,000,000. As I examined the Order, the wave of amazement that had engulfed me rose higher, bearing me buoyantly down the hall, down the elevator, and floating, all smiles, past the guards I'd gotten to know over the past year, out the doors, into the bright San Jose afternoon.

The Kinko's across the street from the courthouse became our command post. The first thing I did was get a stack of fax cover sheets, and started faxing the Order to all of the banks and securities houses that held Cohen's assets. I also arranged for immediate filing of the Order in the title records of the Rancho Santa Fe house and the Godinez house.

Gary rented a workstation and started downloading congratulatory e-mails. His cell phone rang constantly, as callers he'd never talked to before in his life interrupted each other to offer congratulations. We had barely finished lunch, and the world knew. Not, of course, the world at large. Not my relatives, like my Aunt Pearl or my brother Aaron; not my fellow lawyers back in Oregon, not my friends and acquaintances. They wouldn't find out until I told them. No, this world that knew all about our victory and that was suddenly clamoring at our door was a world I had never really thought about. It hadn't mattered to me when I was pursuing Sex.Com. I hadn't ever thought about it, but now we had arrived in Cohen's world – the world of online sex.

Although I'd spent nearly two years battling to acquire the crown jewel of Internet pornography, I knew little about the top players, or how they garnered so much loot. I was about to learn that Sex.Com produced extremely high returns on investment for a small number of very wealthy people, and they all wanted to keep those high returns coming. Indeed, as the phone callers made clear, there was nothing they wanted more than to be very nice to the new owners of Sex.Com, and to keep their advertising running without the briefest lapse.

Sex.Com was now our business, and Gary had an idea that seemed logical, but I had always avoided considering. He wanted me to be the lawyer for our company. Things had changed, and he urged me to step into a new role. I objected that I had a lot of discovery left to do to unravel the whole money web, and recover what we could from the wreckage of Cohen's machine.

Leaning forward to emphasize his words, Gary said, "Don't you understand? You don't have to do that anymore!" I could quit working on subpoenas and discovery, trial preparation and all that other stuff. I could leave that for the hired guns—Wagstaffe, Marty Moroski, and Pam Urueta. There was plenty of cash to pay them, and I was needed in the position of General Counsel for Grant Media, LLC.

So we made plans. Plans that ran rough-shod over the year-end holidays. We had to make the scene with a lot of people. People in New York, Toronto and LA, who ran companies with names like Crescent, Orgasm, and New Frontier. We had planned to end our victory by selling the name to the big-time adult media people, whoever they were, but now, as they all came calling, fawning, and obsequious, a different idea took hold. We could do this. We could run Sex.Com. Why not? We were smart, tough, and had proven ourselves in battle.

We were big in porn, and porn was riding the biggest wave in history, the earliest of early adopters of a technology that barely had a name. Suddenly, it seemed the name would have to be Sex.Com. I suspect that this vision had seized the entire porn world simultaneously, giving a big jolt to an industry that, despite its cutting-edge image, is actually dominated by some very old ideas. By unseating Cohen, we had accomplished the largest single power shift the porn world had ever seen. We had also done it in the face of great skepticism from the porn world itself. Ron Levi, Seth Warshavsky, and their pet lawyers Joel Dichter and Katie Diemer, had backed away from the battle, possibly bought off by Cohen with traffic and cash. Gary had turned down deals with other porn magnates, like Serge Birbrair. From the perspective of hindsight, many of the porn players felt as if they had placed their bets badly. The guy that they'd all laughed at as the self-proclaimed "Big Dummy" had turned out to be the Big Winner. Would Gary punish them all by actually converting it into a "woman-friendly" format, as the mainstream press had reported? That idea struck most pornographers as possibly the dumbest idea in the world, like letting your prize horses sit out the Kentucky Derby because you didn't want them to get tired. Quite simply, their world had been turned upside down, and inquiring pornographers wanted to know–what would we be doing with the site? We had them in the palm of our hand.

If this was baseball, we had knocked the ball out of the park, and it was time to take a victory lap of the bases. First base would be the Big Apple, to meet our new webhost and advertising seller, Yishai Hibari, whom Gary had chosen to run the website and collect the advertising wire transfers in exchange for fifteen percent of the take, paid monthly. The fifteen-percent number was considerably less than the proposal offered by Jonathan Silverstein and various others who had approached Gary immediately after the November 27th victory, so it seemed all right to me. Yishai thus received an immediate share in the venture equal to my own, just for being the bagman. Of course if I'd known how to hook up a job like Yishai's, I wouldn't have become a lawyer.

CHAPTER FORTY-SEVEN

WITH FRIENDS LIKE THESE, PART 2

WE MET YISHAI IN A VERY STYLISH, expensive Manhattan bar and restaurant with sky-high prices. He's a handsome Israeli man, partial to dark
suits, and according to Sue Whatley, our ear on the street, the subject of
mafia jokes. Ron Levy seems to take particular pleasure in murmuring
that he never speaks ill of Yishai because he doesn't want to sleep with
the fishes.

The night we arrived, Gary and I were to meet Yishai at a very fancy
restaurant where Gary surprised me by knocking back several large gin
and tonics, while I drank a few beers. Yishai didn't drink alcohol, and
had an apologetic air, as if it were unfortunate that the world forced us
to think about money all the time, but what was there for it? The evening
was pure socializing, and we barely discussed business. He is a classical pianist, and seemed to have a protective attitude toward his wife. We
exchanged a lot of platitudes about family values. When we parted, I felt
like we had gone into business with a very serious man who had favored
me with his most charming aspect. He wore his gentility like a protective
suit for navigating the dark waters of sexual finance.

The next morning, Gary and I walked to a building not far from our
hotel. Yishai met us in an upstairs office where he said they were opening up some new space to accommodate rows of computer desks. In a
large, sparsely furnished conference room, Yishai and two assistants, a
couple of former Mossad guys, gave us a presentation that projected live
feeds from a high-speed Net connection on a big screen. They provided us with detailed statistics about our site that amazed me with their
specificity and abundance. Type-ins were cascading into those magical
six letters like rain into a mountain lake, a lake of pure liquid cash. It was
dizzying. It was exciting. It was partly mine, and everyone acted like I was
a co-owner of a very desirable asset.

But in the midst of the exhilaration, a dark tinge invaded my mind,
and grew deeper as the hours passed surfing the Net on the enormous
browser in Yishai's Manhattan conference room. The big screen shim-
mered with the energy of millions of minds cascading in from everywhere,

colliding with the images and words that populated Sex.Com. From our digital vantage-point, online humanity appeared as a vast throng of eye-balls speeding through a functionally infinite universe of colors, images, text, and video. The statistics Yishai provided showed nearly a million hits daily, sorted by the equivalent price per click being charged to each of the short list of buyers, some of whom were in for $50,000 per month.

The statistics also told a dark story. Although the site was nominally under our control, we were still selling traffic to the same people who had been buying traffic from Cohen, except for Jordan Levinson, whom Gary had insisted on dropping at once, rejecting Yishai's entreaties on his behalf. The largest advertisers were Wired Solutions, Yishai himself, and Ron Levi, who had been buying traffic from Cohen through a straw man when we took over the domain. They were all running the same gross-out contest that had evolved during the Cohen days, a race in which graphic artists competed to find the lowest common denomina-tor of human desire. Was it a fresh face receiving a rain of semen from a rigid penis all over her innocent face, splattering her eyes, and cheeks, matting her lovely young hair with slime? Perhaps it was a short video clip of an anal sex routine accelerated just a bit and pinched into a three-second loop. There were so many ways to say the same thing, and Sex. Com was the only place pornographers could say it to the whole world, without restraint. Yishai believed in Cohen's stupid, direct approach, and feared any attempts to improve on it. Although Ocean Fund press re-leases had once crowed about a website "a thousand pages deep," Co-hen had actually kept the website to one page, with six banners costing fifty-thousand dollars each, and a single row of text links that sold for between six and nine-thousand dollars apiece. The one-page banner-farm format kept the cyber-real estate scarce, and accordingly expensive. Cohen set his rates, then let the industry integrate his charges into their pricing. Levinson said that with Cohen, it was always "his way or the highway." All advertising revenues were paid in advance by wire transfer, and gratefully so. Serious pornographers were happy to pay for the traf-fic, especially those with the graphics skills and large image libraries to deploy the smut wonderlands that took the millennium by storm. Cohen had also given advertisers total freedom to post any picture or text link they thought would score a click, which kept the advertiser's conversion rates high, and ad rates similarly so. You might say that, by combining totally free speech with a completely free market, Cohen had found the sweet spot at the top of the profit pyramid. Certainly Yishai's report, with its short list of big numbers, made it clear that the status quo at Sex.Com was very profitable.

Cohen's version of Sex.Com was popular for another reason that fans of open markets might appreciate—the lack of intrusive government regulations. Cohen had never reported any of his transactions to the IRS, the Treasury Department, or any other agency of government. This leads to the possibility that some of the millions of dollars that Cohen had pumped through the Omnitec account was simply being laundered from various illicit sources, and may not have reflected real advertising revenue. After all, even AOL had to admit to doing hundreds of millions of dollars in "wash" advertising deals that were simply a way to kite checks for astronomical sums. Cohen was always dabbling in ways to inflate his income and skim a profit, and he wouldn't have blushed at the opportunity to launder a few bundles of drug or gun money. This might account for occasional fluctuations in Sex.Com's monthly revenue, like the month in 2000 when Omnitec received a million in deposits, a substantial upward deviation from the standard 400K. So you never know–maybe Cohen really did have some friends in Caracas who were gunrunners–I never went to see.

Even discounting total Sex.Com revenue somewhat for the possibility that Cohen was actively exchanging black money for white, there were plenty of real clicks being sold to pornographers for their conversion value. In those days, before Google had gone into the business of selling clicks, the term "conversions" was heard almost exclusively in porn circles. Conversions, as most every person knows now, are simply sales, cash transfers via credit card for website signups, that in those days usually cost $20 to $30 dollars each before merchant fees. Profit is calculated based on a simple formula, because certain website traffic will convert at an ascertainable rate. Some traffic is utter garbage from a pornographer's viewpoint–converting at low rates, or not at all. The question is, of course, who is doing the clicking? And in the case of people seeking porn-site conversions, how old is that person, and what is their sex? According to Fernando of Wired Solutions, Sex.Com traffic converted at unheard-of rates, suggested to him that the bulk of visitors were young and sexually inexperienced, typing in the most obvious Internet address to find the object of their desires. In the aggregate, they were clicking at the rate of around 200 clicks per second, and converting at rates sometimes as high as one out of fifty – an unheard of rate during a time when conversion rates of one in two-hundred and fifty were considered extremely profitable. Fernando was a corpulent Latino whose face filled with delight when discussing the unbelievable conversion rates he had seen with Sex. Com traffic. It made me quite uneasy.

When we met in New York to formally sign the hosting and commissions deal with Yishai, we discussed ending the gross-out contest still taking place on the page. Since such agreements don't always look right when you put them in writing, we verbally agreed that within thirty days, advertisers would no longer be allowed to display "penetration" or "girls who look underage." We agreed to immediately stop running text links that smacked of criminality or conduct generally acknowledged to be depraved, like incest and bestiality. Aside from these small adjustments, we weren't changing the site at all. We were afraid to scare off advertisers, and since the word on the street was unclear about Gary, we needed to reassure the markets. Yishai wanted to pour a pitcher of ice water on the idea that Sex.Com might become a "woman friendly" site, as we had suggested in our press release and court filings. Haha, very funny! As Steve Sherman had told me during our breakfast meeting—"Get real, this is pornography!" The end result of the meeting with Yishai was that the Cohen format stayed in place. One page of banner ads, a list of advertisers you could count on two hands, and pure profits of at least $400,000 per month. Not a formula you want to tinker with.

Toward the end of the day, Yishai took us to meet his boss, Richard Martino. They talked about how their company, Crescent Communications, was about to buy a midwestern phone company. They took us on a very boring facilities tour, which consisted of views of eight accountants housed like cattle with their computers, calculating all day long. On the way out of our meeting with Richard, Yishai pulled me aside. They would be happy to pay $15,000,000 for the name – half now, the rest in payments.

Back in the hotel room Gary and I were occupying jointly at Yishai's expense, I told Gary that Yishai had offered to buy the domain. He responded as I'd expected, utterly disinterested, and said he was going out. I was alone in New York City. I took a shower. I lay in the tub, letting the numberless drops cascade off my body into the narrow beige porcelain concavity. The hotel tub was small and cramped in the supposedly fancy hotel. Apparently, regardless of how much money we were going to have, Gary would still be extremely parsimonious, and the facilities could still be banal.

But I had a much bigger problem. All the money in the world would not change the fact that I was getting rich on the exploitation and degradation of women. I was very tired, and felt like crying as I lay in the tub, feeling that every drop of water was a click of someone accessing an image of some girl being photographed forever like a captive animal, and some poor sucker's cash rolling down the drain. I felt like the sewer, collecting all those unwanted moments and mistakes made by young, foolish people with basic needs for love and money. I felt for the women and men, embracing each other lovelessly, doing things they'd balk at doing at gunpoint, just for a little cash. I felt like I was riding with my rich friends on an ocean liner floating on a sea of garbage. I lay in the tub a long time, wasting water and listening to it gurgling down the drain.

CHAPTER FORTY-EIGHT

WHAT A FINE CHRISTMAS!

LEAVING NEW YORK, GARY AND I HOPPED A PLANE north to Toronto, crossing into the comparatively relaxed atmosphere of Canadian airports and hotels, where I suddenly realized Gary and I were really keyed-up. I had adopted his habit of walking bent forward, leaning into the wind of the omnipresent opposition, pressing ever onward. Our impatience didn't quicken the slow pace of the Canadian airport clerks, who questioned us mildly and used ball point pens to fill out new airline tickets after they bumped us off our flight for snow up north. It felt like a plot designed to cause the brains of time-conscious Americans like Gary and myself to explode with rage and frustration. Get a printer!

In the Canadian customs waiting area, I practiced relaxing my mind while closely studying a display case of all kinds of stuff you can't import into Canada, like rhino horn, endangered birds, live snakes and other Asians-themed novelties. The display looked like it had been assembled by a seventh-grader for Science Day. It was dull and obvious, but far more interesting than the concrete floors, metallic surfaces and scuffed vinyl of the baggage depot. We were eventually asked to queue up and be subjected to a quick, skeptical eye from an official servant of the Crown, before being admitted to Toronto, the city of snow and concrete.

In the cab from the airport, Gary and I fiddled with our cell phones, answering calls and inflating our self-importance as we rode through the dark. Sue had set us up to meet Dave Vanderpool from Python and Meir Strahlberg of Orgasm and Date.com. We met in their large spacious offices, where racks of caged servers pumped cash in a clean room, and rows of computers awaited the workers who would arrive again tomorrow to optimize and upload sexy pictures to the Net. The layout was more interesting than the stable of accountants Yishai had shown us in New York. We talked about Date.com, and Gary collected kudos for creating Match. com. After getting acquainted, we left the office and walked down quiet, dark streets to an opulent bar with huge ceilings and black floor-to-ceiling wall drapes. Men were smoking cigars and leaning back with exaggerated ease. There were few women anywhere, and none at our table.

I played my role as consigliore to the big man at Sex.Com, and received encouragement for my performance from everyone except Gary, who was noticeably off his feed. But our companions were jolly enough, and while we sat in the opulent, sophisticated lounge, Gary tried to seem interested in the conversation. Sitting back sipping a pint of good, Canadian draft, I contemplated the appearances of our industry colleagues. Demian, who worked for Meir, was devilishly handsome in goth attire, long black curls and a goatee. Dave was a tall, blonde impeccably groomed Northern European sophisticate who looked like he would be comfortable anywhere the elegant are found. Meir's delicate frame was smoothly packaged in preppy clothes. He made eye contact, and used delicate gestures and words when he spoke to me. The three made good company, and seemed to prove that minting money on the Internet needn't turn you into a grim servitor of cash like Yishai or his boss, Richard Martino.

We dined at a large, round table stacked with silver, china, and starched napkins carefully folded into fan-shapes that looked like chickens roosting on our plates. There we sat, five knaves dining like kings, and discussing the electronic skin trade. Demian talked knowledgeably about "content," what pornsites sell, saying more is always better. Orgasm.com offered several hundred thousand images, streaming videos, a silly astrology column that lampooned sun-signs for their sexual foibles, and various other gimmicks. Suffice it to say that having a dirty mind seemed to be an asset in this business, and discussions of the product led to the inevitable conclusion that inducing masturbation among the clientele drove profits. Hence, the slogan for Orgasm.com was "keeping Kleenex in business . . ."

I thought perhaps we'd have some fun with these guys, but Gary's mood went completely sour sometime during dinner, and he decided to go to bed early. If I'd thought about it, I might have deduced that forced breaks in Gary's pharmaceutical regimen, such as those imposed by air travel, might be causing the downturn in his mood that had been evident for the last several days. After Gary left, I headed out to the streets with Meir, Dave and Demian. They teased each other like kids as we navigated the icy sidewalks and heaps of dirty snow. Dave was minding the business, though, and quickly flagged down a cab that we piled into noisily, jostling and joking. The club they'd chosen for our evening entertainment offered up two floors of nubile women gliding about in revealing outfits, and lounging with customers on large couches and chairs. When they weren't working the customers one-on-one, they danced sensually in brass-railed enclosures, like imaginary creatures trapped in bottles of colored light. When the music stopped, they were freed from the spell, and moved about the railed stages, squatting on six-inch heels to collect their tips from the floor, while murmuring thanks with their beautiful mouths and eyes.

Demian made the most of our entrance. The boys were obviously known for their generosity. We all settled down among soft cushions and chatted while various women came up to talk with us and hang out. They even seemed to actually want to talk to us. Given who I was with, I figured they did a certain amount of recruiting here, so the goodwill I felt might be genuine. After engaging in the obligatory good-natured ogling and salacious talk, we settled into a mood of professional relaxation. I chose a golden-skinned Maltese woman with almond-shaped eyes and a lovely smile as my conversation companion. I rarely want anyone but my wife to push her ass in my face, and once I made it clear that she could relax, that I was having a good time just sitting next to someone as pretty as she was, and that my friends were paying the fee for her idleness, she was good with it. I suspect that most exotic dancers have kids, and this young lady fit the mold. We talked about her little boy, and how she enjoyed her work because it allowed her time and money to care for him. I drank several more Canadian beers, and after a couple of hours, the place was closing, so we left. The party broke up on the sidewalk, with Demian taking off by himself to walk home, weaving slightly around the mounds of snow. Meir and Dave flagged down a taxi and dropped me off at the hotel, on the way remarking that in this city, the cops keep an eye on the prostitutes to make sure they're okay.

Back in the hotel room Gary and I were sharing, he snorted and gasped through his fitful dreams. I don't know about now, but in those days, he slept poorly, and while I'm not a light sleeper, it could keep me awake listening to him struggle with basic respiration. But the beer wrapped me in a blanket of oblivion, and when I awoke, it was a new day, and we were on our way back to the States.

From Toronto, our plane drew a great big diagonal line southwest across the continental United States, landing in LA, where we had been invited to attend the Christmas party for New Frontier, the only publicly traded U.S. company dedicated to selling sex online, and trading on the NASDAQ under the symbol NOOF. Gary and I had been talking with Greg Dumas of New Frontier for months, going back to the days when Gary was trolling for bankers to help with legal fees. Of course, like all the other smut dealers, New Frontier hadn't taken us seriously, or responded in any meaningful way to our funding overtures, but hey, that was before the victory. Nowadays, wherever we went, it was all a big chorus of, "*We love* you, Man!" So that's what we'd grown to expect, and why we were here, a couple of days before Christmas, looking for a rented hall near Sunset and Vine. I was on my own turf, and found the location easily in the rental car, but as had become the norm, Gary seemed bored and distracted.

I soon realized that we had been invited to the classic year-end LA company party, where corporate bigwigs and their wives are distributed evenly among the circular banquet tables, rubbing elbows with middle managers in a ritual atmosphere of artificial bonhomie. It was so familiar. We had the Nazi-style bouncers with muscles bulging under their black t-shirts, sporting cropped blonde haircuts and surly faces. There was a spread of shrimp cocktail, a vast array of cheese cubes, veggies with dip, and an open bar. Folks were eating under the bug lights out on a patio, where rented propane heaters dispelled the chill of the ocean breeze blowing up Sunset Boulevard.

I had endured similar events a half-dozen times during my years in the LA lawfirm scene, and immediately sensed that this was going to be one dull evening. My expectations were fulfilled with a vengeance, as Gary and I were virtually ignored in the glow of self-love radiating from the NOOFers. Whether blinded by the glare of the radiant heaters that warmed the outdoor dining area, or simply the glamour of their own splendid empire, not one bigwig did what Gary expected—stop everything, move people aside, and seat him at his table as a guest of honor. Apparently, Greg Dumas had failed to circulate a memo about how to court Gary. Not one person approached with a rapt look to ask him big questions and bestow their admiration.

As the evening crushed down on us, I absorbed the poignant absurdity. New Frontier had actually outdone itself with the music, supplementing the DJ's sonic output with what has now become a commonplace, but was then rather unique—a handsome, energetic male dancer, his naked upper body toned by the southern sun, his lower body swathed in an Indian-style wrap, feet as bare as if he had been performing on Venice Beach. He was beating a big conga drum, dancing, singing along to the recorded music, his face shining with ecstasy. He was like an ad for health, youth, beauty, and celebration.

A throng of office-help swirled below the bare-chested dance-leader. The messenger boys and photocopy guys were outdoing themselves in their black suits, deploying clichéd male dance postures to ensnare the skinny LA women who are only magnetized by moves they've seen a thousand times before. The event inverted class relations for one night, during which the subordinates demonstrate how much they enjoy the event, in contrast with their bosses, who are so stiff they never make it out to the dance floor, or just take a few turns for the sake of the night. Their uptight asses shake weakly as their silly smiles say it's all good fun, the boss can never dance—that's not how it works—and everybody's dignity survives intact.

I sat on a thumping speaker above the dancing crowd watching Gary from a distance. I'd left him hounding a couple of New Frontier execs about "Where's my escort?" Looking around the room at the abundance of top-shelf booty, I could understand Gary's take on the scene. I don't think he seriously meant he expected an escort–he hadn't asked for one in Toronto, where the service could've been easily and lawfully provided. He was just ribbing the self-stuck, ignorant NOOFers—"Isn't this a sex company? Aren't we in LA, ground zero for sex and money? Isn't it Christmas? Don't I own Sex.Com? Where are my presents?"

Any serious hopes for a linkup between New Frontier and Sex.Com was doomed that night. Some weeks later, I heard from Gary that New Frontier had offered to buy Sex.Com for three times yearly revenue in stock, approximately $24,000,000. Since New Frontier rose markedly in 2001, this would have been a nice deal, but if the company really had any interest in courting Gary, it wasn't visible that night. Too bad–New Frontier had legitimacy, and even though it had over fifteen-thousand domain names, Sex.Com had better web-traffic, and much higher conversion rates. New Frontier was also a public company with relatively transparent finances and big contracts to supply adult cable-TV programming. Cross-marketing through Sex.Com would have given them an instantly recognizable brand in an industry where aside from Playboy and Hustler, brands don't matter. Sex.Com, with its unforgettable six letters and Internet cachet, could have become the third most recognizable name in the minds of sexually curious men everywhere. My old friend Steve Marshank strongly advised me to make this deal happen, and I didn't listen. But as Steve Cohen was fond of saying, "If wishes and buts were apples and nuts, Oh, what a fine Christmas we'd have."

CHAPTER FORTY-NINE

"S" IS FOR "SEND"

FROM L.A. WE RETURNED TO SAN FRANCISCO to face an inevitable, tension-filled exchange. It had been nearly a month since we got control of Sex.Com and with the assistance of Richard Idell, Gary had formed Grant Media, LLC and established a bank account into which Yishai had already deposited $385,000. Gary had been sitting on a bill for eight-hundred and fifty hours worth of legal work I had done on credit, since around July of 2000, when Gary's money got scarce, and what he had went to costs and Wagstaffe's firm. I hadn't said a word about the money since November 27th, so when we got back to Gary's new house on Third Street, I had to raise the issue.

I only had about a four-hour layover in the bay area before my flight left for Oregon, so the exchange was time-pressured. After we got back from the airport, I sat down with Gary in his bedroom, amid the chaos of jumbled bed clothes, heaps of clothing and the usual snowfall of papers covering his battered gray desk. I sat on the bed, and Gary sat on his office chair while I explained that we needed to do our 15% split now, and I wanted to be paid $10,000 in costs that I'd advanced. Also, before we won the name, Gary had said that we would both have signature authority on the account. It was time to give me signature authority. Gary's lips became tight, as he shook his head and said, "No."

Gary said before we figured my cut, I should pay him back for all the money he'd paid Wagstaffe and other lawyers to help with the case. I figured I owed him 15% of that expense, but he didn't agree, and said I owed him all of Wagstaffe's fees, several hundred thousand dollars. Our written agreement didn't say who would pay if Gary hired more lawyers, so we had a bit of a problem, but I couldn't wait to resolve it. We reached a temporary resolution by agreeing we'd leave $85,000 in the account, and divide the remaining $300,000 between us, with me receiving $45,000, fifteen percent of 300K. My unpaid hourly fees would wait, and so would Gary's claim for reimbursement of Wagstaffe's fees.

I waited outside Redwood Bank on Montgomery Street in Gary's car while he wire transferred the forty-five thousand to my account. When he got back he gave me the pink receipt for the wire transfer. I was much relieved and thanked him for the payment. The atmosphere between us was troubled as he drove me back to the airport. In the familiar atmosphere of the Crab Pot restaurant on the SFO departure level, I reflected on my situation, and ate a crab sandwich on white drenched with Tabasco sauce, preceded by a bowl of clam chowder. A week's worth of tension had built up inside me, so I had an oversize glass of beer, then another. Watching the airliners and service vehicles prowling the tarmac outside the restaurant windows, taking passing notice of the TV news on the screens behind the bar, I encouraged myself to relax, but it was a tough sell.

When I got back to Oregon, I was able to pay some bills, and began considering the process of closing down my law practice to take a job as house counsel for Sex.Com. The more I thought about it, the less I liked the idea. The meeting with Yishai and the look of the website scared me. Word was getting around among the lawyers in town that I had won the Sex.Com case. Sooner or later it was going to be discovered by one of the enemies you make in some profusion when you practice law in a rural area. Some lawyer might report it to the Oregon State Bar and make an ethics complaint, saying that owning an adult website that displayed free fuck movies without the barest age-verification requirement, was conduct "likely to expose the legal profession to disrepute." Money comes and goes, I realized, but you can be a lawyer your whole life, and as I now knew more clearly than ever, a lawyer can spin straw into gold, given the right opportunity.

So I started writing Gary an e-mail which began with "Thanks for the offer of a job," and ended three pages later after a long discussion of a lot of my internal gripes about his behavior. I didn't plan on sending it right away. I'd written at least a half-dozen e-mails that I'd never sent to Gary, venting my frustrations first, then adopting a more thoughtful approach after considered reflection. I had planned to do the same thing with this one—get it off my chest, then come back to it and say only the important, essential stuff. I usually composed large documents in Word, and without thinking about it, I had written the whole thing in Outlook Express. After venting for I while, I went to do a shortcut save, and ZIP! The email was gone. It went. Gary had it. Oh SHIT. In Word, CTRL-S means SAVE. The CTRL key is right next to the ALT key, which was what I hit, and in Outlook Express, "ALT-S" means "SEND."

CHAPTER FIFTY

EL DORADO

"In El Dorado-town there is a great bullfighter.
His hair is red as blood,
His eyes are screamin' blue.
And when the gate goes up,
The crowd gets so excited.
Then he comes dancin' out,
Dressed in gold lame'.
He kills the bull
And lives another day."

Neil Young, *Eldorado*

IN ARIZONA, THE POWER OF PRECIOUS METAL has shaped the people and the land. My mother grew up in a town called Morenci, that once had the world's largest open pit copper mine. We went there only once. The town was a big hole in the ground, with tiny trucks maneuvering down a spiraling road into a huge, flat pit. We drove past the few buildings that lined the perimeter road ringing the enormous hole. I asked my mom where her house was, and she gestured toward the center of the gaping chasm, laughingly responding with only a single phrase, "Oh, it was out there, honey." We never discussed it again.

People have seen mirages of great wealth in the desert. As a child I learned of Pizarro, who went seeking a utopia and ended by kidnapping the Inca God-King and ransoming him back to his people for a roomful of gold. After accepting the gold, Pizarro killed the Inca king anyway, ending the life of a man known to his people as "The Son of the Sun." Pizarro himself was murdered a few years later by his co-venturers, who thought, heaven knows why, that he was too greedy. I heard other tales of gold, like the story of the Lost Dutchman Mine in the Superstition Mountains east of Phoenix and Mesa, where a goodly number of folks have died inserting their lives into a puzzle of their own making.

I was most affected by The Treasure of the Sierra Madre, by B. Traven. It was the first novel I ever read, at the tender age of four, and my unforeseen choice of reading material caused some concern among the grownups. The cover of the paperback edition I'd found on my father's bookshelf showed a gang of grizzled miners wearing clothing worn out from hard labor, battling each other amid the ruins of their mining camp, each one clutching a gun and a bag of gold. From rents in several of the bags, precious gold spilled in long thin triangles. As I read the story and understood the plot, it broke my heart to see the bright dust piling up in mounds on the desert soil. The men had extracted it through months of backbreaking labor that had, nevertheless, been filled with the joy of mutual effort. I wanted to end the madness that had caused these men, flush with the fruits of their labors, to unleash hatred and violence upon each other, when all they had to do was share. I wanted to stop the gold from spilling on the ground, or catch at least a little of it in my own cup. Perhaps I was pained so deeply by the story because of that very love for gold that destroyed the miners in B. Traven's book.

Like a poisoned arrow, my email went straight to Gary's heart. He was on the phone to me within seconds. It was not the sort of thing he liked to receive. I did not know what to tell him except that I hadn't intended to send it, and argued that the contents were not that inflammatory after all. In truth, I had somehow obscured from myself how gravely I had injured myself. A bizarre twist of fate had revealed me out of uniform, less than perfectly loyal in spirit. I now have no clear memory of that time period, when the magic I was handling exploded in my face. I only know that I went on, because the damage had been done and the only way was forward.

There were two dedicated intercessors–Sue Whatley and Phil Father, who now held a nominal two percent interest in Sex.Com, Gary's gift to Phil for being his partner in Kremen, Father & Partners (there were no partners). It now seemed like a good thing I had decided to attend the Internext trade show in Vegas during the dawning days of January 2001. At first I thought I'd skip it, and leave it to Gary, Sue, and Phil. But after hanging out with the Python and Orgasm people, and spending quality time with Yishai, I thought perhaps I should show my face at the trade show.

Gary had given Sue Whatley the job of exploring the big players in the online porn business. She had identified the usual suspects–Luke Ford, the gossip columnist, Ron Levy, the King of CyberErotica, Jonathan

Silverstein, a perennial player, Serge Birbrair, and various others. The go-ings-on at Internext were apparently somewhat risqué, or so I was lead to believe, which is why I at first thought it would be more lawyerly to not attend. When I changed my mind, and decided to go, Gary was grumpy about it, and said he would *allow* me to come. And that had been before he got my draft email. Now that Microsoft Outlook Express had spilled the beans about my discontent with the new regime, Gary simmered on medium high all the time. He ignored my emails or replied so tersely it was clear he was freezing me out. Still, I figured I'd make the trip, and Sue rearranged our flight and room plans easily. Gary and Phil had booked rooms at the Hard Rock Hotel, where ostensibly there were more chicks. Sue and I would share a suite at the Venetian, the convention venue.

So there I was, in the lobby of the Venetian Hotel and Casino, with its huge, curving portico, and doormen in pseudo-Italian outfits, equipped with wireless mikes that enabled some of them to sing operatic airs while hailing cabs. It was all dissonant and dazzling, in that offhand way Ve-gas has of jumbling megalithic glitter into a supposedly cool thing—the Strip! In this glamorous environment, Sue and I were short on glitz. A tall woman, Sue wore big, black, platform-soled boots, and concealed her entire person under a full-length pink flannel coat that looked a lot like a housecoat. Wearing Dan Post boots, black Levis, and a tired leather motorcycle jacket, I didn't look like I needed to change companions. She was dowdy and I was scruffy. We were perfect for each other. As we stood in the long line snaking up to the desk, we observed crowds of young men in leather sport-coats, wearing jewelry, occasionally looking up from absorption in their cell-phone conversation to hail the person they were talking to. *They* seemed to be there for "the Show," as industry-types refer to the yearly Internext bash. There were geeky types, gothish people, and occasional gaggles of chicks who looked like they might be passing out literature or adorning a trade-show booth.

Sue and I checked into the room, which wasn't a suite, but was a split-level big enough to appease my desire for a small slice of luxury. After freshening up, we headed back downstairs to face my first post-email meeting with Gary. Extremely stressed is how I would describe my condi-tion. On the elevator ride to the casino floor, a young man and woman, both impeccably attired, were going down with their bags. The woman was a breathtaking brunette around twenty-four, with hair like chestnut-colored silk falling to well below her shoulders. The young man had sandy brown hair, wore clothing that was casually high-class, and looked like he belonged behind the wheel of a Porsche.

The brunette asked us "Checking in?"

"Yep," I answered, with a smile.

With a slightly rueful expression, she said, "We're checking out." She paused, then supplemented this with an explanation, "We've been here a long time." Silence. The gentleman was reasonably handsome, but seemed drained of virility. What was this sad story all about? A dentist who had left wife and kids, being jerked back to reality? An oil scion who'd just run through his trust fund, responding to a warning call from his accountant? Something had turned out badly, probably at the gaming tables. The elevator doors opened, and the sounds of the casino flooded in – batteries of slot machines chiming out the promise of abundant returns for those eager to achieve the unlikely goal of instant riches. We crossed the gaming floor to the Grand Lux Restaurant, where Gary and Phil were waiting. On the way, we saw scores of the young industry players dressed identically in black-on-black, leaning against craps and roulette tables, looking slightly bored with what they hoped seemed like big bets.

Inside the Grand Lux, we found Gary and Phil in a booth. Phil rose to meet us solicitously, while Gary remained seated, his clenched right fist planted firmly on a hardcopy of my excessively candid email. He had grown a goatee, and someone had joined it to a comb-over that accentuated his bald spot. He looked like maybe he had hired a stylist, so I complimented him on the look. He responded with an acid smile that suggested I did not mean it. Shallow breaths heaved his shoulders, as if stoking a fire in his chest. In the booth that seated four, I sat diagonally to Gary, maximizing the available distance between us, in an effort to avoid spontaneous combustion.

Into this situation, Sue and Phil maneuvered expertly like a couple of bomb squad vehicles covered with blast cushions, spraying foam everywhere. Both were extremely obsequious to both Gary and myself. Phil asked me to reconsider my decision not to join the company as an employee, which was of course flattering, because I wasn't sure Gary wanted me as a Grant Media employee, anyway. It seemed that Phil had prepared the ground well, though, because he was focused on getting me back into the company. I had to be okay with that, because I was sure Gary would not make it easy for an absentee partner. Within twenty minutes, the atmosphere had cooled considerably. The igneous heat that had suffused Gary's body retreated into a tiny point of nuclear heat, gleaming in the recesses of his eyes. In my heart, I fervently hoped that I could withdraw the sudden mis-step that had abruptly landed me on the wrong side of the Rubicon.

We finished our dinner, and with rising spirits, headed up to our room for more refreshments. We were putting the past behind us, and Sue was now in control of our agenda. The first stop. she informed us, was Yishai's party, on the upper level in a white-tablecloth Italian restaurant Yishai had rented at a reputed cost of $50,000. Not bad for a business expense, and less than a month of his share of Sex.Com revenue. It was so nice knowing we were helping him stay afloat. As Gary and I strode through the Venetian mall under the big, fake sky they've painted on the ceiling, past the landlocked gondoliers in their marble-lined canals, he threw his arm around me and looked into my eyes, enthusing, unbelievably, "Isn't this great?" To which I was only able to agree. Hoo-ya! We were team Sex.com.

Yishai's party was just like Yishai—so upscale and lavish that you could mistake the guests for actual rich people. Polished silverware, white table cloths, spreads of higher-quality fare, and plenty of good-quality wine and champagne. It was not much of a surprise to see Joel Dichter. But when my eyes focused on his conversation partner, and I realized he was talking to Katie Diemer, it was *dejavu* all over again. Since they were the only people I knew there, I said hi to Joel and Katie. Joel seemed amused at my presence at the party, and Katie said, "Well, this must be quite a feather in your cap." Ah yes, the feather in my cap. I had almost forgotten about it, worried as I was about the color of the cap itself, which I was certain had started out white, but was looking increasingly grey, or even darker. I acknowledged her compliment and took my leave of the compromised pair.

Then came another bizarre exchange, as our host Yishai importuned me by seeking amnesty on behalf of Jordan Levinson, Cohen's Sex.Com bagman. Jordan, who had been scarfing up a percentage of advertising sales, was blameless, Yishai explained. Hardly. I knew Jordan was one of the younger members of a family of seasoned fraudsters with their roots in phone-sex (euphemistically called "audiotext" in the industry) and phone-fraud. His uncle, I believe, was one of the celebrated rate-goug-ers at Crown Communications, a company that the FTC had taken down a few years back. I wanted to go to the bathroom and see if someone had written "DUMBASS" on my forehead, because why would I want to keep doing business with Cohen's confederate? Nevertheless, Jordan now stood before me, impeccably garbed in black-on-black, beseech-ing me to please understand that he had never been in sympathy with Cohen, and *really wanted* to keep buying traffic. Jordan had been buy-ing less than $10,000 per month of traffic through small text links that reputedly converted at a very high rate, so there was plenty of money still on the branch for him, waiting to be plucked, even though he was al-ready stuffed with stolen Sex.Com money. He asked me to please not sue him. I was disoriented. Yishai was our partner now, and being a turncoat seemed to be the way of things around him. I looked around. Where was Gary? Sue sidled up to tell me that Gary was, at this very moment, telling Katie Diemer that he would sue her. Accordingly, the fight with Levinson would still be on as well. Levinson's peace overtures were poorly timed, and left me feeling as confused as a field commander receiving a call that should have been routed to the spy guys.

I felt completely out of place wearing a tattered motorcycle jacket amongst all these well-dressed desperadoes. I stood alone, looking list-lessly at the little round tables covered with wineglasses and plates bear-ing abandoned wedges of brie, cut veggies, and fractured water crackers. I felt like I had lost my sleek profile. My black jeans were crumpling down, bagging about the knees, and the heels of my boots felt big and heavy. Gary was still sporting the rumpled sweatshirt that gave him his Michelin Man profile, but it wasn't radiating any Silicon Valley geek cachet. It just looked like he was cheap and clueless, especially with the new hairdo and goatee. Sue was humbly moving about in the midst of all the refined vampires with downcast eyes. Christ, I thought, Gary should have bought her a coat. Phil Father was elegant in his own black-on-black outfit, but was obviously just window dressing. I had to face it—in this crowd, the Sex.Com crew was *nikulturni*. The experience must have depressed Gary, too, because when we left, he and Phil headed back to the Hardrock Café, ostensibly to look for chicks.

As night turned to morning in the sunless caverns of the Venetian,

I stuck with Sue, whose ever-accommodating shy smile, knowing eyes, blond curls, baby-like features, and throaty laugh increasingly reminded me how nice big German girls can look. She was playing a lowbrow, supersized ingénue, and managing to draw more favorable attention than I would have expected. She was blossoming in the scene, making connections in person with people she'd been gabbing with for months on the Net. She didn't look like a model, which was a plus, because we avoided awkward exchanges and were able to answer inquiries by jointly presenting ourselves as the Sex.Com lawyers. Besides which, she was comfortable in an environment where sex, sex toys, fetishes, bestiality, and other marginal subjects fed bottom line. Sue was quickly becoming one of the boys, mixing easily with important players, and I was very thankful for her knowledge of the business, about which I was still fundamentally clueless.

Industry insiders usually turned adoring when we said we were the Sex.Com lawyers who had beheaded Cohen, the old dragon. It had been an upset victory, because no one in the industry thought Gary had a chance of knocking Cohen off the throne. Paul Wolfowitz should've been there to see what it's like to be received as liberators, because we were the toast of the night. We were receiving accolades for making the world safe for ordinary, decent smut peddlers. I got a sloppy kiss from a porn star. We were the new face of Sex.Com, and a kinder, gentler face it seemed, no doubt, as long as you were looking at me or Sue.

Left to ourselves, Sue and I wandered through hotel lobbies, across gambling floors, into restaurants and bars, collecting kudos, networking and passing out Sex.com business cards that Tara had printed for us back in Oregon. They had vintage erotica pictures on them and looked humorous and light, but a little ambiguous. Eventually we made it back to our room and turned in for the night. The next morning, Sue had arranged a big meeting with Ron Levy, at his request. We were supposed to hook up with Ron's people on the show floor for directions.

The next morning, Sue and I were up, taking care of business. The trade show exhibition floor was enormous. About three hundred booths vied for attention in a room big enough to store a couple of jumbo jets. Above us hung thirty foot banners displaying enhanced blondes overprinted with logos in blue, pink, yellow and silver rendered in visual perfection with high-tech printing. Website logos were everywhere, notable for the extreme obviousness of their appeal — "Hardcoremoney" — "Silvercash. com" — "Cyber Erotica" — "Porn Profits" – "Babenet" — all rendered in bright colors and dynamic characters. The air was shimmering with skin tones, bright colors and metallic sheen. Precise, crisp images of idealized females are the product, and they received pride of place at this exhibition.

Visually, the scene was titillating, but the audio track was tedious. The theme music for the sex industry is a blend of featureless beats that demonstrates disrespect for all legitimate musical forms. At the Cyber-Erotica booth, you couldn't get away from the tired sounds, because Ron had hired a half-dozen slightly past-prime Barbies to bump and grind to the rhythmic dreck that oozed from banks of black loudspeakers. The exhibition of tired hip-swiveling, listless shoulder-rotation, arrogant chin-pointing, and bored pouting would sap anyone's enthusiasm for the sex business. Where, I wondered, had they found these women? They lacked funk, spunk and everything else that would have enlivened their presentation of God's basic handiwork. No wonder Viagra was so much in demand.

The desultory dancers adorning the CyberErotica booth were appropriate, though, because Ron Levy is oblivious to everything about sex except its ability to generate conversions. Call it professional focus. And Ron had a proposal he wanted to present to Gary in the secluded comfort of his hotel room. We approached a member of the scurrying posse of Ron-worshipers clustered around his trade show booth, the largest on the floor. We met Ron's Canadian lawyer, and he gave us the room number and directions to Ron's extremely expensive room, which was off in some exclusive wing of the hotel. Ron was ready, so I called Gary and Phil to request their presence at the Venetian. Phil said he'd be getting Gary moving, but it might be tough.

I think Phil had to use a winch or other device to get Gary out of bed, because he looked about as bad as he did when Dorband asked him if he ever took drugs that might affect his memory. Whatever he'd ingested, it seemed to have obliterated all memories, going back to childhood. I felt his pain. He could barely talk, and I was sure that whatever he was hearing, he wasn't understanding. He looked like a sick dog that might have to be put down, because it was just suffering too much. Gary had always gotten sweaty palms when he thought how it would go with Ron. It was by now part of the lore of the case that Ron had invested $150,000 in Joel Dichter's representation of Gary. Rumor had it that Ron felt some sense of entitlement based on that investment, even though Gary had fired Dichter and Diemer years before, declaring the whole deal a dead letter.

I wasn't worried at all. We owned Sex.Com. If Ron wanted to make a deal, we could evaluate his offer just like Yishai's or NOOF's or anybody else's. It would have been nice to have Gary's brain operational that morning, but for the moment, it wasn't taking calls. Gary was going where he was led, up the elevator and down the long halls of the Venetian to the wide double doors of a suite that Sue told us Ron was renting for $4,500 per night.

Admitted to the suite by a black-T-shirted CyberErotica servitor, we walked into a large white room where Ron was sitting at the head of a conference table a short walk from the entryway. Two packs of Marlboro Lights were stacked to his left, and he occasionally adjusted their position with his left hand, squaring them up parallel with the edge of the large, white table. We sat at a comfortable distance from the great man, Gary and Phil on one side, Sue and I on the other. After getting Gary's approval in the form of a light nod, I took over as the speaker for Sex.Com. This wasn't difficult, because Ron made what seemed like a reasonable proposal – CyberErotica would license the Sex.Com name for $400,000 per month, and would pay us 40% of all the money over that amount that CE brought in from the website. It was a one-year deal, renewable. Ron had no paperwork to review, but if we were interested, he'd have his lawyer write it up. I said sure, write it up, and with that, the interview was over. We finished our coffee — way too strong — and were back out in the hall. For me, it was just one more experience with astronomical numbers and blasé pornographers. I was getting used to this. Gary, relieved simply to have a stressful meeting behind him, caught a cab back to the Hard Rock with Phil.

I accompanied Sue out to the front of the Venetian so she could have a smoke, and there we met a balding, sixty-ish English guy, puffing his unfiltered cigarette with earnest enjoyment. Sue introduced the fellow, who was dressed as unstylishly as we were. His name was Mike Sweet, aka, "The Dirty Old Man," a Canadian porn star. Mike had the laconic style of a fellow who has no real point of connection with the social aspect of the industry, claims he knows zip about chicks, money transfer, etcetera. His partner, Steve Sweet, he said, had brought him to Vegas for the show. He didn't know what it was about, didn't care. Mike droned on stylishly, exuding grandfatherly amusement for the whole affair. Within six months, I would be working for Mike, and I would be privy to his true name, his true passions and just how difficult a job it is to be an aging porn star. Mike has a fascination with military history, and an extensive knowledge of many of the more frightening arts of persuasion. He has, on occasion, paid pain-resistant models one-dollar-per needle-insertion. That's Canadian dollars. The top earner took home $200 bucks. When I got to know him, Mike became scary—not like Yishai, or Ron, or Gary. Scary in his own way, because his mind went into places that I feared I was never meant to go. But at the time, he seemed like a sweet old porno grandpa, involved in some kind of bizarre and profitable family enterprise.

At a lunch meeting later that day, Sue and I met with Fernando, Ben and Mike from Wired Solutions, which had been buying $150,000 of traffic from Cohen's Sex.Com and had maintained that level of buying after Gary took over. These were, by definition, customers, so we wanted to treat them well, and show an interest in their business. Fernando was a moderately obese young man of Latino ancestry, who at that time owned a place in Barbados, which he said got very claustrophobic after a few days. Ben was a Massachusetts prep with a yen for ecstasy that some said might be available from a certain blonde Sex.Com team member. He and Sue made fast friends. I hit it off with Mike, a wiry techie who worked at the Wired Solutions headquarters in Santa Fe. He had a lot of questions about the lawsuit we'd just won, and volunteered plenty of information about Wired's business. Fernando gushed about the conversion rates for Sex.Com "type-ins," clicks that originated from direct requests for the domain, typed directly into the address bar of the surfer's web browser. Unlike search engine clicks, Fernando explained, type-ins to Sex.Com were coming from very young people, who had just figured out how to navigate using a web browser, and were therefore highly susceptible to backbrain stimulation induced by the sexual imagery flashing on the website twenty-four hours of every worldwide day. Suddenly, I started to worry all over again about the ethics of the present condition of the website. It was looking smarter and smarter to consider a partnership with some established player to manage Sex.Com, someone other than

Yishai and Richard Martino, perhaps like Ron or Fernando, who knew how to make a bundle without getting in trouble. I wished that Gary were there to hear some of these things, so we could discuss them together, but I was beginning to intuit that Gary didn't want to be my partner in this business.

After meeting with the Wired Solutions guys, Sue and I cruised the showroom floor one last time. Sue was assiduous in collecting all the VIP passes and free drink cards we would need to assume our properly exalted place in the hierarchy of porn magnates during the last night's blowout. As it winds down, the three-day sextravaganza debouches into a swirling vortex of obscene self-love, the aptly named "Pimp and Ho Ball." Staged in a huge ballroom, powered by expensive light shows and computerized beats, populated with skinny young men and hired women, the scene is well lubricated with a healthy injection of free drinks, available of course to those with free drink cards. I had a pocketful that Sue had provided, and stuck to a diet of cranberry vodkas and the occasional Red Bull.

The real fun at the Pimp and Ho Ball isn't the music, the dancing, the achievement awards for excellence in smut distribution, or the drably scripted stage patter between the porn industry leaders and the crowd of sycophantic webmasters. The fun is about getting things sorted by pecking order. There are three kinds of free tickets given out. The regular ticket will get you in the door. A VIP ticket will get you up one set of stairs. A special VIP ticket will get you to the third floor balcony area, where private rooms have been rented by the majors. And in an extremely elevated location, were no one gets in without an invitation from a true skin-trade tycoon, there is a room where it is rumored you can smoke a joint with Ron. But Sue was the only Sex.Commer to allegedly get into that room, and it's still a rumor to me.

That night, I spent most of my time with Ben, the Wired Solutions ecstasy-head, who seemed to enjoy my company, after Gary drifted away and Sue went looking for Ron's secret hideaway. Up in a private room I met the most intelligent, genuinely attractive woman I'd discovered at the show–Jamie Sweet. She was Steve Sweet's girlfriend, and therefore obscurely related to Mike Sweet, aka The Dirty Old Man. Jamie and Steve were dressed in pajamas, and were fun and easy to talk to. It's strangely cosmopolitan to stand, casually talking with a woman in her pajamas, while leaning against a bar where an anatomically correct, flesh-colored simulacrum of a female ass has two Corona bottles stuck into it, one protruding from the simulated anus, the other from the snug, rubber vagina. I delicately removed the beverage containers from the sex toy as an act of politeness, which Jamie acknowledged with a little laugh. We had a nice chat about sexual freedom and the liberating power of erotica. She introduced me to Steve, over six feet, probably a hundred and eighty pounds, dressed in a leopard print bathrobe and silk pajamas. Steve's shark-like grin, military-style buzzcut, and impressive build bespoke a powerful man with abundant personal charisma and ready access to large sums. I liked him immediately, although I knew nothing about him. He briefly expressed admiration for my litigation prowess, then left me to chat with Jamie, which I kept right on doing for the next half-hour, until Ben and I decided to drift on to some other place.

I found Sue, who had been up in the ganja den with Ron, so she said. We parted company with Ben, who went in quest of a new source of serotonin to heal his overstimulated dopamine receptors. The hours drained away like dark water, leaving us on the faintly brightening shores of a Las Vegas dawn. Susanne and I had checked out of our hotel already, because in some sort of half-assed cost-saving, Gary had only booked his room for the last night. So on the last night of the fun, Sue and I were the homeless Sex.Commers. My plane was leaving sometime that morning, so with our luggage in tow, we caught a cab to the Hard Rock Hotel, there to enjoy what remained of Gary's meager hospitality.

Gary's room at the Hard Rock was much smaller than what Sue and I had at the Venetian. She and I showed up with our luggage at around 4:30 in the morning. Gary was wadded up in the bedclothes like a hundred-and-ninety-pound infant with a comb-over. He looked tortured. Phil was exhausted, and offered us the couch and mini bar. My boss, my partner, my client, snored, snorted and shifted his body repeatedly in the room, which was slowly brightening.

I stood on the balcony and looked toward the bright lights of the Vegas Strip. My brain felt tenderized from lack of sleep and all of the yelling I had done to make myself heard while conversing in smoke-filled rooms drowned in hip-hop noise. The lights ringing the profiles of the hotels and casinos seemed to shimmer with beauty, with hope. In the dusty dawn, the colored lights twinkled brightly in a world where I had membership in the upper crust of low occupations.

The six-letter mantra that had fueled my obsession for nearly two years was still overbearing in my mind, but now, it seemed to exude fulfillment. It was the gleaming sun of morning that was about to rise over the summertime of my life. I had made it. I had done something in the world of money, power, and influence. I had mounted the heights. Standing in my heavy boots, which I hadn't removed from my feet in at least twenty hours, I felt well able to move ahead into the new world I had helped to conquer. I would get on with some of the white hat stuff. We would change Sex.Com for the better.

As I turned these thoughts over in my mind, they began to turn me over. I felt divorced from the earth as persistent thoughts of self-importance lifted my spirits. Nevertheless, after three days of outshining Gary with the people who were responsible for making Sex.Com valuable, I had a strange presentiment. As glamorous as it was to be a warrior, I might be a liability in time of peace.

Looking out over the Vegas skyline, hearing Gary thrashing his sheets in an effort to find a niche of unconsciousness in which to stuff his mind, I remembered the way the fire in his eyes had retreated, but not disappeared. Taking refuge in sleep and intoxication, he had hidden from me ever since the brief reconciliation in the Grand Lux. Hearing him snort and convulse his way through fitful dreams, it did not, frankly, look good for me. I knew what I dared not tell myself. Gary had come to mistrust me. His pain was breeding inside him, darkening his mind with suspicion, jealousy and hatred. He suspected me because I'd expressed secret thoughts. He was jealous of me because I had a wife, kids, a house, and now, money too. He hated me because I was starting to enjoy my new position as a principal in Sex.Com, and he hadn't approved my ascent to that role.

Whether it was preordained or not, I knew from that moment forward that soon we would be adversaries. Lying there, lost in the darkness of a fitful sleep, Gary was hiding from his power, from the terrifying adulation of an amoral crowd, but even as he did, the power of Sex.Com was filling him up like water fills a hollow space underground. The power of Sex.Com had no love for me or anyone. No longer the slave girl whom we had liberated, she now appeared like the whore of Babylon, bestower of all earthly pleasures, enslaver of her devotees. She had Gary completely in her power, and was seducing him utterly with her most powerful, one-syllable mantra, the mantra known only to one person, now pounding away in Gary's heart over and over again – mine... mine... mine... and every now and then... *all* mine.

The sun was rising on a new world, filled with gold and its power. It was my first morning in El Dorado. Outwardly dressed in crumpled black clothes, stinking with cigarette smoke, inwardly I looked up to behold a golden sun at its zenith, blazing in a cobalt sky. I heard the crowd's cheer as the barred gate across the arena slowly rose. The bull charged through the gate on pounding hooves, tossed his horns this way and that, then found me. When the bull charges, I remembered, the bullfighter stands his ground. The bull, not the man, must move. The bull trotted up to face me from a near distance. He lowered his head, scuffed the sand, and looked up at me. I saw the red coals hidden deep in eyes that did not recognize me. I gripped my sword and planted my feet.

CHAPTER FIFTY-ONE

ROAD TO RUIN

AS I WALKED OUT OF THE HARD ROCK HOTEL to find a cab, the sun rose full above the eastern horizon, and the hard light scrubbed the glitter off the town. I saw the cheap stucco walls, potted oases, empty parking lots and ubiquitous billboards offering big meals, big payouts, and big entertainment. After three days of being pummeled by boring beats in smoky atmospheres flowing with free drinks, I was ready for home. As the cab rolled down sun-scoured avenues, the driver reminisced in generalities. He began with, "People in this town..." and concluded with, "They're all into that Ecstasy." To which I responded, "Tell me about it!"

After Vegas, communications with Gary decayed, and black tension seeped into my life. Wagstaffe's office continued to report to me diligently, informing me about trial preparation in deferential letters. On the surface, I was cocksure and optimistic about the future, planning to continue meeting with prospective partners and helping Gary sort through their proposals. On the surface, Gary and Phil sent me e-mails about various business opportunities with industry players, soliciting my remarks. Under the surface there was little sense of interest on their part, and I felt like I was on suspension.

After Vegas, I promptly went looking for trouble and found it. I became obsessed with changing the look of Sex.Com. Everyday I checked the website to see if the changes we had agreed on back in New York had been made yet. And every day I found the same old gross-out contest. I started emailing and calling Yishai every other day or so, to ask him why the banners were still showing all the radically distasteful shit that they had always been showing. I called Wired Solutions and asked why their ads were still so raunchy–hadn't Yishai told them to tune it back? They told me that Yishai had said it to them, but his own banners were still as nasty as ever, so they couldn't afford to back off the hardcore while he was still pushing it.

Feeling that I'd been saddled with this relationship with Yishai, I started insisting in emails to Gary that he had breached his promise to control the appearance of the website, and demanding that we give

Yishai the required thirty-day notice of our intention to end the relationship. I tried various angles to create points of division. I told Yishai
I couldn't have Joel Dichter in the relationship. No worries, said Yishai—Joel was not indispensable. Joel called and said he was resigning
as Yishai's lawyer with respect to Sex.Com. When I couldn't complain
about that, I came back to the nasty content issue, and wouldn't leave it
alone. After being in Vegas with all the click-mongers, I thought I knew
something, and I couldn't believe that our website was obliged to be
the absolute sewer of Internet sex. We were the premier type-in domain
on the entire Internet. We could do better than to spatter our white hat
with mud. Boy, was I dumb.

The entire thing exploded on January 15th, Martin Luther King
Day, in San Francisco. I was heading back from Reno with Tara and Ana,
where we'd stayed for a few days as the invited guests of the owner of
XXX.Com. He had pitched me a proposal to manage Sex.Com, and I
was trying to organize a meeting so he could talk to Gary and Phil about
it. Actually, I'd tentatively arranged for Gary to meet us in Reno, but he
dropped off the map that weekend. He wouldn't answer his cell phone,
and when I finally got hold of him, his mood was foul. He'd spent a miserable weekend entertaining an auburn-haired woman he met in Vegas.
When I asked him about the experience, hoping he'd had some fun, his
answer was filled with bitterness: "Total waste of a day. She made me
go and see her kid." He sounded disgusted, convinced that once again,
he'd been used for his money.

As if seeking my own destruction, I directed myself straight into the
path of Gary's anger. Knowing that he was spoiling for a fight, I told him I
was coming to San Francisco to do business. I told him I had been moni-
toring the appearance of Sex.Com, and nothing had changed. The gross-
out contest had to end. I wanted Yishai's contract cancelled, and since
our agreement required thirty days notice to cancel, the 15th was the day.
I told Gary I was on my way with a letter that I wanted to send to Yishai. I
might as well have danced on an old pirate's bunions.

Tara, Ana, Gary and I met at a sushi place up the street from "Dogpatch," Gary's new house on 3rd Street. He was keyed up to an intense
pitch, perspiring heavily. His energy had turned to iron. As we sat at
the table, I tried to speak, but conversation skated off him. He was a
gauche, graceless, bellowing beast. Suddenly, my cell phone rang and

I answered. While I was talking, Gary devoured the sushi off my plate. The call was from a bonehead spam outfit that was trying to pressure Gary into a deal by threatening to launch their own website, which they intended to call "TheNewSex.Com." The caller was an obvious jackass, and when I told Gary who it was, he exploded—"Tell that guy if he calls me one more time, I'll fucking sue him!" I ended the call, and tried to placate Gary, but he just stormed out, leaving me with an empty plate and a sense of doom.

Hungry, rattled, and humiliated in front of my wife and daughter, I followed Gary back to the office and continued to beleaguer him with demands to review and approve my letter canceling Yishai's contract. He read it, but wouldn't approve it. We revised it until there was nothing left, and then he told me he would write and send his own letter. Then he disappeared from his office. No one could find him, so we left and got on the freeway for home. Three hours later, as Tara and I drove north on I-5, with Ana riding in the back seat, Gary called. The conversation was short and one-sided. It ended with Gary shouting "See you in court!"

CHAPTER FIFTY-TWO

THE SHATTERED MIRROR

"Whom the gods would destroy, they first seek to anger."

LUCIFER CAST FROM HEAVEN MIGHT HAVE BEEN MORE ENRAGED than I was after my ouster from Sex.com. But as his cry of rage ripped the sky, God's favorite angel took a third of heaven's stars with him into exile. I had only my wife and children, Peter and myself to share the sad news. Sue promptly threw her lot in with Gary, moving to San Francisco. My outrage was unbearable. Had I not triumphed? Had I not been hailed as a conqueror, with adoring crowds acknowledging my role as Gary's general in the halls of the Venetian, while magnates inclined their heads in respect?

In two months I'd gone from unknown lawyer to top-flight litigator to porn mogul to ousted Sex.Com partner. I had been counting my millions since I first saw the pipeline of cash from Union Bank Fort Lauderdale to Wells Fargo Anaheim Hills. They were mine already, by contract, and I intended to have them. I couldn't go back to my former life as a country lawyer. I had resigned from the list of federal public defenders, cancelled my yellow pages ads, and ended my lease with Peter.

I had made a dreadful miscalculation. My self-flattering mirror was shattered, and the broken shards reflected a frightening visage. Grim lines of determination sealed over stark hollows of grief. A mild smile occasionally softened my look of steely obsession, but no one gained my attention, because my mind was now totally obsessed with a grey chess-board of claims to be made and rebutted, allies to be gathered, and a war chest to be accumulated. I had begun to think harder than I had ever thought before, and what I thought was an unending stream of aggression. I would destroy Gary, humble Idell, and redeem Sue from captivity.

I could hear Gary taunting, "Now you find the lawyers. You pay the fees. You wait for motions to be decided, then postponed. You try facing the mechanized firepower of the hired guns! Enjoy!" And I took up the challenge, filing a lawsuit against Gary for breach of contract, and moving to withdraw as his counsel for nonpayment of fees.

One man pointed me in another direction. When I appeared in his court before the trial with a motion to withdraw as Gary's counsel, Judge Ware's features drooped in sympathy as he gently asked me why I was leaving now, when I had been there from the beginning. I drank up that small draft of recognition, like the last flash of water in the parched bed of a disappearing stream.

Judge Ware counseled us in chambers to mediate our dispute. We mediated. I hired an expensive and well-respected lawyer from Ashland who had once interviewed me for a job in LA when he was a partner at a New York law firm. He was not cheap, but the mediation had to be done properly, with a name lawyer. My lawyer negotiated well at the mediation, and we got up to a number that, in retrospect, would have been a good result. But on that day, I couldn't accept it. The atmosphere was poisoned. I had imposed only one condition on the mediation - that Richard Idell not be there. But Idell ended up talking to Gary on the cell phone all day, throwing sand in the gears with one piece of negative advice after another, until we just had to get the hell out of there. My lawyer's bill was over seven-thousand bucks for a few days of representation, so after I paid that bill, I realized I had to convince some lawyer to take forty percent of fifteen percent of Sex.Com, or the game was over.

CHAPTER FIFTY-THREE

NORTH OF THE BORDER

"The way leads not back, toward innocence, but onward, deeper into sin." Herman Hesse, *Steppenwolf*

WITH MY LAW PRACTICE SHUT DOWN AND NO MONEY COMING IN from Sex.Com, I had a bit of a money problem. I'd gotten two months of fifteen percent of the profits, so I was up by ninety-grand through Christmastime, then watched the stack disappearing like a woodpile during a cold winter. I was depressed as hell, sleeping 'till eleven every day, buying trinkets for entertainment's sake, throwing the occasional party for local friends to brighten my mood, and researching the sex industry online for the first time. I decided to educate myself about online law and business. I started a website for my wife as an experiment, and she took to it with a lot of enthusiasm, so we spent our days pecking at our computers together, while I tried to figure out where my future was going to come from.

Spring appeared on the horizon, and in March I started looking for work. I called Steve Sweet, the man who looked so good in a bathrobe at the Pimp 'n Ho Ball. He was up in Vancouver, the headquarters of Sweet Entertainment. When I called, he at first teased me by suggesting I actually wanted to talk to his girlfriend Jamie, but I told him that no, I wanted to talk about working for Sweet Entertainment.

Canadians have a long tradition of selling contraband to Americans. Edmonton, north of the Midwestern United States, was a bootlegger's paradise in the nineteen-twenties, the railhead for an underground railway that delivered countless barrels of whisky to speakeasies in Chicago, St. Louis, New York, and other parched areas. Canadian banks got fat with loot deposited by Bugsy Moran, Al Capone, and Joe Kennedy.

In Vancouver, the legal, cinematic, and financial infrastructure was all in place to build a thriving Canadian adult film industry. The Canadian attitude toward sex is flexible. Canadian law forbids only the depiction of extremely degrading scenes combining violence with sex and submission. Canadian girls can be very beautiful, and in Vancouver, BC, the native film industry had familiarized many a young lad with the techniques of video production. Canadian banks maintain offshore operations in former British territories, like the Bahamas, Bermuda, Antigua, and Barbuda, thus providing one-stop money-laundering and tax avoidance services for those smart or rapacious enough to pursue such "asset protection" strategies.

Canadian pornographers operate websites in the US and charge for memberships in American dollars. Back in 2001, each American dollar bought nearly two Canadian dollars, so every thirty-dollar signup to a Sweet Entertainment website generated nearly sixty Canadian dollars. As a result, Sweet Entertainment, operating out of Vancouver's sprawling whore-and-heroin district, hauled in very large bucks.

In April 2001, Sweet Entertainment was hosting the second annual "West Coast Webmasters Convention," an event that had made quite a splash in its first year. Lawyers willing to talk to pornographers about the legal aspects of the business were big draws at these adult industry trade shows, so Steve Sweet was enthusiastic when I offered to speak at the event, and urged me to come up for the three-day bash. Sweet would sponsor my hotel room at the event venue, and there was free food and drink courtesy of the sponsors all day and most of the night. It was a two-day drive from Ashland, and the first opportunity since Vegas to see if I could get any altitude in the online sex business.

My ambivalent feelings toward porn had grown and grown. I was now facing some painfully discovered facts about the sex industry and myself. If I did not keep my hand in the sex industry, my claim to own fifteen percent of Sex.Com would evaporate. I had learned a lot from Gary about putting together an army, and like Gary, I hoped to find someone to finance my efforts to recover control over my share of the business. In the meantime, the online sex industry was the only place I could charge people three hundred dollars an hour for my work, and find clients glad to pay it.

But would anyone hire a guy who was suing his own client? More to the point–would anyone in the adult industry risk offending Gary, the lord of Sex.Com, by hiring me? I staved off despair by remembering an aphorism of Balthasar Gracian's: "A wise man makes better use of his enemies than a fool makes of his friends." Behold, the new owner of Sex. Com had already made enemies in the industry. Word was, the site was turning from a supernova into a white dwarf.

Gary had no interest in networking with porn kingpins, and quickly exhausted Ron Levy's patience with proposed amendments to the four hundred thousand per month licensing proposal. Ron retaliated by abandoning his advertising on Sex.Com, which he had been buying through a straw man at the rate of fifty thousand per month. Ron's withdrawal from his role as a secret Sex.Com advertiser was the first vote of no-confidence that Gary received from the online sex business, and would not be the last. Gary dumped Yishai as his webhost and advertising agent, so Yishai stopped buying traffic, and there went another hundred-grand a month. After Gary implemented a redesign with zero visual appeal, Sex.Com became an industry laughingstock for its ability to scare off porn-seekers. As industry flack Kimmy Kim, a dead ringer for a used-up Joni Mitchell, remarked in my presence – "Say whatever the fuck you want about Steve Cohen, he knew how to make money."

Gary was becoming notorious as an industry outsider who could turn gold into lead. His background as a highly educated dot-commer made the criticism more delicious for porn insiders who, in the wake of the dot-bomb stock market crash of 2000, could brag that they were making more money online than Pets.com had lost. Sex.Com seemed to be headed for what would have once seemed impossible to achieve – obscurity.

As a result, clicks from Gary's Sex.Com weren't converting to paying memberships the way Cohen's clicks had. One of the people who had lost money buying traffic from Gary was Steve Sweet. Thus, I was able to use Steve's animosity toward Gary to jump-start our relationship.

I prepared a lecture for the Sweet event that I called "The Seven Commandments of Adult Webmastering." I'd probably revise the lecture if I gave it again today, but it went over fairly well at the time. The gist of it was actually lifted from a principle enunciated by Napoleon Hill in *Think and Grow Rich*, my Dad's favorite self-help book. Only wealth that is honestly gained can give one security, comfort, and satisfaction. I advised the assembled crowd of some eighty or ninety webmasters to let honesty be their watchword, to deal with honest people, and to be cautious with respect to the obscenity laws.

I avoided the approach followed by the established porn lawyers, who shook down some pornographers with a protection racket by promising that the Bush administration was going to crack down on Internet porn and throw all the big players in jail. While I had been very aware of my own vulnerability as a lawyer-owner of a website that was operating with blatant disregard for the obscenity laws, I saw no reason to believe that a purge of the Net-porn business was in the offing. The business simply produced too damn much money to shut down. The credit card companies would never allow it. Since porn was likely here to stay, I argued that the people who do the dirty work could gain legitimacy by acting legitimately.

There was also a future beyond porn, because those who made money in online adult would have a head start on making money in straight commerce, as it matured. I compared the early Internet economy to that of San Francisco during the Gold Rush. In 1849, most merchants sold mining tools, liquor and sex. Today, those industries still exist, but have a smaller piece of the Bay Area economy. Similarly, the Internet had discovered sex first, but its role would inevitably shrink as the Net attracted more and more straight businesses. My advice to the pornographers was to stay honest, stay profitable, stay free, and be around to harvest the really big money that would come as the Internet became the world's global marketplace. People applauded and smiled at the end of the lecture, and a few came up to talk with me afterward.

Soon I ran into Ben from Wired Solutions, the smooth north-easterner with so much intelligence, charm and breeding. His first question was, "Did he fuck you?"

The life of a loser is full of such pleasant exchanges.

"Yes, he did," I answered.

Ben immediately announced, "I knew it!"

Not really a fun start to the encounter, but Ben was sympathetic, and helped to lift my spirits at the convention, talking me up to everyone we met. He was a high status pornographer, and if he said I was the shit, then no one was going to argue with him. We settled down in Ben's hotel room, crowded with wheeler-dealers networking with their cellphones, sucking down bottles of Canadian beer, and wondering where they would locate their favorite substances there in Vancouver. Ben introduced me to everyone as the incredible lawyer who had won Sex.Com and yet ended up empty-handed. It's not the easiest intro to deal with.

As the evening's inebriation project got underway, Ben volunteered that he was willing to testify at any proceeding on my behalf. I didn't think Ben had been privy to anything that I would need testimony about, and had to ask him, "Testify to what?" Ben answered that, one night at a strip club in Santa Fe, while they were both wired on crank, Gary had explained to Ben how he was going to fuck Charles out of his fifteen percent of Sex.com. He said another lawyer was going to step in and take the credit, make it look like Charles had breached his agreements, and Charles would be cut out. Receiving this information was like adding some heavy metals to a cocktail of battery acid and hazardous waste - I hardly noticed the change in flavor, but it was possibly more bitter.

I absorbed the news and tried to balance my emotions, put on a game face, and do what I'd come to do - set myself up as a lawyer in the industry. I had only one chip to ante up, or I could go back to defending drug dealers in Southern Oregon. There was only one identifiable group of clients who would be meaningfully impressed by meeting the lawyer who won Sex.Com, and they were all around me. Using Ben as a life-support device for my credibility, I circulated among them.

I liked the people I was meeting. Almost all of them were Canadians, young, good-looking and good-humored. Like Bonnie and Russell of Streetlight Productions, Tom Sweet from Sweet Entertainment, and Zak Zarry of Porncity. Each one expressed their appreciation that I had brought a bit of justice to a corrupt business. These folks clearly weren't going to be stuck in porn for the rest of their lives. Zak aspired to be a lawyer and seemed likely achieve his goal. Bonnie and Russell sold their business for a healthy chunk of change a year or so later. Tom Sweet and I sized each other up professionally during a brief chat outside a night club. As I understood it, he was Steve's brother, and thus at the top of the Sweet food chain, so I tried to make a good impression.

Eventually, around midnight or so, I ran into Ben again on a dance floor where pornographers were milling about without attempting any dance steps. The lights were swirling and music was pounding all around us as he shouted into my ear that he'd just gone up to see the top porn czars way upstairs, including Ron Levy, Ron Gould, and other people whose names I didn't know. He had told them the whole story about me and Gary, that Gary was no good, and no one should deal with him. And he would testify! He would testify! The Ecstasy was really kicking in, and I knew that whatever Ben said now, it was the dopamine talking. It was sad. In this place filled with frivolity, anxiety and greed, my best friend was a rave-drug addict with delusions of grandeur.

Later that night, as we settled into the three-til-dawn shift back in Ben's room, and the manic waves subsided in his mindstream, he revealed why he wanted to destroy Gary Kremen, whose trip to Santa Fe to meet the Wired Solutions people had nearly derailed Ben's sleaze career. Ben explained that Gary had invited Ben to leave Wired Solutions and go to work for Sex.Com. Ben told Gary he was interested. Then Gary, apparently deciding that he would benefit most by injecting chaos into the situation, told Ben's boss Fernando that Ben was willing to jump ship. Fernando, seizing the opportunity to trace little incision lines on Ben's soft belly, forced Ben to admit his disloyal sentiments and beg for his job. Endowed with a blueblood's taste for vengeance, Ben lusted for payback, and once again, in an apparently sober condition, swore that when I needed his testimony, he'd be there. I had high hopes that perhaps, at the right moment, he would provide the testimony that would prove that Gary had in fact planned my destruction.

It was also interesting to know that the top guys were attending the Sweet event, a sure sign that the Canadian porn community was important to the industry as a whole. One prominent person who had not yet been seen at the conference was Gary Kremen. Sometime that first night, I ran into Sue, now playing Nurse Feelgood to Gary, who said Gary was in his room, in an abysmal condition, possibly near death. She was embarrassed to be seen in this role, but by disclosing confidences about Sex. Com, hoped to win my approval. She was dying to get away from him, but needed money, she said. He was paying her five thousand a month, more than she'd ever been paid as a lawyer, and she wasn't lawyering. I wanted to hear more about Gary's mental and physical health being on the skids. After what I'd recently heard from Ben, Gary couldn't be close enough to death to satisfy me until he was actually in hell, roasting on a spit. She said that, given how he was abusing his body with controlled substances, she was worried about it all the time, and had a dream where he was lying dead with a mass of foam emerging from his mouth. The image confirmed my then-current impression of Gary as a huge insect that predated on warm-blooded beings.

I had to wait until the second night of the conference to see my dearest enemy at the really big bash Sweet hosted at a conference center someplace across the Lions Gate Bridge, on an island with a beautiful view of Vancouver. The party started around two in the afternoon, so I drove across the bridge and settled in early to enjoy the views across the water from the ranch-style convention center. It was much better than even the nicest lawfirm all-day picnic, with excellent free food and drinks, white tablecloths, silverware, and real wine glasses. At these affairs, rich dilettantes mingle with the techies, photographers, and financiers who spin profit out of digital images and sophisticated tracking programs. Steve Sweet was there, the big shark with the toothy grin, and briefly welcomed me to the event before going on to mingle with others.

It was fun and scary to be in this world, and not on a leash. I wondered — could I get my spoon in here somewhere? I was free to do what I could with this wild, untamed energy, but with a few top guys controlling the big money, and most of them as eager to avoid conflict with Gary as they had been to avoid conflict with Cohen in his day, I feared I'd be blocked at every turn. I was standing outside on a deck with a view, sipping wine, when someone came up and told me, significantly, that Gary had arrived. Some people had apparently been anticipating this moment. Would we meet? Would we fight? Sex.com, like a volcano with a history of past eruptions, was making noises again. Neither of us had need of a scene, however. I approached Gary as soon as I spotted him, noting without surprise that he seemed healthy as a horse. Sue had obviously been exaggerating his condition in an effort to cheer me up. We exchanged insincere pleasantries, then I returned to circulating through the crowd, sipping drinks and swapping business cards.

Eventually it got dark outside, and people started settling into friendly groups at candlelit tables. I hadn't found anyplace to settle down until a tall, older guy with a craggy face and posture slightly bent at the waist, asked me if I'd like to join him and his friends for a drink, if it wasn't beneath me to drink with some poor webmasters. This was the first reference I'd heard to any class distinctions in the big happy family of pornographers. Thus I met Ed, a humble Canadian webmaster who has no doubt by now got title to that piece of island property he was planning to buy off the coast of British Columbia. Ed was completely independent, and had an unglamorous view of the industry. He'd started out in cabinet making, he told me, but when his knees, elbows and back got creaky, he learned computer repair. He did that for awhile, then discovered it was easier and more profitable to make free porn sites, and sell the traffic to the big paysite owners. He was making $10,000 Canadian a month at that time, although as the years went by, he continually reported declines in profits-per-website, as more competitors entered his field.

Kind, good humored, and aware of his limitations, Ed figured that since he didn't design the world, he couldn't account for people's inclinations. His goal was to drive porn surfers to click the "Join Now" button at a big paysite that would send him a commission. His goal was summed up in an industry aphorism — "Tease, don't please." Ed explained that most webmasters made sites that were too attractive. They not only "teased," they "pleased." Since webmasters only earn a commission when surfers *leave* their website to sign up at a sponsor's paysite, Ed wanted his sponsor's website to look far more attractive than his own. As a result, Ed's sites were some of the ugliest on the Net.

Sitting with Ed and his friend Carol, my drink consumption kept ahead of my paranoia and sense of alienation. For Ed, it was a presumed good that we were all alive, enjoying free beer, food, and pleasant companions. We all have stories to tell, stories worth listening to, and although at the end of the night, we each face the darkness by ourselves, we can watch out for each other along the way. As the evening drew to a close, around one-thirty in the morning, we went to the parking lot, but as I headed towards my car, Ed and Carol suggested that I ride the bus back to the hotel. He offered to meet me the next day and drive me out to pick up my Camry during lunch. I accepted his offer as the only wise choice, but one obstacle had to be overcome. Sex.Com had sponsored the bus, and Gary was sure to be on it.

Canadians, however, take driving under the influence of drink very seriously, much more seriously for example than auto break-ins, which are ubiquitous and rarely punished. Since the Mounties are known for always getting their man, I didn't want to be that man. Once on the bus, I discovered that the only seat left was right next to Gary Kremen. I sat in it. We were both three sheets to the wind. Like two soldiers wounded in battle from opposing sides in the war, temporarily unable to kill each other, we did not talk about the battle. When I got back to the hotel, I had another beer and crawled into bed around three or four in the morning. Around lunchtime the next day, Ed drove me out to the island in an old T-bird. I picked up my car and returned to the hotel.

CHAPTER FIFTY-FOUR

THE KINGDOM OF SWEETS

ON THE LAST DAY OF THE VANCOUVER SHOW, I wanted to hook up with Steve and Jamie, the beau and belle of the ball, but they were keeping a low profile. I asked one of their black-tee-shirted family-members, easily identifiable with their "SEG" logos in red and white, and all surnamed "Sweet," if I could get an audience. A brief meeting was arranged, after which Tom Sweet took over as my guide. We visited the Sweet production studio in the Hastings district. The operation was housed in a two-story walkup location off a grimy street. There were two levels of buzz-through security, narrow halls, and low ceilings. The uniform color scheme was military gray. Steve's office was narrow like a closet, and people had to practically line up to see him. Steve's desk was a piece of second-hand furniture, and through the window behind his swivel chair you could see an industrial skyline, complete with cranes, factories and smog. The de-cor said loud and clear, "Don't ask for a fucking thing."

The studio was a single room with different "sets" on each wall, and multiple doors that locked up tight as a drum when shooting was in progress. The actresses, not the props, are the focus of attention in these productions, which were directed and filmed by the ever-affable Rey Damasco, a charming man of Filipino ancestry. Rey, who of course went by the name of Rey Sweet, could put the most skittish filly at ease with respect to her intrinsic sexual charms, the proper use of sex toys, the ease of feigning orgasm, and many other details essential to a prop-er adult film performance. Skilled in the use of the amazing Buttcam, a gimmick camera that Steve had designed to literally explore the inner recesses of the human body, Rey had obtained deep internal views of the elimination canals of many people. If he ever decides to go into medicine, he'll have a head start on the other guys when it comes to diagnosing colon cancer.

Sweet's real gimmick, though, was simulated torture. This was where Mike Sweet, whom I'd met back in Vegas, earned his keep. His dungeon was realistically created. The floor was thick with wax, the walls had been painted to simulate blood smears, and the worktables and walls were adorned with whips, hooks, and weights. From the ceiling hung pulleys and chains. The only seats available looked very uncomfortable and had straps and buckles on them. Thus it seemed I'd stumbled into the lair of a twisted family headed by a dungeon master. Not the only torturer on the payroll, however, Mike was assisted in the business of punishing the guilty by Paige, a blond dominatrix with precise and exacting skills, and a pair of blue jeans entirely stitched together up the inside and outside seams with safety pins. Paige had the unique distinction of not being a Sweet. Her stage name was merely "Miss Pain," and in addition to running a site called MissPain.com, she was the official webmistress for SadoSlaves.com, a scary-ass website if ever I saw one.

The Sweet dungeon tempted one to entertain strange notions, which had to be the appeal of the whole bondage and domination scene. The allure was not entirely lost on me, and I experienced brief confusion when Paige suggested that I join her for a session in the dungeon. I declined with a laugh, and told her I'd have to take a rain check. Though the safety pins had me tuned up to a responsive pitch, being hoisted off the ground in chains, even by an attractive blonde, would still have to be forced upon me. Of course, being filmed in that condition would be so damaging to my own image as a dominating male that I couldn't entertain the notion seriously, even for purposes of career advancement. Although there is a California lawyer who is also a porn actor, and the California Bar association takes no umbrage at the fact, somehow I doubt that the Oregon Bar would adopt the same liberal attitude.

When I got back from Canada, I kept in touch with Tom Sweet, making myself available to consult on some Sweet issues. It wasn't long before I had snagged a copyright infringement lawsuit. Steve was a big believer in pursuing copyright infringers, and a Texas company called E-Race had made the mistake of lifting about three-hundred Sweet images for their own use at a website called PersonalPorn.com. The E-Race partners compounded their error by failing to take Steve's demands for settlement seriously. Sweet Entertainment Group had hired a copyright lawyer in Century City to file suit about a year before, but aside from escalating bills and demands for payment, Steve and Tom hadn't seen much progress toward the goal of crushing their opponents.

I was in Phoenix having breakfast with my brother, his wife, and Tara, when the call came in from Tom Sweet. I was frankly elated, and my brother, a career prosecutor, was astounded. How on earth, he wondered, could I live in this fashion? He'd worked for the City of Phoenix for nearly thirty years, he said, and would be utterly lost if he didn't have that place to go every morning. I, however, was like a bird, he said, and flapped his arms like wings to demonstrate how strange my metamorphosis into an aerial performer seemed to him. Admittedly, the whole lifestyle had an edge to it. Tom had authorized me to drop in on his LA lawyer and find out what the hell was going on.

Two days later, Tara and I were in LA, reviewing the files of *Sweet Entertainment Group, Inc. vs. E-Race*. Fortunately, they revealed a great deal of lackadaisical work on the part of the Sweet lawyer, and I was able to give Tom an effective and alarming pitch. The case was mired in delay, and Sweet had been billed for the cost of fixing two major errors committed by their lawyer, who had not been sending them complete reports about the progress of the litigation. Deadlines to complete discovery were running out, and the future of the case was not positive. The Sweet lawyer was politely apologetic, and while he hoped to get paid his outstanding bill, could tell that he was losing the client. I received authorization from Tom to copy the whole file and plan to take over the litigation, then pending in Orange County Federal Court. My retainer of ten-thousand dollars would be in the mail. Looking for trouble had paid off again.

During the next couple of months, I started kicking E-Race's ass with discovery, and soon had the principals of the company sitting in their lawyer's conference room in LA. Tom Sweet came down to savor the pleasure of observing their discomfort. Instead, peace broke out in the middle of the deposition. Frank Walley, one of the E-Race principals, and one of the best salesmen I have ever met in my life, simply stopped the show, and asked if he could make an off the record proposal. If Sweet would acquire E-Race, all the problems could go away. There was plenty of money to be made, he said, and being sued by Sweet had not been a picnic. They were ready to share. Tom was receptive, got on the phone to Steve, and got authority to negotiate once I completed the depositions. We finished the depositions relatively quickly, since their lawyer interposed no objections and let me learn the things I needed to for purposes of keeping the litigation in an aggressive posture. We were done with the testimony by four o'clock, and then adjourned to drink tequila across the street and hammer out the makings of my first porn-industry merger.

A few weeks later, Tom and I flew to Dallas to perform due diligence on our acquisition target. The first day there, we had lunch with Frank and his wife in an expensive peasant-style Italian restaurant with tasteful décor. Frank's wife is a classic Texas blonde who can't believe what men have to do to make money. Frank kept trying to lure us away from our homework by urging us to stop grinding the paperwork and take a trip with him out to the racetrack, where we could find out what it feels like to drive the E-Race Porsche at a hundred-and-sixty miles and hour. It was a cool smokescreen, but Tom and I stayed on task. We could see why Frank had attempted to deflect our attention from the books. E-Race had been mismanaged rather radically, and although its cashflow was good, its expenses were way out of line. Tom and I agreed we couldn't acquire the company. The best we could do was cherry-pick the assets and leave the liabilities on the table, which ultimately is what we did.

The trip to Texas confirmed that Tom and I had good rapport, even down to little things like using the onboard GPS system in our rented SUV to negotiate the Dallas freeways. Tom is a highly ambitious intellectual, and working for Gary had been a two-year post-graduate program in how to deal with such people. A few weeks later, I received a job offer from Sweet to be the company's General Counsel at ten thousand US dollars per month, with the hope, but not the requirement, that I would eventually move to Vancouver.

CHAPTER FIFTY-FIVE

THANK GOD, ANOTHER ENEMY!

I WAS DELIGHTED TO REPORT TO MY NEW LAWYER that I had landed a job. For forty percent of my fifteen percent, I had managed to rope an old UCLA pal, Jim DeSimone, into representing me in my lawsuit against Gary. Jim had not been a close friend of mine in law school, but I respected his integrity. He had been one of the few law students to join the protests that forced the Regents of the University of California to eliminate South African investments from its securities portfolio, as part of the international movement to free Nelson Mandela and end apartheid. After law school, Jim went to work for Centro Legal, the legal aid clinic where he'd volunteered during law school. After a few years doing public service, he partnered with Ben Schonbrun to practice civil rights and employment law from Ben's beachfront office on the Venice boardwalk. Jim and I got to know each other better after he took that job, because I did the same type of work at Mazursky, Schwartz & Angelo. We had run into each other at bar events and the courthouse, and exchanged the occasional war story.

I actually hadn't even thought of calling Jim until one day when I saw a news article on the Internet about a case that Mike Seplow, a younger lawyer at the firm, had recently settled for a couple million dollars on behalf of a homeless man who was picked up on the streets of LA, misidentified as a New York felon, shipped to New York, and allowed to rot in a mental hospital for two years before the case of mistaken identity was sorted out. I was working on a similar case, that of Roger Benson, who suffered a long stint in a California jail because Oregon misidentified *him* as a felon. Once I was on the phone talking to Jim's partner Mike Seplow, I realized he was a very intelligent lawyer, and it occurred to me that Jim's firm might be interested in taking on my own case.

The case was a tough sell, but Jim is ambitious, and had the employment lawyer's skill of mastering the scores of essential facts necessary understand the case. To some extent, he was seduced by the sleazy glamour of the story and the intellectual sophistication required to master it. Jim was the number two partner at Schonbrun, DeSimone, Harris, Seplow & Hoffman, and so could put the weight of a California firm, and an agreed-upon expense budget, to work on my case. I took Bob Kuenzel, who had served as an excellent placeholder, off the pleadings, and put Jim's firm on.

As was apparent to Jim when he signed on, in my haste to file suit against Gary, I had sped right past an important rule of California lawyer law. Before you can sue your client, you have to ask them if they'd like to engage in non-binding arbitration. If they say no, you can sue them. If they say yes, you have to arbitrate. I knew this, but I also knew there was a more general rule that in a lawsuit based on a written contract, you can sue to attach funds in a defendant's bank account, even if you are supposed to arbitrate the dispute. I had been eager to file a motion for attachment, because I had a written contract, and there was about $45,000 per month that I was entitled to under that agreement. I had written up most of the motion, supported it with all of my evidence, and just needed to have a lawyer finish it up and file it, and Jim did file it. But my strategy produced no benefit. Richard Idell, stepping in quickly to take advantage of my mistake, moved to stay my lawsuit until the matter had been arbitrated by the State Bar. Judge Whyte put the lawsuit on hold and sent us to arbitration. Not surprisingly, he denied the motion for attachment as well. I was beginning to understand the meaning of the old saying that some things can be accomplished quickly only if you don't try to rush them.

Jim prepared for the arbitration diligently, poring over binders of documents. He read my October 4, 1999 agreement with Gary repeatedly, and understood its provisions thoroughly. As a result, he repeatedly lamented a minor omission that was to have a huge influence on our joint expectations. The agreement failed to comply with a California statute that requires contingent fee agreements to explicitly state that the percentage fee is "negotiated, and not set by law." Obviously, the October 4th agreement was extensively negotiated, incorporating as it did all manner of clever provisions that Gary and I had discussed in detail, including the novel financing-by-going-public mechanism. Gary himself had proposed the 15% fee, so it was particularly galling that Idell had found this Achilles heel in the agreement. And the consequence of my error was fatal, because any agreement lacking the essential language was unenforceable, illegitimate, and gave me no rights. A minor error in the fee agreement threatened to undo all my plans.

Of course, even if the agreement was unenforceable, I was still entitled to the reasonable value of my services. The reasonable value of my services would be calculated based on the skill I showed in getting the result, the amount of benefit I'd brought to my client, and the expected fee that other lawyers would charge for getting that result. That left some room for hope, even if my written agreement proved worthless. The way I calculated it, I'd helped Gary recover the world's most valuable domain name, worth at least eight-million dollars a year. I'd helped Gary acquire the three-million dollar Rancho Santa Fe mansion. I'd shown considerable skill in saving the case from dismissal at the last moment, and prevented it from ever being dismissed again. I had rehabilitated Gary's image from wannabe pornographer to white-hat hero. I had been sued for $50 Million and shrugged it off. I had procured the services of State Farm to stave off Cohen's lawsuits. I helped prove Gary's case so thoroughly that Judge Ware thought a trial unnecessary.

I had also devised the plan to have Cohen arrested, an achievement that may seem minor until you realize that civil lawyers never arrest the opposing party. Only a prosecutor can request the court to issue an arrest warrant, and in those pre-Patriot Act days, the prosecutor still had to allege that the defendant had committed a crime. Ignoring this obstacle, I devised the answer—we would bait Cohen into doing the only thing that could get him arrested—defying a court order to show up in front of Judge Ware. To get a warrant issued for Cohen's arrest, I told Gary, we merely had to convict Cohen of a small misdemeanor called "failure to appear." When a judge orders a person to show up in court, and they fail to appear, he issues a bench warrant. It's automatic—the easiest warrant to get. Judge Ware had manifested an interest in Cohen's whereabouts during the November 27th hearing, so it was easy to get him to order Cohen to appear, which had the foreseeable result of Cohen failing to appear and Judge Ware's issuing a warrant for his arrest. By the time I sat down at the arbitration table on January 22, 2002, Cohen had been a fugitive from justice for nearly a year, cementing Gary's victory unshakeably.

Cyrano de Bergerac would have understood. Cyrano was an incomparable swordsman who looked for trouble wherever he could honorably find it, and found it everywhere. Like Cyrano, I had become rather bitter about my fate. I felt I'd won the prize, delivered Sex.Com to Gary like we'd always planned, and now I got to watch other lawyers consume my share of the pie in exchange for cutting me out of the deal. Cyrano was bitter because he won the love of his cousin Roxanne only to confer her affections upon his fellow Musketeer, Christian. Like Cyrano, who couldn't reveal the entire truth of the affair to either Christian or Roxanne, I too was bound by duties of confidentiality to refrain from revealing secrets that might have given me leverage against Gary.

Despite or because of his repulsive physical appearance, Cyrano moved from conflict to conflict, cutting a path with sword and poetry through a world peopled by fools, knaves and lackeys. In the aftermath of my split with Gary, I too had a sufficient supply of enemies, most of whom had at least been nominal allies. Foremost among my former allies was Richard Idell, the San Francisco lawyer who represented the famously cutthroat rock impresario Bill Graham, presumably in the delicate business of cutting the legs off drugged-out entertainers who had overstayed their fifteen minutes of fame. Graham was so famously cruel that even today, twelve years after his death in a 1991 helicopter crash, you get a lot of hits if you Google "Bill Graham" and "asshole." I am sure he found his ideological mate in Richard Idell, whose frigid soul pops open only long enough to reveal the kryptonite, nitroglycerine, and arsenic that substitute for his heart, lungs and liver.

Idell and I first met in his office on Bush Street at the greasy edge of Chinatown. These days he's got a better address on California Street, but remains well known in San Francisco for his bulldog litigation style. Physically and temperamentally, Idell reminds me of a wolverine. He's barrel-waisted, neckless with a short jaw line that operates a pair of lips that have never smiled in my presence, but sneer even better than Cohen's. A graduate of Golden Gate University School of Law, he had the grit and spit of a self-made man.

The Wagstaffe team had got the memo at last, and were singing a completely different tune at the arbitration than had become their habit during the heady months following the big win. For a while, in a dim prehistory that none of the Wagstaffe team could ever recollect, there had been a wild, crazy moment when they all believed that Charles Carreon really was a fifteen percent owner of Sex.Com. That's how delusive it got. Sanity had been restored however, and Wagstaffe's firm had liens for hundreds of thousands of dollars in fees on Gary's Rancho Santa Fe house. There was work in abundance as Kerr & Wagstaffe pursued every avenue of collection against Cohen, and in general satisfied Gary's desire to pursue a policy of armed strength against all comers.

Pam Urueta had been enlisted as a sapper to undermine my character. It seemed she had recovered a memory that she had once heard me say I was burned out, and didn't want to try the case. I snapped at her in the waiting room, and was forced to apologize and make some evidentiary concession, or it would be reported that I had assaulted her with profanity. Poor Jim was humiliated by my out-of-control antics, and gave me a lecture in the bathroom. It was really kind of funny, because he went into this whole passionate Italian advocate routine that was straight out of TV. I wondered how many of those routines I'd developed for my own repertoire of client-control mechanisms.

I was learning once again a painful lesson in litigation. Until you've been there, you have no idea what it will be like. I thought my achievements were indisputable. Unfortunately for me, there is no job so well done that it cannot be improved upon in retrospect by a team of lawyers, and Wagstaffe did a fabulous job of dissing me with affectionate recollections, as if I'd been Gary's handler, a wild guy useful for soaking up Gary's wilder enthusiasms, given to taking a boatload of unnecessary discovery, and unfortunately, responsible for a couple of acts of serious malpractice.

Malpractice? Yes, malpractice of the high-dollar amount kind. Alas, it turned out, once Gary got to running down all the bankers with subpoenas, that on November 27th,, Cohen had transferred $1.2 Million out of the Wells Fargo Anaheim Hills Branch, in violation of the orders that I faxed to Wells Fargo's attorney in San Francisco. Wells Fargo of course was denying having received the order "in time" to prevent the transfer. This was probably true, since Cohen later told me he'd gone down to the Anaheim Hills branch of Wells Fargo in person, and transferred the money the morning before the hearing, just to be safe. Now Gary was suing me, and Wells Fargo, for the money. Those were some of Wagstaffe's glad tidings.

Additionally, he testified, in retrospect I had screwed up by not suing NSI for "negligent damage to personal property." Unfortunately for me, Katie Diemer's Second Amended Complaint included a claim for "negligence" against NSI, and now Idell was arguing that I malpracticed when I didn't carry on with that claim in the Third Amended Complaint, because, he theorized, a negligence claim would have given us an additional leg to stand on with Judge Ware.

Gary's criticisms of my performance were bogus. With respect to the money that disappeared, I'd done everything possible to fax the order to Wells Fargo at the earliest possible moment, and Cohen had simply gotten the drop on us. That last unpreventable theft merged with all the millions that had already been piped offshore, and were also small in proportion to the large sums Gary was now receiving monthly from Sex. Com. And as far as my failure to allege negligence against NSI, I knew Gary would ultimately win on appeal, making it all a moot point.

I was keen to prove to the arbitrators that I had been the architect of victory. I knew I'd benefited Gary in a unique and thorough way that overarched the accomplishments of all Gary's other lawyers. If my contractual entitlement went down in flames because I'd left magic words out of the October 4th agreement, I would be asking the arbitrators to award the reasonable value of my services, so it made sense to build my case around a single principle – I did my job.

I didn't figure I could call a better witness on this point than Bob Dorband. Jim was incredulous when I suggested that we call Cohen's lawyer to the witness stand. Wouldn't his words be discounted as sour grapes? Wouldn't he seem to be the wrong person to have as an ally? No, I assured Jim, no one would ever look at Bob Dorband and discount his testimony. His word on the subject of my skill and ability would be true, and the truth will be believed when spoken by Bob. I had received Bob's promise to testify during a lunchbreak at the two-day trial he defended on behalf of an absent Cohen. Bob's comments on that day made it clear he was now doubly convinced that every accusation of deception he'd directed against Gary had been true all along. He now saw exactly what he would have prophesied coming true in spades. It was telling that I was getting sympathy from a man who represented Cohen. Bob and I could have commiserated about our client-inflicted wounds, but we never have. Bob is a knight I have only met on the battlefield, encased in iron, a foe to whom mercy is alien, and yet accords me respect. His testimony was as good as I could have hoped.

JIM: Up until the time that Mr. Carreon came into the case, what was the procedural status of the case?

BOB: There had been several complaints filed and we had filed a motion to dismiss against each complaint, in turn, and basically won all those motions.

JIM: And what was your expectation as to the outcome of this case?

BOB: After the second amended complaint was dismissed, I thought that was probably going to be it, that they probably would not be able to re-plead it successfully.

JIM: And it was replead successfully?

BOB: Yes it was.

JIM: Who filed the third amended complaint that was pled successfully?

BOB: Mr. Carreon.

JIM: When Mr. Carreon came in the case, did you have to change the way in which you were litigating the case?

BOB: Mr. Carreon was much more aggressive.

JIM: And in terms of his aggressiveness, was it appropriate or inappropriate?

BOB: It was very appropriate.

JIM: And in terms of taking your client's deposition, who in your estimation questioned your client most effectively in this litigation?

BOB: Of all the attorneys that questioned Mr. Cohen, I would say Mr. Carreon was the most effective.

JIM: Who propounded all the discovery to Mr. Cohen, Ocean Fund, and YNATA in this case?

BOB: As far as I can recall, it was Mr. Carreon.

JIM: And in terms of who was responding to your discovery on behalf of Mr. Kremen, which attorney was handling that?

BOB: Mr. Carreon.

JIM: There was a lot of paper in this case, to say the least?

BOB: A ton of paper.

JIM: Did you have a view as to how Mr. Carreon handled those thousands of pages of paper?

BOB: He handled it very effectively, as effectively as any attorney I've dealt with in cases where there's a lot of documentation.

JIM: Were you the attorney primarily responsible for preparing the opposition to Mr. Kremen's motion for preliminary injunction and summary judgment?

BOB: Yes.

JIM: And were there declarations submitted with attached evidence in support of those motion?

BOB: Yes

JIM: And in terms of the attorney who was submitting the many pages of exhibits that supported those motions, what attorney was that?

IDELL: Objection – lack of foundation, vague and ambiguous.

CHIEF ARBITRATOR: I'll allow it if you know.

BOB: I know it was Mr. Carreon.

JIM: And the evidence submitted by Mr. Carreon, did you believe that that played a critical role in Judge Ware's eventual ruling?

BOB: In my opinion, yes.

JIM: Did you and Mr. Carreon have a cordial relationship?

BOB: Yes, we did.

JIM: Did Mr. Carreon ever discuss with you whether he was willing to try this case?

BOB: Yes, he did.

JIM: Did Mr. Carreon ever indicate to you that he wasn't going to be the trial counsel in the case?

BOB: No.

JIM: Did you have the impressions in your dealings with Mr. Carreon that he would be trial counsel in this case?

BOB: Absolutely.

Jim: And what did you base that impression on?

BOB: My discussions with Charles. We would actually have discussions on occasion bout actually trying the case, and in a sort of collegial way, we would talk about how fun it was going to be and that it was kind of a crazy case. And also, my observations of Mr. Carreon in terms of how he was handling the case day-to-day, he was always involved in it, as far as I can tell.

JIM: Did he ever appear to be tired or burned out to you?

BOB: I couldn't say that. No, he never did.

JIM: You were the lawyer for Mr. Cohen at the trial in this matter, correct?

BOB: Yes.

JIM: How long did that trial take?

BOB: It was less than a day and a half.

JIM: Was it a bench trial?

BOB: It was a bench trial.

JIM: Did Mr. Cohen appear?

BOB: No.

JIM: Did you call any witnesses?

BOB: No.

JIM: Were there any liability issues on the facts tried?

BOB: No.

JIM: What issues were dealt with at the trial?

BOB: It was purely damages at that point, and all the liability issues had been decided on summary adjudication, and there were orders entered as a result of contempt sanctions that pretty much precluded our presentation of anything. It was basically, I just sat there.

Bob had flown in from Portland to give his testimony, and when he was done, we adjourned for the day. I will always remember the feeling of sympathy for the adversary I felt when Bob was worn down by the hail of lead, and Cohen left him with no case to defend. Those days were behind him, though he acknowledged without explaining too much, that they had taken their toll on his personal life. After Gary won the trial, he had sued Bob, who then left the Duboff firm to work for Safeco managing an insurance defense shop in Portland. I wished him well and bid him goodbye. My closest enemy had done me all the good he could.

Peter Carini, my closest friend, also flew into town to testify at the arbitration. Since Gary had impugned both my willingness and ability to try the case, the Chief Arbitrator allowed Peter to testify about his knowledge and opinion concerning my trial abilities. Like Bob had, Peter first testified about my willingness to try the case, that had been cast into question by Pam's recovered memories:

JIM: What did Mr. Carreon say on the topic of whether or not he would be trial counsel on the Kremen vs. Cohen matter?

PETER: He was definitely going to be the trial counsel.

JIM: And what did he say that led you to that conclusion?

PETER: Not only what he said, but what he was doing. Oftentimes during that period of time, we'd be working up themes and working up strategies and tactics to be utilized for a jury trial, and we were working on it together. I was interested in doing the case because it was just a great case. I mean, just from a litigator's perspective, going into court against Cohen, it was like a field day. It was incredible, an opportunity you wouldn't want to miss if you were a trial lawyer.

Peter also gave his opinion about how well I tried cases, based on our work together:

JIM: Have you tried cases with Mr. Carreon?

PETER: Yes.

JIM: What are your observations of Mr. Carreon as a trial attorney?

PETER: He's excellent.

But it's one's performance as any adversary that is the most convincing test, and Peter found a succinct way to describe my abilities:

JIM: Have you tried cases against Mr. Carreon?

PETER: Yes.

JIM: And that's when Mr. Carreon was a district attorney; is that correct?

PETER: That's right.

JIM: And during that period of time, how was his work as a prosecutor?

PETER: He was a feared prosecutor.

That's high praise from a man as insensible to fear as Peter. I was proud to have two Oregon lawyers come down to the Bay Area to vouch for me. I had hoped to have a third Oregon lawyer show up, but Sue Whatley was hiding out in Oregon, supposedly on the lam from Gary but probably avoiding me by absenting herself from the Bay Area during the hazardous time period of the arbitration. She had promised repeatedly to come San Francisco and testify for the hearing, once after I personally delivered her a subpoena, but when the day came, she didn't make the trip.

My ecstasy-head friend also failed to show. Ben, who had direct evidence of Gary's admission to axing me with malice aforethought, and had sworn eternal loyalty to my cause for one blazing moment in Vancouver, had also been subpoenaed, and also absented himself. After first calling Jim DeSimone to ask for plane fare, Ben then had a New York lawyer contact us to make threatening excuses for his non-appearance. I sensed Fernando's big, fat hand squashing my plans, while Gary looked on with delight. It was all too gross.

Cyrano knew how little a man can expect from his friends:

Watching you other people
Making friends everywhere
As a dog makes friends,
I mark the manner of these
Canine courtesies and think
"My friends are of a cleaner breed—
Here comes, thank God, another enemy!"

MY FIFTEEN MINUTES OF SHAME

VANCOUVER, BC IS DOMINATED BY A HALF-DOZEN GLASS RESIDENTIAL TOWERS, which are monuments to the unique housing needs of the Chinese elite who bailed out of Hong Kong when Mao's minions took over the metropolis a few decades back. Designed to fit the special needs of the exiles, every apartment has a solarium. In February 2002, Tara and I were living in a luxurious two-bedroom apartment overlooking a soccer field and the marina. We were alternating two or three weeks a month in Canada with an equal amount of time in Oregon, making the ten-hour drive in two-day relays. My son Josh was living at home, and took care of the place during our absence. It was a long drive, but we had fun getting our apartment together and living in a small, cosmopolitan city where we could eat out anytime, take walks by the water, and be out of the USA.

Being out of the USA had seemed like a good idea ever since the towers fell in broad daylight on that very bad day in New York City. It had been a crime so big that even after they connected all the dots, the FBI and the Department of Justice could find only one pathetic madman to charge with the crime. We were getting war instead of prosecution, and war on everyone but the people who'd crashed the planes. I asked my friends to consider what would have happened if seventeen Cubans, rather than seventeen Saudis, had piloted the hijacked airplanes?

My biggest problem came when I saw *three* office buildings fall neatly on that nine-one-one day, collapsing like decks of cards in the palm a demonic dealer. Because only two of the collapsing buildings had been hit by airliners. At that moment, I had the distinct perception that the emperor was wearing no clothes. Then the forensic evidence was spirited away, the landlord made a killing, and the mayor and police chief went on to mine the security industry for the new gold–paranoia.

Yes, as I quarreled with my former partner over the spoils of an empire of smut, the world toppled over the brink. We slipped from the dot-com crash into the Enron implosion, into a new world of terror where we would never be bored again. Fox turned up the volume on the hero machine, the president girded for war, and the cheerleaders in Congress seized their pom-poms and started spouting slogans with a will. None would be last to their feet in swearing allegiance to the homeland and its protectors. The peace dividend Clinton had left behind was suddenly as safe as if Cohen had gotten hold of it. Sex had been eclipsed by death, the fire of lust by the lust for destruction.

Yes, the bad craziness was upon us, and it was eclipsing even the darkness of my own situation. There was plenty besides my missing share of Sex.Com to be depressed about in the good old USA. It was a relief to speak to Canadians, who shook their heads in woe at the unsurprising news that the Americans were on the warpath again, and this time, it was forever. And I had work to do.

Working for Sweet Entertainment Group was turning out to be quite an education in many things I probably should have learned before I signed on. Tom was not Steve's brother, and Mike was not an elder relative. Steve was a black belt in Thai kickboxing who had taken a few months out of his porn career to help his teacher, famed in Vancouver as "The Blade," build his martial arts school. He enjoyed eating sushi in restaurants where he affected the manner of a porn paterfamilias, buying endless amounts of everything anyone wanted. He sponsored employee trips to the local amusement park, where he would dare everyone to ride the scariest rides, and clearly had the most fun of anyone.

For me, joining a pseudo-family of kooky and somewhat legendarily outrageous pornographers seemed likely to be a profitable lark. Aside from turning down Steve's request that I adopt the name of "Charlie Sweet," I was fully on board. At the 2001 Internext show in Vegas, I was there wearing an SEG t-shirt, adding Gary Kremen's former legal muscle to Steve's team. Ana, now 21, came along for the trip. She wore a Bebe pinstripe suit to the Pimp 'n Ho Ball and when asked, told everyone she "was a pimp." My friends vied for the right to protect her from lowlifes, and Steve had only five words of advice: "Stay out of the business." She took his advice, but had a great time at the show, which was one big carnival to her.

The job had long stretches of what were supposed to be fun. One night during August 2001, I was sitting on the beach in Florida at night with a number of pornographers. Darrin Babbin was there with a smiling black woman who laughed easily. Darrin, who looked nerdy with a black moustache and big glasses, was drinking Jack Daniels from a 1.5

liter bottle with no apparent effect. He told me he started out playing piano for the Christian Broadcasting Network, and was now working for Sex.Com in search-engine optimization, but Gary's scene was a zoo, and Darrin had already accepted a new job at New Frontier. There were other sleaze luminaries sitting by the lapping shore in the indolent night. Joe Elkind, a famous cokehead with the schnozz to prove it, had induced a foolish young thing to blow pot smoke down his throat, easing the labor of sucking on his own joint. Joe was briefly distracted when he had to discipline one of his bodyguards, who had gotten into a little scuffle on the hotel grounds, but it didn't mess up his mood. Oystein Wright of Mansion Productions, a tall Norwegian in the software business, was there with a caramel-skinned beauty. It was a pleasant gathering.

At some point, between his slugs of Jack and pulls of reefer, a young man whose name I don't remember, asked me if I really was the lawyer for Sweet. I pointed to the SEG logo on my t-shirt and told him that, yes, I was. Sweet's most popular product was a series of short films called SweetLoads. He asked me if I'd watched Sweet Loads. I told him that I hadn't watched the movies, just the site tour. He seemed incredulous, and with his eyebrows raised for emphasis and his face nodding, advised, "You should watch them. They're incredible. I've watched them all two or three times."

So, the next time I had a high-speed connection, I watched a couple of the Sweet Loads vignettes. It was my introduction to the POV genre, for point-of-view, which in porn, describes the practice of shooting your own video with a handheld camera while having sex. In each movie, the set was simply Steve's grey office. The first victim was a big blonde with large tits, who reminded me of a cow. Her mascara and the whites of her eyes showed large below her pupils as Steve insisted that she keep looking up at him. It went on and on, looking like difficult work for the woman. The girl looked miserable and humiliated. I watched another video, and it was just the same. I stopped at two, and couldn't understand how anybody could watch them all, much less twice. There were dozens of them, and Tom later told me that not a one of the girls got paid a penny to do Sweet Loads videos. They were "auditions" for movies that Steve never intended to make.

One day in early February 2002, Steve got all excited about a new deal we had to pursue with a self-made pornstar named Max Hardcore. I had never heard of Max, but Rey had explained to me that his content was hugely famous on video, and had the raw qualities that would make it a natural for a co-marketing deal with Sweet. Sweet, I realized, was a leader in all things gauche, and had pioneered such innovations as shoving baseball bats, large fruits and vegetables, and other household items into the sexual orifices of their models. I could hardly imagine what tremendously novel way of using women's bodies Max had devised that would drive Steve's interest in him to such a pitch. But I would soon see, because Steve had bought plane tickets for us to fly down to LA and meet him the next day.

Max Hardcore was the most charming misogynistic bastard I have ever met. Steve and I flew into LAX on an early flight, then jammed down the freeway in a tiny SUV to arrive early at Max's house in the Pasadena hills east of LA. It was a beautiful morning, and the weather was lovely. Max's webmaster met us, showed us the house and the hot tub. It was pretty good-sized, nicely laid out, no porn in evidence anywhere, and the feeling of sex everywhere. Max, I learned from the webmaster, was a fucking machine who scripted, performed and directed the shooting of all his own work. Right about that time, the great man rolled up in his lowered white pickup truck, wearing a white cowboy hat and mirrorshades.

He and Steve hit it off famously. It wasn't a question of whether they would do a deal, but of what it would be. Max described some of his signature screwing styles, which included of course pissing on his partner, using surgical equipment like a speculum to dilate her vagina, and having her drink milk from the cup so created through a length of clear surgical tubing. He had a favorite model to work with, named Catalina, about whom he couldn't say enough good things. She had my silent admiration. Anyone who could make a career out of fucking a jerk this big had to be tough. Max always referred to women as sluts, even Catalina, in marked contrast to Steve, who always called them content, and liked to give lectures about "how to treat your content." Very impressive, unless you've watched SweetLoads.

Like Steve, Max liked to register his intellectual property. He had registered his own trademark, "Max Hardcore," which he proudly displayed, pulling the official registration from a file folder to display the gold-embossed treasure he'd received from the US Patent & Trademark Office. He also assiduously copyrighted everything, designed all of his own video covers, and retained all of the rights to his work. He only licensed his productions for a term of years, and never sold a title, because, he explained, porn never gets old. "Take it off the shelf for a few years and then reissue it, and the sales come right back." I had to admit, I was getting an education from a guy who had managed to beat the odds by a considerable length–male porn stars are utterly disposable, but this man was in control of his career.

Still, it was scary to be sitting there in Max's study watching him get on with Steve as if they were father and son. They spoke each other's language. They liked the same things. They had each dominated hundreds, maybe even thousands of women with their voices and their looks, their air of command. I was learning secrets I had never wanted to learn.

Once I asked Steve directly, "You're the devil, aren't you?" In return, he only gave me that sharklike grin. As I watched Steve and Max magnetizing each other with mutual admiration, I asked myself what my mother would think, seeing me here with these men. I asked myself why I was cementing deals between two misogynists who had their own unique reasons for hating women, and only needed me to seal the deal with contractual language. Sure, I could do it, but did I want to broker a merger that would flood the Internet with more nasty shit? Suddenly, the words burst into my mind, "Can money be this important?" I was seriously pondering this question when the Mexican maid came up to let us know that lunch had been served.

It was a lovely lunch. She had laid out a spread of cold cuts, cheese, fresh sliced tomatoes, lettuce, and open jars of mayonnaise and relish. The plates and silverware were sparkling clean, and the lettuce was crisp and freshly rinsed. There was good bread. By way of enjoying what good there was in life, I put together a tasty sandwich and bit into it. Delicious. Steve was headed for the kitchen table when his cell phone rang and he stopped. He stepped outside to take the call.

A short while later Steve returned to the kitchen, very pale. The police had raided the shop in Vancouver. The employees were all standing in the hall in handcuffs, while the cops searched and seized. We had to go back to Canada immediately. We hurriedly excused ourselves from the meeting with Max. As we were leaving, Max made a touching offer. Did we, you know, *need* anything? I assumed he meant a little session with a mirror and a straw, which we declined. He didn't detain us any further then, just encouraged Steve by saying that he'd been to jail more than once, and to hang in there, that it would all come out right.

Although I thought Steve should think twice before flying back that night, because he might be arrested at the airport upon arrival, Steve is too much of a field commander for that sort of thing. After a little dithering about his own safety, and much more anxiety about what his troops might be thinking, he overruled my cautionary advice, and we flew back to Vancouver on the first available flight. It is not, I realized, that the devil has no character. It is just that he has a different agenda.

There were no cops at the airport when we returned, just Jamie and her brother Thor, a serious, sedate geek who seemed to work at Sweet so he could keep an eye on his sister. The next day we went to the shop, and everyone was there. We rejoiced that no one was in jail, assessed what was lost, and started figuring what it would take to get back to work. A lot of equipment had been seized and had to be replaced. But no one had given any incriminating statements to the police. Steve rose to the occasion like a wartime leader standing in the ashes of his fortress. But my time with the organization was effectively over.

A week after Steve and I returned, I got word that my dad had passed away in the Eastern Star Nursing Home in Phoenix after two years of silently taking his meals through a tube in his stomach. He had never understood the meaning of Sex.Com, or how it had kept me from visiting him more than a few hours in his last two years of life. We made a quick round trip from Vancouver to Phoenix to attend the funeral, then packed up the apartment and returned to Oregon. It had taken only ten months to exhaust my fifteen minutes of shame.

CHAPTER FIFTY-SEVEN

ENFANT TERRIBLE

ON AUGUST 13, 2002, JUDGE ALEX KOZINSKI TOOK THE BENCH in the Ninth Circuit courtroom in downtown San Francisco to hear oral arguments in *Kremen vs. Cohen*. Kozinski is a maverick, which was apparent to everyone when Reagan appointed him to the Ninth Circuit bench in 1985. Widely admired for his brusque rhetoric, he had graduated from UCLA Law School a mere ten years earlier, thus becoming the youngest appointee to the U.S. appellate bench. Born of Rumanian immigrants in Los Feliz, a Latino suburb northeast of LA, he was known for writing clever, biting opinions, and suffering fools with very poor grace.

Perhaps foreshadowing the outcome of the case now before him, about ten years earlier Kozinski had authored the blunt opinion that gave Cohen a pyrrhic victory in his appeal from the San Diego bankruptcy fraud convictions. Kozinski's opinion reversed one of the three convictions and remanded him for resentencing by Judge Judith Miller. The same Judge Miller who Cohen had called a "cunt," something she probably hadn't forgotten when he stood before her again a couple of years later. Despite Cohen's appellate victory, Judge Miller sentenced him to the same term of years as she had at the conclusion of trial. For some reason, Cohen thought his first encounter with Kozinski boded well for the outcome of the Sex.Com case.

Cohen had taken up the habit of calling me occasionally to incite my animosity toward Gary and to share his plans for causing Gary pain and expense. Sometimes, when he was very proud of his cleverness, he would disclose his litigation plans, and in such a mood he told me about his lawyer's theme for the appellate argument. It didn't sound like a good theme, and I was sure he'd never use it, so I was surprised when Cohen's lawyer stepped up to the podium in the beautiful Ninth Circuit chamber and spoke his opening line.

The atmosphere was hushed and decorous for what those involved knew was a momentous hearing. Several reporters, and bigwigs like Phil Sbarbaro of NSI, were in attendance. The appearance of the courtroom was truly splendid, the most dazzling I have ever seen. The stonemasons and cabinet-makers of the FDR era had outdone themselves creating a temple of justice. Everywhere the eye wandered it settled on sculpted marble and fine woods carved with complex designs. The lights were concealed behind stained glass. The three judges, with Kozinski in the middle, sat in high-backed leather swivel chairs, black-robed and charged with power, surveying the lawyers and the gallery from their exalted position.

Mike Mayock, who had argued Cohen's criminal appeal years before, addressed his opening line directly to Kozinski. To my immense surprise, he said just what Cohen had told me he would say: "Judge Ware was sucker-punched."

Kozinski's brow immediately furrowed, and a cloud gathered over his head. While Mayock was drawing his breath, Kozinski checked his advance with an abrupt response: "Wait a minute. You can't come here and call the District Judge a sucker."

Mayock tried to dig his way out of the hole Kozinski had put him in. He hadn't called Judge Ware a sucker, he pleaded.

Kozinski kept him on the hook. Yes he *had* called the judge a sucker.

When a judge speaks to a lawyer that way in open court, it's like being hit in the forehead with a fencepost. His brain stalls. If he's lucky, he does the right thing from pure instinct. Mayock wasn't lucky. His instincts failed him, probably because there was no right thing to do. A sucker punch hits the sucker before he has a chance to defend himself, and it was obvious to everyone in the opulent chamber that Mayock had been suckered by a master. Kozinski finished him off with a dose of disdain, demonstrating utter disinterest in his argument, allowing him to drown in disgrace. Cohen told me that Mike had a heart attack a short time later. Unlike past occasions when Cohen had reported that he or his lawyer had suffered a heart attack, this time I think it was true.

Jim Wagstaffe was up next, arguing for affirmance of Judge Ware's verdict against Cohen, and a reversal of the summary judgment for NSI. The atmosphere in the court relaxed as Wagstaffe efficiently recounted the story of how Cohen had stolen Sex.Com, laundered the proceeds through offshore banks, and was living in Mexico, a fugitive from Judge Ware's arrest warrant. Machiavelli said that victory makes everything all right, and it certainly was true of Gary's case against Cohen. Gary had gone from fighting an uphill battle to coasting downhill, and the nods from Kozinski and his fellow judges made it clear that Wagstaffe had little to worry about from Cohen's appeal.

Wagstaffe moved on to the appeal against NSI. Judge Ware had concluded that domains were a form of intellectual property too evanescent to form the basis for a conversion claim, because they weren't "merged with a document." Thus, Gary's search for a "document of title" had expanded. In the trial court, I had pointed to the registration documents Gary filed to obtain Sex.Com, and the falsified documents Cohen submitted, combining Gary's name with Cohen's email address to "spoof" NSI. They had looked like "documents of title" to me, but Judge Ware had not even considered them. Wagstaffe took my argument further, pointing to the entire Whois database as the fundamental document that makes all domains a form of personal property.

Through Gary's growing influence, he had gotten a variety of cutting-edge legal organizations to support his fight, like the Electronic Freedom Foundation, that had never been interested in the cause before. Kozinski and his fellow judges had received numerous amicus briefs attacking NSI's arrogant position, but more than scholarly legal opinion was in the air.

A wind of change was blowing through the courtroom, as the barometer of public opinion came into harmony with the facts of Internet life. What had been esoteric in June 1999 when I joined the case, and remained obscure in May 2000 when Judge Ware dismissed NSI, had since become common knowledge. Computer printers were on every desktop, ready to turn online documents into hardcopy. In truth, printing itself was irrelevant, as electronic documents had become ubiquitous. Our society had moved beyond reading its email to drowning in spam. The very word "document," was losing meaning as people Googled for facts they once would have looked for in books, newspapers, libraries or archives. Taxes were filed online, paper airline tickets were an anachronism, and even the federal courts were requiring lawyers to learn the new "e-filing" system. By fall, 2002, Internet domain names were being registered at a rate that was accelerating exponentially, generating millions of dollars in registration revenue. Meanwhile, NSI was still trying to hide behind the lack of a "document."

The danger of Internet fraud had also ceased to be theoretical. Newbie websurfers everywhere were falling prey to Nigerian inheritance scams, offshore casinos, and phishing scams that forged whole financial websites to extract precious personal data. Identity theft had become the fastest-growing crime in the nation, aided by insecure databases and loose verification procedures. Forgery and false impersonation were becoming the signature crimes of the computer era, and the courts were beginning to see more cases like Gary's, where con artists directed their deceptions not to the owner of property, but to those in charge of their property – the banks, the credit reporting agencies, and of course, the domain name registries.

The domain name business had also changed. NSI had lost its monopoly on domain registrations, and with it the mystique of being a government contractor performing a unique function. Nor was it any longer a wet-from-the-womb dot-com brimming with electronic cash. It was a mere small-cap subsidiary of a big company called VeriSign, for which domain registrations were a drop in its revenue bucket. New companies like Godaddy and eNom had made mincemeat of NSI's registration business by cutting prices and providing a decent level of customer service. NSI's argument that it would be too burdensome and costly to impose oversight obligations on registrars had been shown to be ridiculous.

Kozinski received Wagstaffe's arguments welcomingly, asking questions that brought out the strongest points in Gary's favor. When Dave Dolkas stood up to argue NSI's defense of Judge Ware's decision, Kozinski's mood changed. When Dave said there was no document of title, Kozinski's response wasn't polite. What about the Whois database? NSI had total control over that record. It was printable. It recorded the names of domain name registrants, and all of their information. Why wasn't it a document? Wasn't it NSI's property? Wouldn't NSI have a claim if someone injured that property? Dave seemed puzzled. Maybe, he ventured, it would be trespass? Kozinski seemed appalled by the response. Dave's habitual thinking patterns had apparently reached the limit of their utility.

Kozinski's questioning then moved Dave further into unfriendly territory – the topic of the forged letter. Ellen Rony's analysis finally received its due. Citing what Ellen had called "red flags" that should have raised questions, Kozinski rejected Dave's argument that NSI couldn't have discerned fraud from the face of the letter. He pointedly asked if it wasn't strange that a company called "Online Classifieds" would lack an Internet connection, as the forged letter asserted. As the pace of Kozinski's

298

attack on NSI's position moved to a brutal conclusion, Phil Sbarbaro, his bald spot jerking and his pin-striped suit a jumble of conflicting lines, began shifting uncomfortably in his seat. By the time Dave sat down, NSI's position had been utterly rejected by the enfant terrible of the Ninth Circuit. Phil sprang from his seat and darted from the courtroom, pushing through the massive red leather doors without reverence for the dignity of the court. Although I called to him as he blew past, "Hey, Phil," he was not interested in exchanging pleasantries with an old enemy, and ignored me completely.

After the hearing, I congratulated Wagstaffe on his argument, and maneuvered my way around Idell. I was standing by the ornate elevator, wrapped in an old-fashioned cage, when Gary came out.

Gary swung his bulk a little side to side and tossed me a question, "Whaddja think?"

I answered politely, "I think it was good for you."

Tara, who had appeared at my elbow, leaned forward to interject "I think it was great for Charles!" Like giving a vial of nitroglycerine a sharp rap, her remark had an instantaneous effect.

Gary's eyes exploded into bulging orbs of rage as his reply flew forth from his goatee-encircled mouth: "Well, you really fucked up Wells Fargo! Idell has the proof!"

Ah yes, the bittersweet pleasure of hedging your bets. Gary's victory over NSI was tainted by the painful thought that he had just lost leverage against me. I had been vindicated by Kozinski's endorsement of my reasoning. The court could now lift the stay of my lawsuit, and he would no longer be able to accuse me of malpractice for not filing a stupid negligence claim against NSI. Negligence! How absurd. For after all, what could NSI have negligently damaged but Gary's *property*? As I had always said, Sex.Com was either property, or it was nothing.

Jim DeSimone was delighted to hear about Kozinski's performance, whom he reminded me was UCLA alumnus. I took a few calls from clueless reporters who didn't know how to read a docket sheet and still thought I was Gary's lawyer. Cohen called, but when I told him about Mayock's terrible performance, he still expressed optimism, and looked forward to reading the opinion. Cohen didn't have long to wait, but the panel's unanimous opinion couldn't have been worse for him. If there had been a baby in the bathwater that Mayock had presented to the panel, they ignored it entirely, because all of his arguments were sent uncer-emoniously down the drain with a one-line opinion published in early October 2002. "In light of Cohen's status as a fugitive from justice and his egregious abuse of the litigation process, we exercise our discretion to dismiss his appeal." In response to this news, Gary told Wired magazine, "It shows sometimes justice prevails."

I was hoping that I, too, would receive a little justice from the Ninth Circuit, in the form of an opinion vindicating my position on the property character of domain names, but the distance from the cup to the lip once again proved elastic. When Kozinski's opinion came out, it was not unanimous, and it was not what I had hoped. The other two silent judges apparently got the memo that NSI was supposed to win the case, and tried to derail Kozinski's common-sense efforts to treat NSI like any other civil defendant. In an opinion that didn't attempt to conceal his outrage, Kozinski revealed that his two fellow robe-wearers had decided that the issue he saw as an utter no-brainer—that domains were prop-erty under California law—was actually a great big open issue that re-quired them to solicit an opinion from the California Supreme Court. He was livid, because these judicial nincompoops had actually forced him, the panel leader, to "certify a question" to which the answer was utterly clear. Kozinski thus loaded the certification with an extended rant that listed all of the reasons why the California Supreme Court couldn't be bothered with such a ridiculous request, like its backlog of death penalty appeals, and implied that the matter would now take another three years to resolve simply because his fellow-panelists refused to interpret well-settled California law.

Kozinski and I got the last laugh, though. The California Supreme Court followed Kozinski's advice, refused to certify the question, and kicked the case back to the Ninth Circuit within a couple of months. Koz-inski swiftly issued a new, unanimous opinion, that established that In-ternet domains are property in the State of California, and throughout the Ninth Circuit, from Alaska to Arizona.

THE MIDDAY SUN

By SUMMER 2003, I HAD BEEN LITIGATING AGAINST GARY for longer than I had litigated against Cohen. The bar arbitrators concluded I'd saved Gary's case from certain catastrophe, and performed everything I'd promised in the October 4th agreement. However, they held the agreement legally invalid for lack of the magic words, and awarded me what they figured was the reasonable value of my services. I didn't agree with the results of their estimations, and rejected the award.

Jim DeSimone and I prepared to march forward to trial, but increasingly he was playing Sancho Panza to my Quixote, cautiously asking whether I hadn't considered the possibility that a jury might not award much more than the arbitrators? Wondering if we'd even get a jury, since during the years the case had been pending, invalidating fee agreements had become increasingly popular with the judges. Jim was urging me to wake up and smell the coffee. Schonbrun, DeSimone had spent over twenty-thousand dollars on the litigation, and they weren't eager to throw more cash at a quixotic quest. His partners thought we needed to settle.

Gary, I realized, had the resources to engage in a forever war, and as I viewed the mounting debts I was accumulating, I realized I did not. Because the whole matter was so convoluted and insoluble, one evening at home, I turned to an old friend for advice. I grabbed three pennies and my favorite edition of the I Ching, a birthday gift from a friend in LA. Tossing the three pennies six times, and recording the results in a series of six lines, I deciphered the oracle and read the advice that King Wen and the Duke of Chou recorded in antiquity for the guidance of society. While it may seem strange to consult an oracle, rumor has it that the Japanese were winning the war in the Pacific until they stopped consulting the I Ching. That story may be apocryphal, but it has the ring of truth, and whenever I have faced a big legal career decision, I consulted the big Chinese book.

I had made my first big legal career decision twenty years earlier, reading the I Ching by the light of a kerosene lamp, in a little yurt in the middle of a big, muddy field in Southern Oregon. The children and my wife were asleep and it was as dark outside as if there were no cities anywhere on earth. There was no electricity or running water in the yurt, where we had lived for nearly three years in continuous poverty. The I Ching delivered an oracle that encouraged me to enter the legal profession, predicting that I would reach the heights of what it called "the way of the inferior man." This seemed like a mixed blessing, but the oracle explained that if I wanted to obtain power, I would have to learn the way of the inferior man, because I lived in corrupt times, when inferior men control the heart of society, and superior men have small influence. As somewhat of a consolation, I should know that Heaven favored my following the way of the inferior men, so I could not be blamed. Ever since, whenever I've been offered an opportunity to change jobs, I've usually consulted the I Ching to get an understanding of the options before me.

When I consulted the oracle about my lawsuit against Gary, it told me that by continuing my chosen course, I would arrive at a complete disaster. After an understandable feeling of letdown, I began to feel relieved. There had been something behind that sense of doom that had hung over my battle with Gary. It had been an ill-advised campaign, conceived in the worst crucible of all–pride and passion. Sun Tzu advises but one way to deal with an overpowering adversary–don't fight them. I had ignored that teaching for three years. I'd been in darkness so long, it was as if the sun had stopped on the wrong side of the earth. Now that the oracle had warned me in the clearest terms, I could sheath my sword and make peace.

In June of 2003, Gary and I sat in Wagstaffe's conference room, drinking Bushmills Irish whiskey from big, square water glasses. The settlement documents were being finalized by Wagstaffe, Idell, and Jim DeSimone. My escape was pre-planned. I had booked two flights to Europe for departure the following week and told everyone that Tara and I were going on vacation, and I was settling the case before I left. The gambit had worked. Everyone came to the table and bargained hard. Only Idell seemed pained over the demise of the conflict. Another few months, he was sure, and he could have crushed me. I wasn't giving him the chance. I saw an exit, a bright light at the end of a very long hallway, and I was walking towards it like a condemned man waking from the dream of his execution.

As I sat in Wagstaffe's conference room, I threw the I Ching again. Sitting there, tossing my pennies and writing out the lines, I received a positive oracle. The bright, shining lines advised me to make the most of my situation, to enjoy abundance and bestow warmth like the sun at midday. The oracle had guided me to this place, and now it confirmed my decision to make peace. I hadn't spend much time thinking about how to make peace until then, but in the future, I decided, I would explore this new land. Hidden in the changing lines of the oracle lay a reminder that the sun always passes from its zenith, that summer gives way to fall, and abundance is followed by austerity. I knew that must be true, but austerity seemed far away as I contemplated what the settlement would bring. I was ready to rule a peaceful domain.

I got up from the conference table, went downstairs, walked across the street, sat down next to a beautiful young blonde at a fancy bar, and ordered a beer. She was a Stanford student, an aspiring environmental consultant, and she was having one of those light blue drinks that beautiful young women sometimes drink. I chatted with her for about a half hour about the exciting career she was planning on having. It was great to have not a care in the world. I left the bar after finishing my beer, and walked to the corner market to buy a fifth of Bushmills.

When I got back to Wagstaffe's office, details were still being hammered out by the two Jims, but I was ready to relax, and poured myself a splash of the reliable Irish whisky. Gary asked me for a drink. I hadn't even offered him one, because he doesn't much like to drink, so I knew he was trying to be friendly. I poured him a good shot, and we sat sipping the warm, amber fluid as the sun went down and the spherical lights of the bridge turned to the scalloped hem of a dress edged with pearls.

When the agreement was ready to sign, Gary and I drew out our pens and signed a new agreement, one that put all disputes to rest. It had been a long time since there had been peace between us. It felt good. We decided to have another shot and go eat dinner.

Our lawyers looked at us like we were crazy. After a settlement, the clients do not leave the building together, carrying a fifth of whiskey and wandering out to find a new adventure. But that was Gary, and that was me. We left our lawyers in the glass tower, signed out with security, and walked out past the huge brass propeller screw that dominates the entryway of Wagstaffe's office building.

We picked up my car from the parking lot, and I drove us to Joe's, an all-night cafeteria where Gary and I had often eaten among cabbies and nighthawks. We stood in line for roast beef, mashed potatoes, cole slaw and dessert. We set the plates down on red and white plastic tablecloths, and ate just like we had in years past. Joe's is like that – it never changes, so time kind of stops there. As in years past, Gary spoke to me in sharp, clipped, phrases, as if we'd never stopped being mutual venturers in the world of profit and loss. As if the years wasted in anger had been nothing more than a record skipping a groove, that we had put right at last so we could hear the rest of the song. Things were just like they'd always been, as the juggernaut of a San Francisco night spun around us, heavy with aborted dreams. In the general destruction of everyone's expectations, the fracture of our relationship had been less than a minor matter. Still, we had marked one stone in the edifice of civilization with the scars of our striving.

We finished our food, and Gary invited me to spend the night at his place, so I drove to his house on Third Street. We were pretty tired, so after talking, we agreed it was time to crash. He insisted that I take his room and use his bed, and he would sleep on the couch. There wasn't any brick dust anywhere, and his room was pretty clean. The bed was unmade, but looked fine, so I poured myself some whiskey, and shut the hall door. As I looked around the room, I saw that Gary's room hadn't changed much, except that he now had a row of porn videos on his shelf, many still in the shrink wrap. There was a book by Jared Diamond he'd once borrowed from me and never returned. I felt a silly desire to reclaim it, but let the impulse go.

There was nothing to do, so I turned off the light, and went to sleep with the bay breeze billowing the curtain over the sliding window, wide-open to the west.

When the brightening sky filled the room with soft light, and I awoke in Gary's room, I knew there had been a miracle. It was barely six in the morning. Gary was sleeping on the couch. I wrote him a note and left it in his room, thanking him, wishing him well, and saying I'd decided to make an early start of it. I put my things in my car, carefully backed it out of his narrow garage, and drove north on Third Street. As I sped past the empty dockside warehouses, long, dark shadows alternated with blasts of sunlight that flooded the car with brightness. I got on the freeway on-ramp, pulled onto the eighty west, and headed for Oregon.

EPILOGUE

STEVE COHEN WAS ARRESTED BY MEXICAN POLICE on Friday, October 27, 2005 in Tijuana, while trying to renew his visa. He was turned over to U.S. authorities, who arrested him on the outstanding civil warrant issued by Judge Ware. He refused to comply with Judge Ware's orders directing him to account for and return the stolen Sex.Com money, and remained imprisoned for contempt of court until May 5, 2007.

YISHAI HIBARI runs Profit Plantation, and continues to focus on delivering porn to dialup users at a high markup.

RICHARD MARTINO and his brother Daniel pled guilty in February 2003 to stealing over $650 Million from Internet and telephone users seeking adult entertainment, psychic readings, and other services by billing them for undisclosed charges. As part of his plea agreement, Richard admitted to being a Gambino crime family "capo de regime." On January 30, 2006, he was sentenced to nine years in federal prison.

GARY KREMEN settled with NSI for an undisclosed sum in April 2004, and sold Sex.Com for fourteen million dollars to a company called Escom, LLC in January, 2006. He continues to make efforts to recover some portion of the sixty-five million dollar judgment he obtained against Steven Michael Cohen, but so far has been only marginally successful. Gary sued ARIN, the Association for the Registration of Internet Numbers, in part because ARIN refused to implement a court order to give Gary the IP addresses formerly assigned to Cohen. ARIN claimed the IP addresses are not property.

SUSANNE WHATLEY moved to Florida to become the paramour of Internet porn mogul Serge Birbrair, and got breast implants so large that they were referred to in the industry as "the Twins."

STEVE SWEET was acquitted of all obscenity charges by a British Columbian magistrate, who concluded that, while the SadoSlaves.com content was disgusting, it did not offend contemporary community standards in Vancouver. His alliance with Max Hardcore was solidified, and Max's videos are now marketed through the Sweet website.

TOM SWEET settled his lawsuit with Steve Sweet and started a project to raise a million dollars to start an environmentally sustainable business using web-based marketing and billing. The project is well on its way to success.

MAX HARDCORE, aka Paul F. Little, was convicted on June 5, 2008 on ten counts of obscenity by a Florida Federal jury.

ALEX KOZINKSKI was elevated to Chief Judge of the Ninth Circuit Court of Appeals on November 30, 2007. In June, 2008, he was forced to recuse himself from sitting as a trial judge in a Los Angeles obscenity trial after the L.A. Times revealed he had posted titillating images on his son's website.

PHIL FATHER ended his partnership with Gary Kremen. According to Phil, his two percent of Sex.Com did not provide him with any substantial monetary payout.

TARA CARREON retired from the law business and became the webmistress of American-Buddha.com, which features, among other things, political philosophy, muckraking, satirical erotica, and spiritual cinema.

MARIA CARREON was hired as a legal secretary in New York City by one of the lawyers whose clients were subpoenaed by Ana Carreon, thanks to Sue Whatley, who talked the other lawyer into hiring her. Maria recently gave up her legal secretary career, and now attends The New School for Social Research. Her blogs about life in the Big Apple appear at ByBeautyDamned.com.

ANA CARREON applied to Stanford and was admitted to the Classics program, where she put in two years as a straight-A student. She returned to her home in Ashland to attend Southern Oregon University, where she is studying photojournalism. She maintains a website of her work and photos at Dreampretty.com.

PETER CARINI survived the departure of Maria Carreon as his secretary, hired two lawyers to work for him, and became the undisputed DUI king of Southern Oregon. He bought a large house in a tony neighborhood in Medford, Oregon, becoming the first Italian family to achieve the honor.

JOSHUA CARREON, the only son of Charles and Tara Carreon, and a loving brother to his sisters Ana and Maria, was a kind, gentle man, and a very talented graphic artist. His roots were in graffiti art learned as a skater kid in Santa Monica. He loved to buy stacks of t-shirts that he hand-silk-screened with political art. He also created prints on industrial materials and on fabric, often enhanced with bright painted calligraphic strokes to create striking works of visual art. Joshua was the head designer and reporter for the Ashland Free Press, and took hundreds of videos of musical, political and social events in Southern Oregon. He was killed in an automobile accident on February 16, 2007 in Dunsmuir, California, at the foot of Mt. Shasta, near Castle Crags, and is deeply missed by many friends and family.

Made in the USA
San Bernardino, CA
03 June 2018